FACING THE FIEND

Facing the Fiend

Satan as a Literary Character

Eva Marta Baillie

CASCADE *Books* • Eugene, Oregon

FACING THE FIEND
Satan as a Literary Character

Copyright © 2014 Eva Marta Baillie. All rights reserved. Except for brief quotations in critical publications or reviews, no part of this book may be reproduced in any manner without prior written permission from the publisher. Write: Permissions, Wipf and Stock Publishers, 199 W. 8th Ave., Suite 3, Eugene, OR 97401.

New Revised Standard Version Bible, copyright © 1989, Division of Christian Education of the National Council of the Churches of Christ in the United States of America. Used by permission. All rights reserved.

Cascade Books
An Imprint of Wipf and Stock Publishers
199 W. 8th Ave., Suite 3
Eugene, OR 97401

www.wipfandstock.com

ISBN 13: 978-1-62032-924-5

Cataloguing-in-Publication data:

Baillie, Eva Marta.

    Facing the fiend : Satan as a literary character / Eva Marta Baillie.

    x + 208 pp. ; 23 cm. Includes bibliographical references.

    ISBN 13: 978-1-62032-924-5

    1. Devil in literature. 2. Devil—History of doctrines. I. Title.

PN56.D465 B145 2014

Manufactured in the U.S.A.

To my Family—Danke.

On another day the angels came to present themselves before the LORD, and Satan also came with them to present himself before him. And the LORD said to Satan, "Where have you come from?" Satan answered the LORD, "From roaming through the earth and going back and forth in it."

JOB 2:1–2

Contents

Acknowledgments ix
List of Abbreviations x

Introduction: Setting the Stage—
  The Birth of a Character   1

Part One: The Dwelling Place of Satan

1. Is Satan Evil?   19
2. Satan's Biography: The Origins of the
     Satanic Narrative   29
3. Satan in Story and Myth   50
4. Satan and the Written Word   66

Part Two: Satanic Characters

5. The Restless Wanderer   77
6. The Tormented Shadow   93
7. The Zeroing Zero   110
8. The Creative Eliminator   135
9. The Stumbling Block   154
10. The Transgressor   178

Conclusion: Satan's Salvation or the Redemption Lies
     in the Text   188

Bibliography   197

Acknowledgments

This work is the result of excellent teachers, inspiring fellow postgraduate students, and the interreligious and interdisciplinary dialogue at the Centre for Theology, Literature, and the Arts at the University of Glasgow. Thanks to Mark Baillie, Mark Godin, Andrew Hass, David Jasper, and Sylvie Warnecke.

Abbreviations

BM	*Blood Meridian or The Evening Redness in the West,* by Cormac McCarthy
GB	*The Great Bagarozy,* by Helmut Krausser
HD	*Heart of Darkness,* by Joseph Conrad
LthK3	Lexikon für Theologie und Kirche
MM	*The Master and Margarita,* by Mikhail Bulgakov
TMG	*The Testament of Gideon Mack,* by James Robertson
WJ	*The Wandering Jew,* by Stefan Heym

Introduction

Setting the Stage

The Birth of a Character

Sympathy for the Devil

The character of Satan is problematic; he is the "weak place of the popular religion, the vulnerable belly of the crocodile."[1] Current popular culture makes Satan a subject of its attention. Films featuring the devil are successful blockbusters, books on the occult sell well, and Satan appears in various music genres, ranging from American folk to heavy metal. Outside popular culture, however, and in particular in the theological discourse, there is little "Sympathy for the Devil."[2] The idea of Satan cannot be adequately expressed and discussed in terms of theology. The Christian system of monotheism does not allow a systematic and theological approach to the existence of Satan. In a dualistic worldview, the figure of Satan might have its own system of thoughts and doctrines; indeed, the Gnostics developed their own idea of a system of good and evil in which the personified evil played an essential role. Orthodox Christianity, however, has always denied a dualistic approach to cosmology and avoids elaborating a divine antagonist. Satan refers to experiences of evil, pain, and suffering. Most systematic definitions of Satan or the devil in the tradition of Christian theology come to the conclusion that Satan is a metaphor for the experience of relational evil and temptation, the willful denial of God, the attempt to deny the divine world order. This study approaches Satan as a literary figure, against the

---

1. Percy Bysshe Shelley, "Essay on the Devil and Devils," 265.
2. The opening track of Jagger and Richards, *Beggars Banquet*.

imagistic or now cinematic dimension of Satan. With the preponderance of visual imagery in our late modern period, why is it that the literary Satan keeps emerging? And what can the literary figure of Satan contribute to the understanding of evil? I argue that the literary is the only means by which Satan can survive, and that as a result of the changing literary (and cultural, philosophical, and theological) landscape and our changing perceptions of evil as we move into the twenty-first century, the satanic character must also change.

Satanic figures exist in the oral and written traditions of many cultures. Although varying in appearance and role many attributes are repeated in a great variety of religious myths due to syncretism or mutual influence during cultural developments. For this study, I will focus on the "Christian Satan," that is the concept of Satan developed in the system of Christian theology and modified through folklore and story in the wider context of Western Europe.[3]

The contemporary systematic theology of the Christian churches largely seeks to avoid any mention of Satan as a person:

> Any careless talk of a "persona of evil" reduces—as some examples from the history of piety account for alarmingly—the trans-individual power of evil to a scary or ridiculous "divine" antagonist.[4]

According to this theological approach personifying Satan can lead to simplifications of the dilemma of evil. The quote highlights that the problem of the definition of Satan lies in the terminology of the discourse, semantically and ontologically. Asking the question "Does Satan *really* exist?" inevitably assumes an empirical existence that requires proof through scientific process. There are, it seems, only two possible ways of addressing the issue of Satan for contemporary Christian theology. One is to interpret the satanic figure as a mere symbol for the temptations of the world, the other is to

---

3. This study will only very marginally refer to the influences of "personified evils" in other cultures and religions. The complex discussion of Satan's presence in the pastoral or liturgical reality of the Christian churches can only be touched upon since such an analysis would go beyond the scope of this thesis and refers to many areas outwith the literary perspective taken here. See here, for example, a study on the contemporary talk of the devil in German churches: Leimgruber, *Kein Abschied vom Teufel*.

4. "Eine unbedachte Rede von der Person des Bösen (Teufel) reduziert zu leicht— wie manche Phänomene der Frömmigkeitsgeschichte erschreckend belegen—die . . . überindividuelle Macht des Bösen auf die (grausige oder lächerliche) Figur eines 'göttlichen' Gegenspielers" (own translation). Schneider, *Handbuch der Dogmatik*, 1, 233.

Setting the Stage

assert the personal existence of Satan. Satan as the face of evil, however, evokes interest and fascination and cannot be dismissed.[5]

The catechism of the Catholic Church from 1993 asserts the personal aspect of evil:

> Evil is not an abstraction, but refers to a person, Satan, the Evil One, the angel who opposes God. The devil (*dia-bolos*) is the one who "throws himself across" God's plan and his work of salvation accomplished in Christ.[6]

We find ourselves in a situation where the talk of Satan is theologically and pastorally difficult, but the interest in his personal existence unbroken. A number of studies focus on Satan and his purpose in cultural discourse: Satan has for a long time been of interest for biblical scholars, systematic theologians, anthropologists, sociologists, and philosophers.[7] I suggest that approaching him as a narrative figure could create a new blueprint for an academic discourse on Satan. His realm then, his dwelling place, is therefore not theology as such, but literature and art. It is only here that Satan is given a face and a story:

> All art depends on opposition between God and the devil, reason and energy. The true poet (the good poet) is necessarily the partisan of energy, rebellion, and desire, and is opposed to passivity, obedience, and the authority of reason, laws, and institutions.[8]

Satan's first appearance as a serpent in the Garden of Eden encapsulates the idea this study will investigate further: Satan's essence resides in the story; it is through narrative his character is understood, but it is also his character that drives the story forward. Before its identity was shaped

---

5. In his article on new approaches to the faces of evil, Stefan Orth observes a growing interest in the theological and philosophical debate around evil and the devil ("Antlitzlos und unbesprechbar?").

6. *Catechism of the Catholic Church*, Part 4, Section 2, Article 3.vii. 2851.

7. The standard work in English on the history of Satan in the Jewish and Christian traditions is Jeffrey Russell's edition in 5 volumes (1977–2006). The most recent biography of Satan has been written by Henry Ansgar Kelly in 2006: *Satan: A Biography*. On the topic of Satan in literature, I refer to *The Old Enemy: Satan and the Combat Myth* (1989), published by Neil Forsyth who also more recently wrote *The Satanic Epic* (2003). Another recent publication is *The Devil as Muse* by Fred Parker (2011). Jürgen Bründl's *Masken des Bösen* focuses on the dogmatics of the devil (2000), while Ute Leimgruber's *Kein Abschied vom Teufel. Eine Untersuchung zur gegenwärtigen Rede vom Teufel im Volk Gottes* examines pastoral and liturgical aspects of the contemporary talk on Satan (2004).

8. Ostriker, "Dancing at the Devil's Party," 580.

by Jewish and Christian theologians, the role of the tempter is referred to as that of *nachash*, translated by the Septuagint as "serpent" and later associated with Satan.[9] It is the force that enters into the innocent state of Eden to tempt and promote disharmony. When reading the Bible chronologically, following the Christian canon of the Scripture, we encounter the serpent in Genesis 3:1 as the first real character of the narrative.

> Now the serpent was more crafty than any other wild animal that the Lord God had made. He said to the woman, "Did God say, You shall not eat from any tree in the garden?"[10]

Following the biblical text, the reader learns that the serpent is a creation of God, that it is subtle or crafty, and that it intends to challenge Eve to transgress the divine order. Christian theology has connected the serpent of Genesis 3 with Satan, the great tempter and enemy of humankind.[11] The Augustinian reading of Genesis 3 established that the logic of Eden is complicated by the appearance of Satan and identified the fall of humankind as the origin of all sin. The text gives us no explanation for the motivation of the serpent, but the reader understands the destructive potential of its opening question. Satan sets out to challenge the existence of humankind in Eden, and at the same time, his appearance develops the story. In the Hebrew original the terms נחש *nachash* (serpent; related: hiss, sting, to hiss and whisper as in enchantment, to entice, or to seduce) and ערום *arum* (subtle, crafty, using craft for defense)[12] are attributed to the serpent. The characters of the man and the woman, however, remain undeveloped. Yet the serpent with its specific characteristics is therefore recognizable as a (literary) character.

The story of the fall exhibits the pattern of transgression from innocence to self-awareness; Satan plays an acutely emancipatory role in

---

9. In the ancient Near East the serpent symbolized life, death, wisdom, nature, chaos, and fertility. It was only later, in post-biblical thought, that the serpent became identified as Satan or one of Satan's minions. The snake plays a prominent role in the literature and cults of the ancient world, echoes of which are found in Israel's religion: "A serpent features in the epic of Gilgamesch and robs Enkidu of immortality. The creature's ability to shed its old skin led to the widespread belief that it had learnt the secret of renewing its youth. Furthermore, the serpent was associated with the fertility cult—with the worship of Astarte and with Baal, who was often iconographically represented in serpent form" (Hayter, *The New Eve in Christ*, 104).

10. Gen 3:1.

11. In chapter 3, I will discuss the development of the satanic figure and also the connection between the serpent and Satan.

12. For an exegesis of Gen 3:1, please see Robbins, *Genesis 1–3 in the History of Exegesis*, and Bonhoeffer, *Creation and Fall*. The adjective also means "more naked"; the same root that is used in the word that describes Adam and Eve's situation after the fall.

the story of the fall. He encourages Eve to eat from the forbidden tree and when she and Adam do so, they see and understand: "Then the eyes of both were opened and they knew that they were naked."[13] This transgression, later interpreted as original sin, can be seen as an innate part of the human condition that enables a free and conscious decision of the person.[14] This is where the literary perspective becomes the central viewpoint. The idea that human beings need to face themselves, and accept their inner fears and weaknesses before they are able to become fully conscious of their own identity is a common narrative arc. First published in 1667, it was John Milton's seventeenth-century epic poem *Paradise Lost* that gave the serpent of Genesis 3 a face and developed the text into a character study of Satan, weaving together the Christian tradition and myths from over 1,500 years. It was a study that would influence the image of Satan in literature and art immensely over the next four centuries.

> As to the devil, he owes everything to Milton. Dante and Tasso present us with a very gross idea of him: Milton divested him of a sting, hoofs, and horns; clothes him with the sublime grandeur of a graceful but tremendous spirit.[15]

In his revolutionary nature Milton's Satan is a role model for the Romantics; he is also regarded as the inspiration behind many later works. And it is this revolutionary aspect of Satan's character, his urging of human beings to gain knowledge and to transcend boundaries, that to date appears to have no place in theological debate.

This central aspect of the conflict of good and evil, natural versus social existence within a human being, is addressed through literary renditions that go back to the biblical Scriptures of the Old and New Testament. The biblical references to Satan are ambiguous. The Old Testament only speaks of the Satan in terms of the adversary; the New Testament refers to demons, the tempter in the desert, and the great dragon, "the ancient serpent called the devil or Satan,"[16] but Satan in the New Testament is not a single entity. He only takes his form through creative human imagination. Satan is referred to in different narratives and used as an umbrella term that brings together medical, religious, and mystical experiences. The images and characterizations of

---

13. Gen 3:7.

14. As Paul Ricoeur confirms: "Henceforth the evil infinite of human desire—always something else, always something more—which animates the movement of civilizations, the appetite for pleasure, for possessions, for power, for knowledge—seems to constitute the reality of man" (*The Symbolism of Evil*, 254).

15. Percy Bysshe Shelley, "Essay on the Devil and Devils," 264–75.

16. Rev 12:9.

Satan derive from narratives, gathered throughout centuries. They have been influenced by ancient mythology, by cultural models, and by spiritual experiences. There is no authoritative body of text that we can refer to when we speak of Satan. It is all in the story of human imagination, the story of the archenemy, the opponent, the fiend. In theological terms, Satan is only *accepted* as tempter, evil doer, or dark force in every human life, never *believed in*. Talking about the creation of Satan essentially requires a definition of his existence. Without initiating an ontological discussion on the meaning of the term "being" it is necessary to think about this question. If one wants to take narrative and literature seriously, the only possible answer is: Yes, Satan does exist. "Literature is either the essential or nothing," says Georges Bataille in *Literature and Evil*.[17] For the purpose of this work, I have to assume that Satan does exist through literature and that his presence in narratives is real.

Satan as a Literary Character

While he was writing *Doctor Faustus* between 1943 and 1947, Thomas Mann had a companion at his side: a black poodle called Nico. Is it a coincidence that Thomas Mann had a black poodle accompanying him during his process of writing his version of the old Faust myth? Or was it maybe Mephistopheles himself, appearing to Thomas Mann and inspiring or even enabling him to complete the book that he later called his "Lebensbeichte," because the characters of Serenus Zeitbloom and Adrian Leverkühn resemble the authors in various ways?

The devil inspires authors, poets, artists, and musicians—his true nature in art seems to be creative, even though he is usually associated with destruction. If we want to believe William Blake, the true poet is of the devil's party without knowing it. The various accounts of the devil in literature and art would certainly promote the theory that Satan himself is working on the side of the artist. While the biblical canon leaves us with many open questions about Satan, the literary canon gives more than enough definitions and interpretations of the devil. The devil is the master of the game of illusion, he wears different masks, comes in different disguises—he sometimes appears as a man, sometimes as a woman, sometimes he looks at us as an animal, and sometimes from the mirror. Generally, the devil has inspired the creativity of human beings more than any other character that finds its roots in the Scriptures.

17. Bataille, *Literature and Evil*, ix.

Setting the Stage

We will see in the following chapters that Satan does not have a being of his own. His nature is parasitic, his existence defined by negative terms, and he has no dwelling place of his own, but uses human beings as temporary hosts. His existence is manifested in his actions; we understand evil through the evildoer and Satan's existence becomes immanent in human relationships that are influenced by the idea of mimetic desire and revenge. We do not understand Satan in his ontological existence, but through his expressions. His character is approached through art; we understand his being through stories and myths. The "traditional" faces of Satan are known to us through folk narratives, mythology, and proverbs and find their sources in biblical and pre-biblical narratives. Satan is not a theological character—attempts to formalize his existence in a theological framework have failed in a similar fashion to any attempt to portray God in narrative. Satan's dwelling place is the narrative, the story, this is his kingdom. One of Satan's many names, given to him in the Scriptures, is the "prince of this world"—he exists in our narratives and through our narratives. He only takes his form through human creative imagination.

The relationship between Satan and literature is symbiotic: Satan can only exist through literature and literature needs Satan to keep the story alive. This relationship develops its own dynamic: once created, the figure of Satan becomes independent and eludes any attempt at abstract definition. It seems that at times, the writer or narrator loses control, needing to admit that the satanic character escaped the creative parent to act out the ascribed character traits without restraint. One might argue this is the case with any literary figure—and indeed with any creation: the creator can set the seed, can draft and plan the creature, but once it comes to life, he can merely be a spectator. The same goes for the satanic figure in story and narrative, but there is something more to it than to any other literary figure, as lively and present he or she might be: if we create Satan, we play with the fire—we evoke the expression of evil and the presence of the eternal denier. *"Mal' den Teufel nicht an die Wand"* is an old German proverb that translates as "Do not paint the devil on the wall" or "Speak of the devil and the devil shows up." This warning refers to old beliefs in the invocation of the devil. The temptation to call upon him is strong, particularly amongst artists. To call him or to create him is easy, but it is certainly more difficult to be rid of him again. The solution lies again in the narrative: in the Brother Grimm's fairy tale, to know the name of the demon *Rumpelstiltskin* saves the child of the miller's daughter. Knowing the name gives power and control, and ultimately allows one to defeat the enemy.

The figure of Satan has constantly changed in the traditions of Western art and literature, but has always played a role. He first appears in our tradition in the Hebrew Bible, most poignantly in Genesis and the book of Job, and he then plays his role in the New Testament. After his narrative premier, Satan became a bit reclusive and indeed, until the thirteenth century, he was defined as "an obscure force subject to divine omnipotence"[18] and had not yet developed characteristics. The faces given to him in popular beliefs and myths were versatile, strongly influenced by regional traditions and mixed with the world of magic and sorcery. It was only with scholasticism, the political and ideological development at the end of the Middle Ages, and the opening of the world with the urge to explain and systemize that Satan became a face with clear features, a face that has influenced Western culture and art until today. The biography of Satan was written by the church fathers who tried to incorporate various figures of opposition and different tales into one coherent system of theology and mythology: "On the face of it, the serpent of one tale had little to do with the rebel of a second, the tyrant of a third, the tempter of a fourth, the lustful voyeur of a fifth, or the mighty dragon of a sixth."[19]

We are dealing with at least two main narrative strands that we need to consider when discussing at the story of Satan. Having identified Satan as the opponent or the adversary, we encounter Satan in an *exterior* and an *interior* battle—the former being represented in the cosmic battle of the book of Revelation, the latter being represented in the temptation in the wilderness. This work is interested most in the personal struggle with the opponent, the post-Cartesian Satan. It is not the devil of the Middle Ages who led the cosmic battle, but the one who emerges post Enlightenment. It is the Satan who whispers in human ears—the one who offers knowledge, the evil motivation in us that is described in Paul's letter to the Romans:

> We know that the law is spiritual; but I am unspiritual, sold as a slave to sin. I do not understand what I do. For what I want to do I do not do, but what I hate I do. And if I do what I do not want to do, I agree that the law is good. As it is, it is no longer I myself who do it, but it is sin living in me. I know that nothing good lives in me, that is, in my sinful nature. For I have the desire to do what is good, but I cannot carry it out. For what I do is not the good I want to do; no, the evil I do not want to do—this I keep on doing. Now if I do what I do not want to do, it is no longer I who do it, but it is sin living in me that does it.[20]

---

18. Muchembled, *A History of the Devil*, 12.
19. Forsyth, *The Satanic Epic*, 5.
20. Rom 7.

Setting the Stage

It was Milton who introduced the aspect of the internal struggle into the narrative of Satan's rebellious combat. *Paradise Lost* is arguably the first work of literature that shows concern for the inner struggle of the adversary and acts as a character study of the leader of the rebellion. It is this "inner dragon" that we are mainly concerned with here, but that distinction finds its origins much later in the story.

Narrative and Metanarrative

So, theologically redundant, I was passed into the hands of folklore.[21]

Spufford's statement confirms that the key to understanding Satan's existence lies in the narrative. Without doubt, Satan has been an immensely popular subject for Western literature throughout the centuries. However, where do we begin without becoming entangled in the multiple strands of the devil's literary career? Since the purpose is not to create an anthology, it seems reasonable to select the text according to certain themes and topics that are relevant to the discussion. The method applied to the selected texts in this work is a juxtaposition of theological and philosophical ideas within literary texts. The particular selection of primary texts is thus necessarily subjective, partial, and incomplete.

Initially this study was inspired by Woland, the devil in Bulgakov's *The Master and Margarita* set in 1930s Russia. He is undoubtedly one of the key satanic figures in modern literature; Mephisto in Goethe's *Faust* and Satan in Milton's *Paradise Lost* also belong to the core canon of satanic characters. But alongside these older, well-known, and valued characters, there are some new images of the "old enemy" that are worthy of consideration, since they help shed some light on the ever-transient figure of Satan in contemporary thought whilst reflecting the nature of a postmodern society. The chosen texts for this work are all novels by European or Northern American authors and portray the figure of Satan in recent and contemporary fiction. They illustrate a consistency in the assignment of certain satanic attributes that give witness to a rich symbolic tradition in the depiction of Satan.

The novel as a literary genre is the most appropriate for the subject of Satan. First of all, the novel is a fictional narrative and clearly marked as that. Second, the novel is character driven and has a developmental aspect, and therefore provides the best dwelling place for the satanic, which is constantly changing, dynamic, and open for interpretation. Third, the novel provides

---

21. Spufford, *The Vintage Book of the Devil*, 11.

intimate reading situations. As is seen later, Satan thrives on the personal and relational aspect of evil and the novel requires an intimate relationship between author and reader and at the same time offers an insight into a character's life that goes beyond the descriptive. The term "interdisciplinary" in the context of theology and literature does not simply imply that the story illustrates religious morals, but rather refers to the mutual influence and active interrelation between the two. One cannot engage with theology without understanding text and narrative. Investigating the relation between the two disciplines is more than referring to the tradition of religious texts, songs, and theological abstracts. *Novels* that deal with religious imagery use them not only to "freight their stories with vestiges of a once powerful and compelling past, earnestly or ironically," but they are "asking questions of the nature of religion itself, and rewriting religious understanding out of the cultural interchange between what has been, what is presently, and what can be in the future, an interchange which works across manifold and overlapping spheres of cultural interest and expression."[22] The interdisciplinary approach can be seen as an attempt to write a non-foundational[23] theology in relation to the problem of evil. Traditionally, theology offers a systematic approach to the content of faith, while literature is often regarded as dangerous, subversive, and chaotic.[24] In a world that accepts the death of God and preaches the downfall of institutionalized religion, it seems difficult to approach the question of evil with the traditional theological methodology. For many theological questions, and especially for questions relating to evil, an interdisciplinary approach offers an alternative to systematic theology. Any work in theology and literature tries to facilitate the "understanding of the nature of theology through literature, or even theology itself as poetry of faith."[25]

For those working in the field of theology and religion, the fundamental shift in the transition to modernity in Western culture, including the disappearance of God, is regarded as a "theological seachange that is perceived in literature long before it is even acknowledged or articulated by the theologians themselves. Theology arises from the corpse of organized religion."[26] It is still theology, but disconnected from any ecclesial tradition

---

22. Hass, "The Future of English Literature and Theology," 849.

23. The term "antifoundational" describes any theology that does not build its theory around an unquestionable foundation. I use the term non-foundational to suggest an alternative to a systematic theology concerned with the construct of a rational system. (See also Mills, "The Pneumatological Ekklesia.")

24. Jasper, "The Study of Literature and Theology," 24.

25. Ibid.

26. Ibid., 25.

Setting the Stage

and therefore without the necessity of a system of salvation. For those involved in the field of theology and literature, reading a play, a story, or a novel is a necessary step towards religious understanding. When it comes to the question of the existence of evil, the answer cannot be found in an onto-theological explanation, but needs to be searched for in the field of imagination, expression, and phenomenology.

I argue that evil cannot be understood in its being, but in its expression. German theologian Dorothee Sölle referred to this concept as *realization*: a worldly correlation of what has been given or promised in the language of religion.[27] The form of expression is manifold and includes all forms of visual and expressive art; this work, however, focuses on narrative and literature, the spoken and written word. Historically, the dialogue between religion and literature as an academic discipline has its beginning in the 1940s and 1950s. T. S. Eliot's essay *Religion and Literature* (1935) was one of the first systematic approaches to the subject. The relationship between the two, however, is older and can be either approached from a historical or an abstract point of view:

> Where theology of all sorts, Lutheran, Tridentine, Islamic, Calvinist and, one is tempted to say, Marxist, Freudian or "structuralist," has always differed from literature is in the authority it claims for its ultimate source or sources. "Literature" must surely remain oblique. It has always probed the meaning of human experience with some imaginative vision of how it should be evaluated and, if necessary and possible, changed.[28]

The translations of the Scriptures into the vernacular have acted as a stepping stone between text and theology. But for theology, dealing with text has always been the primary point of reference:

> A serious commitment to literary critical method may, sometimes paradoxically, lead us back to truths which theology has forgotten or has failed to articulate; . . . the forms of literature and art can often quite spontaneously illuminate in startling ways the divine work of formation and redemption; and . . . theology, critically and rigorously pursued, in its turn, continues to offer a systematic and necessary reminder of the things of ultimate concern in literature and literary criticism.[29]

---

27. Sölle, *Realization*, 29.
28. Levi, "The Relationship between Literature and Theology," 17.
29. Jasper, "The Limits of Formalism and the Theology of Hope," 9.

Facing the Fiend

The traditional academic discipline of theology is still very much concerned with a certain religion or even denomination. Any interdisciplinary approach to theology and literature offers a new way of exercising theology that is more open to creativity and less restricted by frameworks of institutions and traditions. When it comes to addressing the big questions of theology on the background of modern and postmodern thought, it seems important not to be restricted by rigid and inflexible dogmatic systems but to use the full potential of theology, which is in its deepest nature inquisitive.

Despite the interdisciplinary approach, this work is situated in and feels committed to Christian theology. It attempts to retell Satan's story through literature, not to explain or justify the existence of evil, but to allow the expression of the "Unspeakable" and therefore defeat the "deathly wordlessness" of pain and suffering. But logos had never been able to provide human beings with the sense of significance that they seem to require. It had been myth that had given structure and meaning to life, yet as modernization progressed and logos achieved such spectacular results, mythology was increasingly discredited.[30] In a study concerned with the relation between literature and theology, the introduction of the philosophical terms of μύθος and λόγος appears supportive of the discussion. Both terms come from Greek philosophy and have been transported into the world of Christian religion and narrative. The words have been interpreted in different ways and have been used to characterize opposite or conflicting approaches in religion, literature, and science. This investigation applies them to describe the problems associated with the satanic character in theology. The term μύθος originates from the Indo-European root *mudh* (to think, to reflect) and initially defined thought in the sense of the content of a speech or conversation. In early Greek philosophy, the term referred to a story or narrative. During the period of Attic Greek, the term μύθος was used to describe stories about gods. Only with Aristotle did the term μύθος become equivalent to fiction: for Aristotle, μύθος is imitation. The term λόγος was introduced into Western philosophy around 540 BCE by Heraclitus, referring in his usage to the basic concepts of all things. In the philosophy of Socrates, Plato, and Aristotle, the term λόγος described the ability of human beings to use their reason and the knowledge of the world. Christian theology develops around the idea of the λόγος. It follows the logos theology that has been defined in the first councils of the church, which has its foundation in the prologue of the Gospel of John.[31]

---

30. Armstrong, *A Short History of Myth*, 122.

31. "Christianity must always remember that it is the religion of the Logos. It is faith in the 'Creator Spiritus', in the Creator Spirit, from which proceeds everything that exists. Today, this should be precisely its philosophical strength, in so far as the problem

Setting the Stage

It was not until Plato and Aristotle that the definitions of μῦθος and λόγος were separated. Until then both had been used in a complementary fashion:

> There was, therefore, a contradiction in Western thought. Greek *logos* seemed to oppose mythology, but philosophers continued to use myth, either seeing it as the primitive forerunner of rational thought or regarding it as indispensable to religious discourse.[32]

Christianity, similar to Judaism and Islam, believes in a God who has played an active role in world history. It is due to the uneasy attitude towards myth in the Western world that theologians have tried to make their religions conform to the rational standards of science:

> Western modernity was the child of logos. It was founded on a different economic basis.... The heroes of Western modernity would be technological or scientific geniuses of logos, not the spiritual geniuses inspired by mythos.... Unlike myth, logos must correspond to facts; it is essentially practical; it is the mode of thought we use when we want to get something done; it constantly looks ahead to achieve a greater control over our environment or to discover something fresh.[33]

The dualism of "myth" and "reason" has been problematic, especially since the nineteenth century, when myth was seen as an obsolete mode of thought. The rational critique of myth begun by the pre-Socratics and furthered by Euhemerus (ca. 300 BCE) was readily accepted by Christians until it came home to roost with the contrast between the mythical Christ and the historical Jesus drawn by theologians in the nineteenth century.[34] In

---

is whether the world comes from the irrational, and reason is not, therefore, other than a 'sub-product', on occasion even harmful of its development or whether the world comes from reason, and is, as a consequence, its criterion and goal. The Christian faith inclines toward this second thesis, thus having, from the purely philosophical point of view, really good cards to play, despite the fact that many today consider only the first thesis as the only modern and rational one par excellence. However, a reason that springs from the irrational, and that is, in the final analysis, itself irrational, does not constitute a solution for our problems. Only creative reason, which in the crucified God is manifested as love, can really show us the way. In the so necessary dialogue between secularists and Catholics, we Christians must be very careful to remain faithful to this fundamental line: to live a faith that comes from the 'Logos', from creative reason, and that, because of this, is also open to all that is truly rational" (Ratzinger, "Cardinal Ratzinger on Europe's Crisis of Culture").

32. Armstrong, *A Short History of Myth*, 102–3.

33. Ibid., 121.

34. Olshewsky, "Between Science and Religion," 244.

the history of Christian theology, it was mainly the work of David Friedrich Strauß in the nineteenth century and then Rudolf Bultmann in the twentieth century that asked for a complete demythologizing of the New Testament and consequently of the Christian faith.[35] Bultmann argued for an existential, i.e., anthropological understanding of the myth instead of a cosmological reading of it.[36]

In postmodern thought, myth has experienced a revival. Many thinkers rejected the opposition of myth and reason or science, arguing that human beings are myth-making creatures, and that myth carries as much truth as empirical or rational science:

> If it is written and read with serious attention, a novel, like a myth or any great work of art, can become an initiation that helps us to make a painful rite of passage from one phase of life, one state of mind, to another. A novel, like a myth, teaches us to see the world differently; it shows us how to look into our own hearts and to see our world from a perspective that goes beyond our own self-interest. If professional religious leaders cannot instruct us in mythical lore, our artists and creative writers can perhaps step into this priestly role and bring fresh insight to our lost and damaged world.[37]

Generally, it is acknowledged that the study of religion should not be an entirely rational exercise, as it concerns the study of "experiences that are obscure and ineffable, because they are beyond speech, and relate to the inner rather than the external word."[38]

Satan is a mythical figure: Almost all characterizations of him do not come from biblical sources, but from ancient, pre-medieval, and medieval mythology.[39] Satan's birthplace is shrouded in myth; his material form has been created through narrative and story. Could we then argue that Jesus

---

35. See Strauß, *Das Leben Jesu*, and Bultmann, "Neues Testament und Mythologie," 15–48.

36. "The actual sense of the mythos is not to give an objective worldview, but it is an expression of how man understands himself in his world. The mythos needs to be interpreted not cosmologically, but anthropologically or better existentially." Own translation of "Der eigentliche Sinn des Mythos ist nicht der, ein objektives Weltbild zu geben; vielmehr spricht sich in ihm aus, wie sich der Mensch selbst in seiner Welt versteht; der Mythos will nicht kosmologisch, sondern anthropologisch—besser: existential interpretiert werden" (Bultmann, "Neues Testament und Mythologie," 22).

37. Armstrong, *A Short History of Myth*, 149

38. Ibid., 109. In Greek Orthodox Christianity, theology was only valid if pursued together with prayer and liturgy.

39. Cf. Part One, chapter 2.

Christ is λόγος and Satan is μῦθος? One claims the authority of a canon of Scripture and the other is the creation of human imagination? The cosmological fight in Revelation 19–20 could suggest this; the vision describes the faithful and true rider on a white horse, whose name is Word of God and he defeats the Beast, traditionally associated with Satan, and throws it into the lake of fire. However, the answer is not as straightforward as that, since this division can only work in an already existing concept of thought and the rider in the vision is also part of the myth. For many, the story of Jesus Christ is as much myth as the existence of Satan. However, the hesitation and difficulties Christian theologians have in approaching the subject of Satan outside the language of myth shows how little the figure of Satan has to do with any rational model of thought or belief. This study highlights how difficult it has been for Christian theology to incorporate Satan into a systematic concept of faith. Like any mythical figure, Satan develops his greatest power *in the story*, and not in interpretation. His power lies in the symbolism of myth and the retelling of it. Humans are myth-making creatures and Satan is a powerful myth, conveying a great deal about the nature of evil in the context of the individual and the community. The Satanic myth is retold because it carries some truth about the reality of evil that is most effectively expressed in narrative.

Part One

The Dwelling Place of Satan

one

Is Satan Evil?

Understanding Satan as a character requires the introduction of a *context* in which the character operates. Our search for Satan's dwelling place takes us to different areas of definition and interpretation, but the most fundamental question at this point is the relationship between Satan and evil. The question of whether the character of Satan is evil or not cannot be answered readily, since the problem is twofold: like any character, Satan has many layers and describing him as evil is an over-simplification. At the same time, the abstract concept of evil depends on contextual circumstances. The best approach seems the one applied to the description of God in the methodology of *via negativa:* Evil is the absence of Good, the absence of relation, the absence of personhood. Still, Satan is traditionally associated with evil; in fact, Satan is commonly mentioned in the context of the origin of sin, he is described as evil incarnate, and as the facilitator of evil acts. And his attraction as a character lies in his dark nature. As a character, Satan mostly has human features; he functions as an anthropomorphization of evil. It also seems as if the abstract concept of evil finds one form of expression through some attributes that we observe in the character of Satan. In particular the observation that evil generally has a face—we encounter it through persons and in relationships. The following provides an overview of the problem of evil in relation to the character of Satan, trying to identify what factors underlie our understanding of him.

Part One: The Dwelling Place of Satan

The Dilemma

Evil is an existential reality of human life. The definitions of evil depend on their context: moral, social, theological, psychological, or legal. Most definitions, however, would agree that evil is anything that causes suffering, pain, and destruction and that is usually connected with wrongdoing and overstepping boundaries. Evil can be the violation of a society's rule of conduct (morality), but it can also be understood as the violation of a universal principle, beyond social customs. The phenomenon of evil is universal and ubiquitous in its experience, although the term is generally used in the context of religion, (social) philosophy, and ethical debates. The questions of what constitutes evil and why it exists are two of the big questions of humanity and are approached repeatedly because of the impossibility of answering them satisfactorily.

Since the rise of the social sciences—psychology, sociology, and psychoanalysis—the explanation for evil has been increasingly sought in the human psyche or in human relationships and social realities, turning away from metaphysical causes for evil. It was Immanuel Kant who marked a paradigm shift in the discussion around evil that influenced all further discussions on that topic. His work determined a shift in the history of ideas from ontology to ontic, from metaphysics to phenomenology. His philosophy of reason initiated a philosophical movement that turned towards the rational understanding of the world and put the human mind and its ability to think and understand in the center of every model of thought. Kant's ideas have to be seen in the context of the development of the natural sciences in the late eighteenth and the nineteenth century: the success of the physical sciences called attention to their method and "new" sciences like psychology and sociology, but also the traditional sciences such as philosophy and theology, had to prove their legitimacy by defining their methods. Evil, however, was for Kant beyond pure reason; it was, like the existence of God, something that cannot be known. He did not abandon the metaphysical argument completely; for Kant, the existence of transcendence was not questionable, since it was beyond the influence of human reason. Kant's thoughts on evil were influential for the contemporary debate in several aspects: Kant understood evil as an immanent problem and focused therefore on the question of evil as a *moral* problem instead of a transcendent and metaphysical issue. He also located the source of evil in the *human will*, defining the term positively, and not merely as a privation of good. For him, evil is a real possibility. In that context, Kant emphasized the role of the subjectivity and the power of the individual's will.[1]

---

1. Cf. Hoeffe, "Ein Thema wiedergewinnen," 11–34, and Sasso, "The Fragmented

German idealist Georg Friedrich Hegel developed Kant's thoughts further and contributed to the development of the modern understanding of the self and the idea that expression is inseparable from being. Hegel was the first to give a secular formulation of the problem of evil. He distinguished three forms of evil: natural evil, moral evil, and metaphysical evil. He related the universal aspect of human life with its social and historical phenomena to the progress of human spirit in history. For him, passions, private interests, and the satisfaction of selfish impulses are the most potent force in people. The Hegelian idea of progress in history is reflected in the *developmental* aspect towards life: Hegel sees in the narrative of the fall more than a myth; he understands it as the awakening of human consciousness from a purely animal-like state. Evil is part of God's creation and the contradiction between good and evil is the driving force of all movement and development. The pain of the fall is necessary for the birth of humanity. In theological words, we could refer to it as the *felix culpa*, the fortunate fall—an expression used by Augustine and still present today in the Exsultet in the liturgy of the Easter Vigil. Hegel states that "The hour when man leaves the path of mere natural being marks the difference between him, a self-conscious agent, and the natural world."[2]

This is a more developmental and teleological attempt to understand evil: humankind is in process of becoming the perfect beings God intended us to be, and not the fallen creatures of sin. John Hick refers to it as the Irenaean type of theodicy, going back to the theology of St Irenaeus of Lyon, who set out a theology that would be distinguished from that of the Latin fathers as the Greek theodicy and formed the groundwork for a Christian alternative to the Augustinian concept.[3] There is not, however, a distinct Eastern Orthodox theodicy compared to a Western theodicy, influenced by Augustine. The Irenaean theodicy forms a framework for later theologians who could not agree with the Augustinian definition of the fall. Irenaeus understands human beings as immature and imperfect beings that need to undergo development in order to reach the state that the creator has intended for them. This is both an individual and a communal development, that is, both human beings and humankind undergo the process of development. Irenaeus regarded Paul's teaching as authoritative and therefore accepted the concept of the fall of humankind and the Pauline interpretation of Genesis that it was through Adam that sin entered the world. For him, however, the fall was not the one event that corrupted God's

---

Will," 2

2. Hegel, *Logic*, §24 addition.

3. Hick, *Evil and the God of Love*, 372.

plan with humankind, but more the expression of the weakness and immaturity of humanity, possibly even necessary for the future development of humankind towards maturity and understanding. Humanity was created as personal beings in the image of God, but more as "working material" than as "end products." That also means that creation is not complete, but is still developing. The experience of evil in the world then can be interpreted as necessary for the process of that development: evil is inevitable, because it will make human beings the perfect creatures that God intended them to be. The world we experience is therefore a place of soul making.

Friedrich Schleiermacher created a similar approach to the question of evil. He saw humankind in the process of acquiring God-consciousness in the environment of the creation. Ultimately, evil and sin serve God's purpose.

The Irenaean theodicy is attractive for modern thinkers, since it avoids question of predestination and the dilemma of God creating free beings who turn away from him and therefore face damnation. The Irenaean theodicy also has a stronger emphasis on the personal relationship between creator and creature.

The problem we face with an Irenaean (i.e., teleological) approach to the existence of evil is the question of how to see the "greater good" in the very reality of pain and suffering. Generally, evil is experienced as something alien, as something that threatens human coexistence from outside. Evil has regularly been associated with an external force responsible for evil actions. But equally, there has always been an awareness of the inherent human ability to act contrary to what seems good and right. Evil is always connected with an ethical judgement. In philosophical terms, these two approaches can be characterized as the metaphysical and the ethical approach to the question of evil. Today we recognize a difference between *existential evil* (such as illness, natural disasters, and accidents) and *human or personal evil*. Most people in the modern Western world would not even attribute the adjective "evil" to natural disasters or accidents, but would rather speak of catastrophes, tragedies, or epidemics. But until the dawn of the modern world the assumption that moral and natural evils are causally linked had not been challenged for centuries and stands in the tradition of the concept of original sin. The fall has historically been considered as an explanation of why human life and our world is not what it should be. The relationship between sin and suffering was regarded as causal; natural evils were regarded as punishment for the sinful actions of the human species. With the Enlightenment and the rise of empirical sciences, natural disasters and illnesses were not associated with sin anymore, but could be explained with natural laws and medicine. Generally, we do not ask anymore why the earthquake, the tsunami, or cholera epidemic happened, but instead we ask how we can prevent it from happening again and how we can ensure that we have the appropriate measures to limit the damage by securing buildings and providing good infrastructures, warning systems, and vaccinations. Evil in our understanding is the willful act of destruction of the self or the other.

Whenever we use the term "evil" to describe a deed or a person, it is usually because we cannot understand the motives behind someone's action. The transgression of the boundaries of a society or humanity in general is considered evil. I want to argue here that the best way, if not the only way, to deal with the existence of evil in our world is *to approach it through its expressions, not through its being*. We encounter the limits of an ontological definition of evil in the very fact that we struggle to define what we mean by saying someone is evil. We may describe their actions as evil, but referring to a human being as evil usually involves a certain inability to understand their actions. Any ontological approach to the question entails a reference to a metaphysical existence or at least to a framework of definitions that lies outside the human realm of ethical decisions. Etymologically, the word "evil" is related to the German word *übel*; both are considered to come from a Proto-German and Proto-Indo-European root, related to the modern English word "over" and modern German *über*, expressing the idea of transgression.[4] In that context, Satan would certainly qualify as evil: transgression is his nature—he challenges, oversteps boundaries, tempts, misleads.

When the world is not the way it should be, we begin to ask why:

> Behind the principle of sufficient reason itself is the assumption that the *is* and the *ought* should coincide.... Metaphysics is the drive to make very general sense of the world in face of the fact that things go intolerably wrong.... The urge to unite *is* and *ought* stands behind every creative endeavour.[5]

If we try to approach the problem of evil, we find ourselves faced with two different problems: There is the issue of the existence of evil in the world and there is our problem of dealing with the issue.

The traditional theological concept is metaphysical and has, since Gottfried Leibniz,[6] been connected with the term *theodicy*. The main point of any theodical discussion is to find reasons why a just, loving, and omnipotent being would allow suffering and pain. Theodicy is the systematic

---

4. Onions, *The Oxford Dictionary of English Etymology*.
5. Neiman, *Evil in Modern Thought*, 322.
6. Leibniz, *Die Theodicee*.

Part One: The Dwelling Place of Satan

attempt to understand suffering in the presence of a good God. While Leibniz is responsible for the terminology, the problem itself goes back to the scriptural roots of this theological thought system: the speeches of Job's friends in the book of Job are the oldest account for theodicy in the Bible. Eliphaz, Bildad, and Zophar try to find justification for Job's suffering by arguing that Job must have sinned in order to deserve divine punishment. God's reaction condemns the attempt to justify the suffering and makes clear that the causal connection between human sin and divine punishment is not the truth: "My wrath is kindled against you and against your two friends; for you have not spoken of me what is right, as my servant Job has."[7] But what is the truth that Job has spoken? It is not a justification of his suffering or a systematic approach to it, but rather lament and accusation. It is the reaction of a human being towards suffering, a way of dealing with it without giving in to despair. This is probably the most basic reason for any theodicy—the need to challenge suffering, deal with the existence of evil, and not to give up despite the fact that not one explanation so far has been satisfying. The question of why there is evil rather than good becomes more pressing in a theistic worldview, since it challenges the motives of the deity, but the question of why evil exists is not solely theological. It is the realization that the world is not the way it should be, and the continuous process of asking why, even though the answers may never be found and we may never be able to understand the motive behind evil. Even then, we must still ask why God permits it.

Whether we discuss the problem of evil in theological or secular terms, the fundamental issue stays the same—the intelligibility of the world as a whole,[8] as Susan Neiman puts it. According to her, it is precisely this attempt to understand that characterizes humanity:

> If you cannot understand why children are tortured, nothing else you understand really matters. But the very attempt to understand it, requires at least accepting it as part of the world that must be investigated. . . . To abandon the attempt to comprehend evil is to abandon every basis for confronting it, in thought as in practice. The thinkers who returned to the problem of evil while knowing the limits of any discussion of it were driven by moral demands. For creatures endowed with reason, love of the world cannot be blind. The intellectual struggle is more important than any particular results that emerge from it.[9]

---

7. Job 42:7.
8. Neiman, *Evil in Modern Thought*, 7–8.
9. Ibid., 324.

For this purpose, the context for our discussion will be that of Christian theology. The problem of evil does not apply to any concept of deity. The issue is more problematic in academic terms for a religion that worships a deity who is equally good and almighty. This is the case for Christianity, which has followed the monotheism of its Jewish roots and generally attributes infinite goodness and omnipotence to God.[10]

The issue has been brought into focus by the Scottish Enlightenment philosopher David Hume in his work *Dialogues concerning Natural Religion* (1779). Hume refers to the dilemma that was supposedly first formulated by Epicurus (341–270 BCE) and was quoted by Lactantius:

> Epicurus' old questions are yet unanswered. Is he willing to prevent evil, but not able? Then is he impotent. Is he able, but not willing? Then is he malevolent. Is he both able and willing? Whence then is evil?[11]

In Christian theology, the figure of Satan has been introduced to solve this contradiction. He has taken on the role of a scapegoat; he is the one who bridges the gap between God's omnipotence and benevolence and the experience of pain in the world.[12]

To return to the story of Job, it is Satan who inflicts Job with unspeakable pain and suffering as a result of a wager with God. But where are the limits of his powers? Is it not a wager with God that stands behind Job's suffering? And is Satan not restricted by God's command to spare Job's life? Satan cannot be the explanation of why evil exists, and after taking a closer look, he also is not evil personified. His character, however, allows us to investigate the phenomenon of evil by putting it in the context of narrative and myth.

Who Takes the Blame?

The perception of Satan as God's adversary, in the sense of being his equal but opposite, comes from a dualist worldview. Christian theology rejects dualism and therefore the existence of two independent principles or substances. Satan, however, has secured himself a role in Christian

---

10. There have always been streams of thoughts in the history of Christian theology that tried to offer different solutions to the problem, such as the dualism of the Manichees or the Albigenses, but mainstream Christian theology acknowledges God as the all-good and all-powerful being and is therefore confronted with the reality of evil.

11. Hume, *Dialogues concerning Natural Religion*, Part X.

12. We will later see that this attempt has only been partially successful and immediately raises new questions about the extent of God's power over Satan.

theology, avoiding clear positioning in the system. Our world is either an ultimately harmonious unity and evil is eventually part of the greater good, or it is determined by the irreconcilable realities of good and evil. Neither of the two thought models is essentially compatible with Christian theology, but elements of both are found in Christian thought. John Hick picked up on that problem with the title of his standard work *Evil and the God of Love*.[13] We will see later how this dilemma of bringing together a benevolent God and the experience of evil in the world has become most prevalent after the European Enlightenment and the rise of modern Western thought. But most theologians in all traditions have had to deal with the existence of evil in some way, and Hick's work identifies the main attempts to explain the existence of evil in the world in the Christian tradition. The ultimate monotheism of Christianity suggests a monistic approach to reality: if God alone is powerful and good then there is no possibility for any rival or contrary reality. Evil then can only be seen as existing in God's realm and under the influence of God's will and purpose: "Evil can thus be domesticated within the divine household and seen as a servant instead of a deadly enemy: and then the theodicist finds himself calling evil good and preaching peace where there is no peace."[14]

Against this approach stands not only the human experience of evil as something that challenges the harmony of creation, but also the Christian message through Scripture and revelation that condemns evil and sees it as the enemy of God and humankind. The concept of monism regarding the question of evil does not sufficiently acknowledge the human experience of evil as destructive and painful. John Hick regards Spinoza (1632–77) as the philosopher who expressed monism in Western thought in its purest form. Spinoza, rationalist and determinist, believed in the perfection of reality. The created world is perfect and thus an expression of the eternal and infinite perfection of God or Nature. Good and evil have no reality or meaning of their own; they are only relative concepts and experiences for the individual. Everything happens by absolute necessity and exists in its own right as an expression of the divine perfection. Spinoza's monism is a logical thought construct, something that is impossible to realize in a practical approach to life. The approach cannot justify evil, since it denies its reality: "In showing that the evils that we human beings experience are the illusory products of confused and inadequate ideas Spinoza has not made those evils any less dreadful and oppressive. For they are illusions only in a

---

13. First published in 1968, this work is still a useful overview for this topic.
14. Hick, *Evil and the God of Love*, 16.

highly sophisticated sense.... Pain, cruelty, and grief are still actual experiences, and they still hurt."[15]

Spinoza's philosophy is a radical and logical approach to the idea of monism in Christianity; most other thinkers who support a monistic understanding of the Christian deity acknowledge that sin, pain, and suffering are real and universally conceivable. The idea of evil as privative and negative, or the perception of evil as nothingness, however, is very strong in Christian theology and is ultimately devoted to the idea of monism. It is not surprising that it was Augustine who first formulated the idea of evil as *privatio boni*. He himself was a follower of Manichaeism before his conversion to Christianity and in his theology he critiques the idea of dualism and the existence of two Godheads, responsible for good and evil in the world.

The most extreme dualistic approach to reality suggests the existence of a benevolent and a malevolent deity, both equally powerful and responsible for their respective spheres.[16] Dualism in some form has been a way for other Western thinkers, also more recently, to approach the problem of evil. Generally this approach refers to Plato's philosophy and his attempt to find the responsibility for evil outside the deity:

> He is responsible for a few things that happen to men, but for many he is not, for the good things we enjoy are much fewer than the evil. The former we must attribute to none else but God; but for the evil we must find some other causes, not God.[17]

Plato introduced the idea of the *Demiurge*, the creator of the physical world who forged it from existing chaotic material. The *Demiurge* is benevolent and tried to create the world as good as possible but had to work with the material given, and that is the source of evil:

> Identical with the matter that imprisons us as embodied beings, clogging and weighing down the soul and impeding it in its search for goodness and truth, so that the philosopher must aim so far as possible at a detachment from the body and its distractions.[18]

---

15. Ibid., 23.

16. Followers of Zoroastrianism (after 600 BCE in Persia) believed in two rival Gods: *Ahura Mazda* is the source of good and *Angra Mainyu* responsible for evil. Zoroastrianism equally influenced Western and Eastern religion and is reflected in early Christianity in the teachings of Mani (b. *ca.* 215 CE) and in the twelfth and thirteenth centuries in the beliefs of the Albigenses or Cathars in the south of France.

17. Plato, *Republic*, 379 C, quoted in Hick, *Evil and the God of Love*, 26.

18. Hick, *Evil and the God of Love*, 27. This idea has strongly influenced Neoplatonism and Gnosticism.

Part One: The Dwelling Place of Satan

Plato's idea has influenced dualistic attempts among Western thinkers who promote the idea of a single, good God whose sovereignty is limited by the matter and therefore the "material" he is working with. Evil therefore would be a consequence of the matter, the energy, or the laws of nature that God has no influence over. The idea of dualism not only contradicts the Christian concept of a God who is an infinite and eternal creator—a concept deeply rooted in the Bible and the traditions of Christian theology—but it is also "metaphysically unsatisfying."[19] Who stands behind the creator and creation if neither is ultimate and self-existent?

Against this external dualism, some thinkers have suggested an internal dualism that sees the opposition to good within the divine nature itself.[20] The limitations of the deity can lie in the self-limitation of God (either when it comes to doing the logically impossible or to dealing with the free will of his creation) but it can also go beyond this by stating that the source of evil is God himself. This, of course, causes great difficulty by creating a "schizophrenic" God who is partly good and partly evil. It also is no proper alternative to the idea of God in any monistic thought model: God alone is the source of everything, the sole creator and omnipotent, and therefore ultimately the source of all things created—good and evil.

Neither monism nor dualism is a satisfying approach to the problem of evil in Christianity. Simply put, a purely monistic explanation would question God's goodness, while a purely dualistic approach cannot sustain God's omnipotence. But both thought models have influenced debates around evil and have served as landmarks for the discussion. The Christian Satan is not a malevolent deity; despite dualistic tendencies and influences in Christian thought, Satan is a creature and therefore dependent on God for its existence. But the story of his successful promotion from a minor member of the divine court into the "dark lord" shows that he was a welcome figure in the development of the early church and its attempts to create a coherent theology around the belief in the *one* God.

---

19. Hick, *Evil and the God of Love*, 29.

20. This is the case for example in *Process Theology*, following A. N. Whitehead and E. S. Brightman.

two

Satan's Biography

The Origins of the Satanic Narrative

There is no one "biography" of Satan. There is no authoritative body of text we can refer to when we speak of Satan, rather Satan appears like a shape-shifter, and every story gives him another face and body, deploying the old stereotypes, but adding new elements at the same time, creating a curious mixture of familiarity and strangeness. The story that is retold here is the story of the Satan who grew out of various Jewish and Christian traditions, a Satan whose origins were inspired by the ancient near Eastern combat myths.[1] The most recent biography of Satan was published by Henry Ansgar Kelly in 2006. His main objective is to set straight which part of the Christian image of Satan is based in the Bible and which part is not. With his detailed account, Kelly seeks to present "a challenge to those who believe that the Bible demands belief in the existence of Satan."[2] He talks about a master narrative that was created around the satanic motifs that appeared in the individual books of the Bible. Even if this is not a work of biblical exegesis, it is, however, vital to take into consideration the biblical origins of

---

1. "These discussions of Mesopotamian, Canaanite, Egyptian, Persian, and Greek conceptions of underworld gods, divine tricksters, cosmic combats, and realms of the dead provide us with a bird's-eye view of the world that surrounded biblical Israel. We cannot draw straight lines between these foreign gods and ideas and Jewish and Christian ideas about Satan, Sheol, Gehenna, and hell. However, we can infer that these foreign ideas were in the air that biblical writers and Jewish and Christian apocalypticists breathed" (Wray and Mobley, *The Birth of Satan*, 90).

2. Kelly, *Satan*, 5.

Satan in order to understand how the master narrative is formed and how it has influenced all the other accounts of Satan in literature.

It was not until post-biblical times that the story of Satan was constructed:

> The most significant retro-fitting that has occurred in the history of Satan is the thoroughgoing re-interpretation of the Satan of the New Testament, identified with the various satanic figures of the Old Testament, as a rebel against God. More than any other, this interpretation has bedevilled the history of Satan, transforming him from a merely obnoxious functionary of the Divine Government into a personification of Evil—a personification that really exists as a person.[3]

As we will see in the following, Satan is born within and reliant upon narrative. One might argue that the search for biblical origins does not help in understanding a complex figure such as Satan or its narrative, but it makes one thing very clear: the image that was formed of Satan was inspired by the biblical sources, but it quickly developed its own life. Influenced by apocryphal works, cultural impacts and myths, theological and philosophical considerations, and the need to systemize, the image of Satan very quickly developed its own dynamic:

> Belief in a demonic being called Satan evolved only over a long period of time. Several factors influenced this development, including the religious syncretism of the ancient Near East, the foreign domination of Palestine, the increased reflection about the origins of evil on behalf of Jews in the Second Temple period (548 BCE–70 CE), and Jewish apocalyptic thinking.[4]

Biblical Sources

The Old Testament

The biblical story of Satan starts in Genesis, but as illustrated, it was only post-biblical narratives that equated the serpent in the Garden of Eden with Satan. The Old Testament does not identify Satan as an evil cosmic being, rather the name Satan comes from the Hebrew word שטן or השטן meaning "accuser" or "slanderer." In the Old Testament, the name is used in different

---

3. Ibid., 2.
4. Wray and Mobley, *The Birth of Satan*, 114.

Satan's Biography

contexts: it can be used to identify a worldly opponent, like the satans of 1–2 Samuel and 1 Kings, or as a supernatural Satan, as in Job, Numbers, or in the trial of Joshua the High Priest in the book of Zechariah. If used with a definite article (*Hasatan*), the title usually refers to the role of an accuser or an adversary. "Satan" by itself can either refer to "an adversary" or stand as a proper name. This distinction is important in the later translations into Greek and Latin. The Old Testament does not know one but several satans and they appear to serve different functions. They appear as terrestrial and celestial agents who oppose, test, or punish people. The Hebrew word *satan* is used in the Old Testament to refer to various human opponents: in Psalm 109, a person complains against accusers and expresses hope that the Lord will punish those who function as satans against them. The word *satan* appears again in the first book of Kings in the context of the adversary who is raised against Solomon (1 Kgs 11:14), and as an attribute to David, given to him by the Philistines (2 Sam 29:4). It is clear that in this context the word *satan* refers to a human opponent or antagonist.

There are four passages (all postexilic, circa sixth century BCE) where Satan appears as a superhuman being, and in all these incidences the word Satan designates a *role* rather than acting as a proper name. The first Satan in the Old Testament appears in Numbers 22:21–35, but he is not identified by his name, more by his action: the prophet Balaam sets out with the Moabites to see Balak, the King of Moab, who is at war with the Israelites. Even though God had agreed to Balaam's journey, he later changes his mind, and sends his angel to *oppose* Balaam "as his adversary" (Heb. *lesatan*).[5] But Balaam cannot see him, only his donkey realizes the obstacle and stops in the middle of the way. Balaam beats the animal several times until it opens its mouth to tell him of the angel of the Lord who stands in the way of the prophet. There is no evil motivation in that opposition: the journey Balaam chose is against the will of God, and the Angel of the Lord (*mal'ak YHWH*) is simply doing God's will by posing as an obstruction to him. Kelly sees in the story of Balaam and his donkey more than a—admittedly—humorous story: "This is a momentous occasion. God has opposed the actions of Men before this, but now, for the first time, He, or His Angelic manifestation, is characterized as an adversary, a satan."[6]

The angel of the Lord, who fulfills the role of an opponent in Balaam's story, appears elsewhere in the function of a divine messenger or herald. Forsyth notes that in some Old Testament passages, the *mal'ak YHWH* is

---

5. This contradiction is usually explained by textual critics with different authors of the two passages.

6. Kelly, *Satan*, 16.

simply an aspect of God himself, "it is what appears to Moses in the burning bush before Yahweh himself takes over two verses later. It also appears as the pillar of fire and cloud that gives darkness to the Egyptians but light to the camp of Israel."[7] Generally, the *mal'ak YHWH*—translated as *angelos* in the Septuagint—is a separate entity exercising God's will. Occasionally in the Old Testament, God himself has to stop the angel's action, like in 2 Samuel 24:16 where the angel is in the process of stretching out his arm against Jerusalem when God stops him. We see here how there is a possible conflict between the Lord and his powerful executioner.

The prologue of the book of Job identifies the Satan as a member of the court of heaven. His function seems to be that of a tester: he advises God to test Job's devotion to him by inflicting misfortunes on him. The book of Job originates from the sixth century BCE; most scholars situate it in the time of the Babylonian exile.[8] The prose prologue was probably added later, and puts the story of the suffering righteous man in a different context: we encounter Satan as tester and God as the one who allows him to harm a man who is truthful to his Lord. The book of Job suggests that celestial beings or angels can perform different functions at YHWH's court, including "singers and applauders, guardians, observers, testers, and even agents of entrapment."[9] The Satan in the book of Job is not God's opponent but is part of his court, walking up and down the earth and observing certain individuals. As a member of God's court he fulfills the task of testing Job's faith and does not appear as God's antagonist, but as his subordinate who can only act with his consent. It is not so much the figure of Satan that seems problematic, but more God's role as a facilitator in allowing Job to be tested. Satan is nothing more than God's agent. The figure of Satan in the book of Job was possibly inspired by the official inspector and informer employed by the central authorities of the time.[10] The Satan of the book of Job is probably the most interesting and well-known satanic character of the Old Testament, and the wager between God and the Satan and his status as one who "roams the earth" have become popular motifs in art and literature.[11]

The next time we encounter Satan as a supernatural being is in the visions of the prophet Zechariah: the prophet sees the High Priest Joshua

---

7. Forsyth, *The Old Enemy*, 111.

8. Habel, *The Book of Job*; Hooks, *Job*; Dell, "Job," *Eerdmans Bible Commentary*.

9. Kelly, *Satan*, 23.

10. Ibid., 26.

11. The prologue of Job inspired Goethe's "Prolog im Himmel" between God and Mephisto in *Faust*. The idea of Satan as a wanderer will be explored more in the discussion of Stefan Heym's novel *The Wandering Jew*.

standing in the court of justice, at his right side stands Satan in the role of an accuser, but before he can fulfill his task, he is interrupted:

> May Yahweh rebuke you, O satan! May Yahweh who has made Jerusalem His own rebuke you! Is not this man a brand snatched from the fire?[12]

As in the book of Job, the Satan of Zechariah appears as part of the divine court, in the function of the "eye of the king: they are on the look-out for both good and bad behavior and they report everything back to Divine headquarters."[13]

The following passage is interesting, since Satan fulfills the role that in an earlier account of the same narrative was attributed to God: in 2 Samuel 24 it is *God* himself who incites David to take census, while in 2 Chronicles 21 *Satan* provokes David's transgression. The first version of the story makes God responsible not only for David's sin, but also for the punishment. The Chronicler, who retells the story of Israel, puts different emphasis on the characterization of David; he is portrayed less as a political leader, but more as the administrator who establishes Israel as a worshipping community with Jerusalem as its religious center.[14] In that context, the story of David's sin is rewritten and it is Satan, not God, who incites David to take census. This change of protagonists protects God from blame and makes the punishment more just:

> For the first time, we find in the Chronicler a Satan who acts independently of divine permission. In this simpleminded theodicy, Satan substitutes for God as the agent provocateur in human affairs, indeed, he ceases to be an agent of God at all and acts on his own initiative.[15]

Biblical scholars commonly link the birth of Satan with the Persian influence on the Hebrews after the Babylonian Exile in the sixth century BCE. The dualism of Zoroastrianism is believed to have influenced the Jewish faith system and therefore contributed to the rise of Satan as opponent and adversary to God. The Scriptures of the Old Testament, however, recognize Satan as one of many supernatural beings in the divine realm whose tasks are exercising God's will, including observing, testing, and punishing human beings. If we assume that the Zoroastrian system had started to

---

12. Zech 3:1–2.
13. Kelly, *Satan*, 28.
14. Forsyth, *The Old Enemy*, 119.
15. Ibid., 121.

Part One: The Dwelling Place of Satan

influence Jewish belief during the time of the Old Testament Scriptures, the analogies are slight:

> The best argument against a strong Persian influence is the fact that the developing Satan concept has not yet been linked with combat mythology.... Rather, the name of Satan for a supernatural being developed originally within Canaanite-Jewish conception of the heavenly court and is linked exclusively to the legal and judiciary proceedings of that court.[16]

We have seen that in the Old Testament, Satan does not appear as a distinctive demonic figure, opposed to God and responsible for all evil. Hebrew monotheism was too strong to allow the existence of a powerful supernatural being in opposition to God. Everything exists in and through God, and good and evil are both expressions of the one God. A rational approach to suffering and the question of why God allows evil have not yet come into the focus of attention, but rather suffering is accepted as part of God's plan for humankind.

The text mentions supernatural beings, connected to God either as members of his divine court, his messengers or executioners, accusers or tempters, or even God's self-expression. Commonly, these beings are referred in translation and interpretation as "angels":

> Job Description of Official Satans: Patrol of the Earth, observe Human behaviour, test ostensible virtue by various means. Be prepared, upon consultation with High Command, to instigate preventative or punitive measures against sinful actions. Function as accusers in tribunal, and announce verdicts against culprits.[17]

It is the function of the stumbling block for humans that was taken up and developed further into the role of an adversary, not only to humankind but eventually also to God.

The Apocryphical Works and Qumran

Most biblical examinations of Satan refer to the apocryphal works to explain the birth of the Christian Satan. Those not included in the biblical canon do indeed give us some clues on the development of the satanic character and the history of textual interpretation; the figure of Satan emerged

---

16. Ibid., 123.
17. Kelly, *Satan*, 28.

Satan's Biography

as a conglomerate of canonical and non-canonical references. According to most biblical scholars in recent times, the library of Qumran gives us evidence of what books were regarded as authoritative reading in Jerusalem around the beginning of the Christian era. The book of Enoch and the book of Jubilees were revered at almost the same level as the Torah[18] and are therefore likely to have influenced the early Christian image of Satan.

As an inter-testamental work, the book of Enoch was written after the completion of the Old Testament Scriptures and before New Testament times, with the majority of the book probably composed in the early second century BCE. The book is pseudonymous work, the author claims to be Enoch, the descendant of Adam and Eve mentioned in Genesis 5:24. The storyline is based on the lustful sons of God of Genesis 6:1–4. In the book of Enoch, the sons of God are known as Watchers, who abandon their duties of supervision over the earth by lusting after human women and mating with them, begetting the Giants. The Watchers are bound in the valleys of the earth till judgment day as a consequence for their actions. The first leader of the Watchers is Semyaz, but on earth the main corruptor of humans is Azazel. God puts the Watchers into dark caves to await final judgment at the end of times, but the ghosts of the Giants survive and keep troubling humankind.[19] The banishment of the Watchers is the only mentioned fall of angels. Early Christian writers identified the fallen morning star or "Lucifer" from Isaiah 14 with Satan, referring to the legend of the fallen watchers: Tertullian (*Contra Marcionem*, v. 11, 17), Origen (*Homilies on Ezekiel* 13), and others, identify Lucifer as Satan, who also is interpreted as being "cast down from heaven."[20]

Composed around 150 BCE, the book of Jubilees is a commentary on, or a rewriting of, Genesis and parts of Exodus. It is presented as a revelation to Moses; God orders an angel to preserve the revelation in writing. In the book of Jubilees, God follows Noah's request and orders the Angels of the Presence to bind the Ghost-Spirits. The interesting figure in the book of Jubilee is Mastema, the chief of spirits. He is not the chief of the Giant-Ghosts, but he has been put in charge of them. His purpose is given to him by God and is clearly punitive and directed against humankind. The punishment: he makes humans wicked by enticing them to commit more sins. He begs God to leave some of the Ghost-Spirits before him, so that he will be able to exercise his authority over the children of men.[21] The Angels of

18. Ibid., 42, referring to Eugene Ulrich's study "Our Sharper Focus on the Bible and Theology."

19. *1 En.* 6–16.

20. Rev 12:7–10; cf. Luke 10:18. See also discussion in Part One, chapter 2.

21. *Jub.* 10:8.

Part One: The Dwelling Place of Satan

Presence bind most of the Spirits in the Place of Judgement, but they leave a tenth of them, "so that they might be subject to Satan upon the Earth."[22] Mastema functions as a pseudonym for Satan—meaning "animosity." Mastema also appears in the re-telling of the *Akedah*: in Genesis, it is God who tests Abraham; in the book of Jubilees, it is Mastema who instigates the temptation and who has a similar role to the Satan in Job. Mastema appears again in the Jubilees version of Exodus, where he assists the Pharaoh in the pursuit of the Israelites: "During the process of rescuing the Israelites from Egypt, the Angels of the Presence periodically restrain Mastema from accusing the Israelites."[23] The book of Jubilees serves as dramatization and development of God's satanic minister: Mastema is in charge of disciplining and testing humanity, exercising powers that could bring him into conflict with God's will to preserve life.[24]

Written generally between 150 BCE and 70 CE and discovered between 1947 and 1956, the Dead Sea Scrolls of Qumran show, in relation to the satanic figure, the first emphasis on dualistic imagery,[25] influenced by Zoroastrian ideas. Recent research has shown, however, that the incidence of dualistic texts within the Qumran library is comparatively minor, with the word *satan* appearing in the Qumran texts only in fragments, and then on only two or three occasions. The most quoted passage for our purpose is the *Instruction on the Two Spirits*.[26] Here, the Prince of Light is opposed to the Prince of Darkness; however, the text does not suggest the existence of an independent Satan:

> It is allowable to look down on Darkness personified, as long as we remember that darkness itself is a part of God's creation. . . . However, even if one were to conclude that the Prince of Light engages in battle with the Prince of Dark, it would not necessarily mean that they are anything other than abstract personifications.[27]

---

22. *Jub.* 10:9–11.

23. Kelly, *Satan*, 39.

24. Ibid., 40.

25. On the origin of evil spirits and dualism in relevant Qumran fragments, see Archie T. Wright, *The Origin of Evil Spirits*.

26. For a discussion of the dualistic thought in the Qumran library, please see Kelly, *Satan*, 44–46.

27. Ibid., 48–49.

Typical for the belief of the Qumran community is the contrast between God and Belial,[28] but the War Scroll states clearly that Belial is a creation of God and therefore no independent personification of darkness:

> The upshot of our tour of the Wadi Qumran, on the shores of the Dead Sea, is that, apart from imported texts like the Book of Job and the Book of Jubilees, there are no active ensoulments of bad behavior. Belial and the Prince of Darkness are passive. They do not seem to be celestial testers or prosecutors or persecutors working under the direction or observation of God. Rather, we see only soulless allegorical or metaphorical figures that go about their single-minded business and then disappear. In other words, there is no Satan here.[29]

The New Testament

Compared to the books of the Old Testament, the New Testament mentions Satan (ὁ διάβολος, the devil, in the Septuagint) more frequently. There are over thirty direct references to the devil, not including other names referring to Satan such as Tempter (Matt 4:5 and 1 Thess 3:5), Beelzebub (Matt 12:24), Enemy (Matt 13:39), Evil One (Matt 13:19, 38; 1 John 2:13–14; 3:12; and particularly 1 John 5:18), Belial (2 Cor 6:15), Adversary (*antidikos*, in 1 Pet 5:8), Deceiver (Rev 12:9), (Great) Dragon (Rev 12:3), Father of Lies (John 8:44), Murderer (John 8:44), and Sinner (1 John 3:8).[30] The diabology and demonology of the New Testament are influenced by Hellenistic Judaism, and the names that describe Satan in the New Testament reflect the influences of both Hellenism and Apocalyptic Judaism on the Scriptures.[31] Jesus performed exorcisms on people who were said to be possessed by demons and he was tempted by Satan in the desert. For him and his followers, demonic possession was a reality. The various accounts of Jesus casting out demons put the communal and social aspects of evil into context:

> Jesus is identifying illnesses, including those caused by Demons, as part of the testing that Satan puts men and women through,

---

28. Von der Osten-Sacken, *Gott und Belial*.
29. Kelly, *Satan*, 50.
30. For discussion on the various terms related to Satan, please see Van der Toorn et al., *Dictionary of Demons and Deities in the Bible*.
31. Russell, *The Devil*, 228.

and the miraculous curing of the sick in the name of Jesus signifies Satan's loss of control.[32]

Since the writings of the New Testament were composed by different authors and in different contexts, there is again no homogenous picture of Satan. However, he still finds here the substance he needs in order to fully appear in post-biblical times. We do have to acknowledge the difficulty in reading the New Testament sources without having the image of Satan that has been developed in Christian theology and myth after the first century AD in mind. In order to give a short overview of the "satanic verses" in the New Testament, I will follow the line of argument applied by most scholars in this context.

Satan's Appearance in the New Testament

The writings of St. Paul are the oldest of the New Testament. Most modern scholars attribute six or seven of the thirteen letters to him.[33] Paul's writing is a powerful testament of the earliest Christian theology and Satan does not feature profoundly; instead Paul was mostly concerned with circumstances threatening the Christian communities he was addressing in his letters, such as moral misconduct, false apostles and preachers of false doctrine, sinful pride, and discouragement. In the first letter to the Thessalonians, Satan appears as a tester, as in the book of Job. The author writes "We wanted to come to you—certainly I, Paul, wanted to, again and again—but Satan blocked our way" and "For I was afraid that the Tester had somehow put you to the test, and that our labour had been in vain."[34]

In the first letter to the Corinthians, Satan has a penitentiary function. Paul is discussing the issue of a man in the Corinthian church who is having sexual relations with his father's wife or concubine. That letter states: "You are to hand this man over to Satan for the destruction of the flesh, so that his spirit may be saved in the day of the Lord."[35] As Kelly notes, "The action that

---

32. Kelly, *Satan*, 100.

33. Romans, First Corinthians, Second Corinthians, Galatians, Philippians, First Thessalonians, and Philemon are generally accepted as Pauline writings. Ephesians, Colossians, 2 Thessalonians, 1 Timothy, 2 Timothy, and Titus are often considered pseudepigraphs and the Pauline authorship, along with the letter to the Hebrews, which has no author and was only in antiquity ascribed to the apostle, is disputed.

34. 1 Thess 2:18 and 3:5.

35. 1 Cor 5:5

Satan takes involves corporal but not capital punishment, since it is aimed (at least by Paul and his fellow-Christians) at rehabilitation."[36]

Second Corinthians 2:10–11 can be read as a warning of Satan's tactics: "And we do this so that we may not be outwitted by Satan, for we are not ignorant of his designs." This is similar to 2 Corinthians 11:13–15, which is a warning of the false apostles: "Even Satan disguises himself as an angel of light." Kelly writes that "at the very least, we can conclude that Paul is saying that Satan encourages dissension among the followers of Christ, and does so in a devious and dangerous way."[37]

In 2 Corinthians 12:7, the purpose of the angel of Satan is a good one; he is given to Paul to keep him from sinful pride: "to keep me from being too puffed up, a thorn was given to my flesh, an angel of Satan, to batter me, to keep me from being too puffed up."

In Paul's writing, Satan appears mostly as a disciplinarian, tester, or obstructer for the young Christian communities and Paul expresses the hope that "the God of peace will soon crush Satan beneath your feet."[38] This sentence has often been associated with the curse placed on the serpent in the Garden of Eden and in fact, Christians from the early days interpreted it together with Genesis 3:15 as a prophecy that the woman (Mary) and her offspring (Jesus) would defeat the serpent. There is, however, no evidence that at this point in the development of the Christian thought the serpent had been identified as Satan.[39] It is more likely again that Paul referred to Satan as an obstacle or obstacle setter.[40] He also warns against being led astray from devotion to Christ, just as Eve had been deceived by the serpent.[41] We can conclude Paul is saying that Satan encourages dissension among the followers of Christ, and does so in a devious and dangerous way.[42]

Among the Deutero-Pauline epistles, 1–2 Timothy and 2 Thessalonians also refer to Satan as an obstacle or adversary in the search for the true Christian belief. The Epistle to the Ephesians sees the devil in allegiance with the powers of darkness that rule this world.[43] The second Epistle of

---

36. Kelly, *Satan*, 58.

37. Ibid., 62.

38. Rom 16:20.

39. The book of Wisdom is the only possible link between the serpent and Satan: "However, through envy of an adversary, Death entered the World" (Wis 2:24). For a detailed discussion, see Kelly, *Satan*, 69–79.

40. See also Luke 10:18–19: "I have given you authority to tread on snakes and scorpions and over all the power of the Enemy, and nothing will hurt you."

41. 2 Cor 11:3.

42. Kelly, *Satan*, 62.

43. "Finally, be strong in the Lord and in the strength of his might. Put on the whole

Peter and the Epistle of Jude[44] mention a historic fall of angels who failed to do their duties.[45] The Epistle to the Hebrews and the Epistle of Jude identify Satan as the angel who controls death[46] and ascribe Jesus the power to destroy him and his power over death, while the first Epistle of Peter warns the Christians to beware of the devil, the accuser, who is like a roaring lion, looking for someone to devour.[47] The ecumenical epistle by James encourages its listeners to stand against the devil, so that he would flee from them.[48] Here, Satan is back in his old role of accuser, trying to lure the individual and community away from the one true faith.

The Gospels portray Satan as tester and the authors follow the satanic tradition of the Old Testament where Satan appears as a stumbling block. The Satan of the Gospels appears on earth to put Jesus through a series of trials as in Mark's Gospel, where Satan appears as an obstructionist: "His first activity is to induce people, including Jesus, to deviate from their duty. His second function is to prevent people from understanding their duty—but Jesus himself does the same thing, as did God and the prophets before him, and as Paul does after him."[49] The context of Mark's Gospel is apocalyptic and Satan appears as the embodiment of the forces of evil that need to be defeated before the reign of God.

Matthew draws a connection between Jesus' enemies and Satan, while Luke puts Satan in charge of the kingdoms of this world: "Satan's role in Luke makes it clear that opportunistic evil forces are indeed active in the world and pose a threat to the Kingdom of God."[50] John's Gospel confirms that Satan is the ruler of the world and that this rule will come to an end and the author of this gospel also places a strong emphasis on the connection between Satan and Jesus' worldly enemies. The key satanic texts in the

armor of God, that you may be able to stand against the schemes of the devil. For we do not wrestle against flesh and blood, but against the rulers, against the authorities, against the cosmic powers over this present darkness, against the spiritual forces of evil in the heavenly places" (Eph 6:10–12).

44. Jude quotes from the book of 1 Enoch and 2 Peter draws on Jude. The fallen angels in Jude and 2 Peter are the Watchers from the book of Enoch.

45. Jude 6 and 2 Pet 2:4–9.

46. "So that through death he might destroy the one having control of death, that is, devil, and free those who in every aspect of life were held in slavery by the fear of death" (Heb 2:14–15) and "But even the archangel Michael, when he was disputing with the devil about the body of Moses, did not himself dare to condemn him for slander but said, 'The Lord rebuke you!'" (Jude 1:9).

47. 1 Pet 5:8–9.

48. Jas 4:7.

49. Kelly, *Satan*, 84.

50. Wray and Mobley, *The Birth of Satan*, 117.

Gospels offer different narratives that have been reinterpreted in various accounts of fiction.

Satan's Story in the New Testament

> And the Spirit immediately drove him out into the wilderness. He was in the wilderness for forty days, tempted by Satan; and he was with the wild beasts; and the angels waited on him.[51]

The Synoptic Gospels tell the story of Jesus' temptation in the wilderness right at the beginning of his public life. After his baptism by John, the Spirit leads Jesus into the wilderness where he fasts for forty days and is tempted by Satan, the shortest account of which is given by Mark. Luke and Matthew give more detail on how exactly Satan tempts Jesus. In Matthew's account, the Spirit leads Jesus out into the wilderness in order to be tempted by the devil (Matt 4:1). The temptations vary slightly in the two texts: in Matthew, Satan first tempts Jesus to turn stones into bread, then to throw himself from the pinnacle of the temple to be saved by the angels of the Lord, and finally he offers him all the kingdoms of the world if Jesus worships him. Luke gives the same account of the first temptation, but changes the order of the second and the third, so that Satan offers glory and authority over the kingdoms of the world and finally tempts Jesus to test the promise of the Father that the angels will carry him in their hands. The satanic temptations work on three different levels; the devil appeals to Jesus' physical needs—after forty days of fasting, Jesus must have been famished. The second temptation in Matthew (the third in Luke) is directed towards the image that Jesus wants to convey in his message—will he come as an almighty and untouchable king or will he live and die as a man? The last temptation is that of power—Satan offers worldly power in exchange for worship. The story of the satanic temptations stands at the beginning of Jesus' public life, before he begins his ministry. It has influenced many works in literature and art and has contributed to the image of Satan. Especially influential has been the personal aspect of the encounter between Satan and Jesus, involving an intimate conversation in an isolated setting, portraying the power of temptation over the human mind and soul. Jesus' encounter with Satan in the wilderness focuses on the personal struggle of the individual with the forces of evil.

At his personal crossroads, when he begins his journey to Jerusalem, Jesus encounters Satan again, but in a different form than in the desert. It

---

51. Mark 1:12–13.

is Simon Peter, his faithful disciple and the one on whom he will build his church, whom Jesus calls Satan:

> Get behind me, Satan! You are a stumbling block to me; for you are setting your mind not on divine things but on human things.[52]

Peter questions Jesus' mission; it is hard for him to understand that the Messiah should be killed:

> From that time on, Jesus began to show his disciples that he must go to Jerusalem and undergo great suffering at the hands of the elders and chief priests and scribes, and be killed, and on the third day be raised.[53]

The Satan of this passage follows up the tradition of the Old Testament where Satan appears as obstacle in the way of Balaam. Peter acts as an obstacle in Jesus' path; however, his motives are not satanic and his attempt to convince Jesus to change his fate is motivated by political reason, concern for the disciples, and friendship.

John's Gospel refers to Satan as the ruler of this world several times (John 2:31; 14:30; 16:11). Jesus' mission is to cast out the ruler of this world: "The Gospel of John tells the story of Jesus' life in terms of a cosmic battle between light and darkness, good and evil."[54] Another passage that refers to a cosmic battle in the Gospels is Luke 10:18–20. Again, the ruler of the world does not appear as cosmic being, but is represented in whoever opposes Jesus' mission. For the author of John's Gospel, the first-century Jewish community fulfilled that role. Even though John sees Jesus' enemies in this world, the language he applies is that of a cosmic battle:

> John's Gospel follows the plot seen in some of the Qumran literature and in the Synoptics by depicting a redeemer figure who will rescue humanity from the grip of Satan. The battle is a familiar one: a struggle of good versus evil, expressed as a war of light against darkness. . . . The Prince of Darkness works through human beings in insidious ways: through demonic possession, illness, and the corruption of hearts.[55]

---

52. Matt 16:23; cf. Mark 8:33.
53. Matt 16:21. Cf. Mark 8:31; Luke 9:22.
54. Wray and Mobley, *The Birth of Satan*, 125.
55. Ibid., 128.

Satan's Biography

Many scholars today see Satan fulfilling a social role in the New Testament, characterizing human opposition[56] with the spiritual warfare waged between God and Satan equating to the conflict between Jesus and his followers and their enemies. Elaine Pagels argues that the figure of Satan in the Gospels is used to demonize opponents of the Christian message, particularly Jews. According to her, it is the Gospel of John that portrays most clearly the social identity of Satan; as here, Satan does not appear as an independent supernatural character as, for example, in a strong temptation scene. John interprets Satan psychologically and theologically as the embodiment of evil in other people, the passion as a struggle to the death between Satan and Jesus: "So, in effect, 'Satan' is used in the Gospel of John as a personification of social rivals, as the rhetoric in the modern world casts a political enemy as 'the Great Satan.'"[57]

Written towards the end of the first century, the book of Revelation (or Apocalypse of John) includes various elements that have been influential in the development of the satanic figure. The book of Revelation belongs to the genre of apocalyptic literature and its symbolism, poetic language, and visionary style had a great impact on its reception in the tradition of the Christian belief system, influencing a number of literary and aesthetic interpretations of the text.[58] In short, there are three textual aspects of Satan that we can draw from Revelation: Satan in relation to the angels of the seven churches,[59] Satan's role in the battle between Michael and the dragon, and Satan as the celestial accuser of humankind. Revelation 12 describes a visionary scene that had great impact on Christian imagery—the woman in childbirth and the great red dragon, waiting to devour the newborn. The woman and child are saved as Michael and his angels fight the dragon, which is also referred to as the serpent:[60]

> The great dragon was hurled down—that ancient serpent called the devil, or Satan, who leads the whole world astray. He was hurled to the earth, and his angels with him.[61]

---

56. Pagels, *The Origins of Satan*.

57. Wray and Mobley, *The Birth of Satan*, 128.

58. The four horsemen of the Apocalypse, for example, feature in two of the discussed novels (*The Wandering Jew* and *The Master and Margarita*).

59. The messages to the seven churches of Minor Asia express the demand to its members to resist and/or repent any temptations to strain from their faith. Satan is again associated with false belief.

60. Both terms are used interchangeably in Revelation 12:13–17 and also allude to the Leviathan, a sea monster from Jewish and Christian mythology, influenced by ancient Near Eastern mythology.

61. Rev 12:9.

Part One: The Dwelling Place of Satan

The Word of God in Revelation 19 appears as a rider on a white horse who captures the Beast from the Sea and the False Prophet and throws them into the lake of fire. Eventually, an angel from heaven seizes the dragon and throws him into the abyss where he must stay for a thousand years, after which he will be released again to "deceive the nations that are at the four corners of the earth."[62] Finally he too is thrown into the lake of fire where he is tormented forever and ever (Rev 20:10). There are a few other figures that have shaped the figure of Satan, such as the Angel of the Bottomless Abyss (Rev 9:1 and 11, in Hebrew *Abaddon*, meaning "destruction"), the Beast from the Bottomless Abyss (Rev 11:7) and the Beast with the number of a man (Rev 13:18).[63] Here we find the blueprints that were later used (amongst others) to create *the* Satan of Christian thought: Satan as the rebel Angel, defeated in battle by Michael, cast out of heaven and eventually bound in hell, but still with the capacity to tempt and deceive human beings.

The Biblical Summary

While the texts of the Old Testament leave the Satanic character undeveloped, the New Testament and apocryphal writings show the first signs of Satan developing his *Gestalt*. The Prince of Darkness appears with personal attributes—whether he functions as accuser, tempter, or punisher. The biblical storylines that deal with Satan are popular motifs in literature and art; however, there is no coherent picture of the satanic figure in the Scriptures and no attempt to incorporate him into a system of belief or to establish him as Jesus' principal antagonist:

> There is no pre-mundane fall of the Angels. There is no connection of Satan with the Serpent of Eden or the sin of Adam. There is no connection of Satan with the Angles who fall at the time of Noah. There is no Antichrist, only anti-Christs, who are Human and are not directly associated with Satan. There is no rebellious Lucifer, only Jesus, the good Lucifer.[64]

The texts leave room for the artistic imagination and development of Satan. Satan's origins lie in the story; he is a fictional character—introduced

---

62. Rev 20:8.

63. The beasts in Revelation are most likely based on the four great Beasts in Daniel 7. The number of the Beast is 666 ($\chi\xi\varsigma$), usually understood by scholars to refer to the Emperor Nero. Historically it was also understood to refer to other possible worldly opponents like the Pope during the age of Reformation, Aleister Crowley, or more generally the governments of this world.

64. Kelly, *Satan*, 172.

to portray whatever appears as an obstacle in human life. His appearance makes the text interesting; it creates tension, provides a template for conflict and personal dilemma. The satanic story, however, cannot be found in Scripture alone; it required the systematization of Christian theology and the input of folklore and myth to create the character of Satan.

(Early) Church Codification of the Myth

> Theologically, Satan's greatest virtue is to serve as a scapegoat.[65]

The process of creating an opponent for Jesus and his message of love was influenced by the attempt to deal with the existence of evil in the world. Constantly struggling with dualism, the early church had to develop a system of faith that acknowledged the existence of sin and pain without ascribing them to God *or* an equally powerful deity that desired the destruction of humanity. To "source out" the ambivalent and paradoxical aspects of the Christian deity seemed necessary in the context of the Christian belief system, but the creation of Satan as a theological construct left many questions open. The reason for Satan's popularity lies less in the teachings of the church than in folklore and narrative. The distinction, however, between allegedly historical and fictionalized accounts of religious themes and events is not always clear. The influences of story and dogma have been mutual. The official biography of Satan was constructed gradually, based on the Scriptures, but also on popular belief and folklore. It is this "new" biography that features in most works of literature and art.

It is difficult to trace the exact development of the satanic story, but with Augustine (fifth century), the doctrine of Satan was more or less constituted. The second-century Apostolic Fathers, among them Saint Ignatius (Bishop of Antioch), Clement I (Bishop of Rome), Saint Polycarp of Smyrna and Philo of Alexandria, represented their church in a time where Christianity was a minority faith in the Mediterranean world. Doctrines were still uncodified and only very few standards of orthodoxy existed. Influenced by Greek and Iranian dualism, and facing threats from outside, the young church was very much concerned with the struggle between the two ways, and Satan was seen as a force that tried to divert the faithful from the path of unity, encouraging heresy and schism. Satan became the leader of the forces of darkness and the Christians saw themselves as opposing them on the battlefield of martyrdom.

---

65. Wray and Mobley, *The Birth of Satan*, 176.

Part One: The Dwelling Place of Satan

With the Christian apologists of the second century, this position changed slightly. Analytical and logical reflection upon revelation started to replace the more mythical and intuitive approach, when Christianity grew and claimed universality. Thinkers such as Justin Martyr and Irenaeus had to compete with Rabbinic thought and Greek philosophy, and this resulted in the canonization of the biblical texts and the establishment of a common theology. Justin was the first to discuss the problem of evil theologically, and his thoughts had a great impact on later centuries. He followed Revelation in equating Satan with the serpent in Genesis (Rev 12:9) and he confirmed that Satan was the tempter of Adam and Eve, the tempter of Jesus, and the Prince of the demons. Satan fell as a result of his temptation of the first humans, and his motivation was envy. This motif was common around the time of the apologists, along with the understanding that Satan was a fallen angel. Irenaeus and Tertullian, two thinkers concerned with human sin and morality, rejected the Gnostic view of the world as the product of an evil creator and established that Satan was—like any other creation—created good and fell from grace because of envy. Irenaeus introduced the aspect of the free will into the discussion. By our own choice, we have given ourselves into the power of Satan.

It was Origen of Alexandria who can be seen as the most inventive diabologist of the early Christian tradition.[66] In his work *Against Celsus* he argues that "the genesis of evils will not be grasped by the man who does not understand about him who is called the devil, and about his angels, what he was before he became a devil, and how he made his angels apostatise along with him."[67] Origen introduced an important new connection to the discussion: the devil did not fall because he envied Adam and the creation of humankind, but because of pride. Origen was the first to clearly identify Satan with the Lucifer from Isaiah 14 and with the quote from Luke 10:18: "Behold, I see Satan fallen from Heaven like lightening." He suggested a movement from light to darkness: Satan as a luminous angel who rebelled against God as a result of his pride and was cast out of heaven. Origen eliminated the story of the Watchers—the angels who fell in the "beginning" along with Satan.[68] He also brought together other Old Testament traditions

---

66. "A great deal of the vivid elaboration of legend and literature on the Devil's nature arises from Origen's initiative in using these texts," (Russell, *Satan*, 132).

67. Origen, *The Apology of Origen in Reply to Celsus*, 159–60.

68 The fall of the Watchers post-dates the fall of humanity. The classical Christian narrative of the fall of Satan, however, happens before the creations of humans. Satan was the luminous angel who rebelled against God because of pride, was cast out of heaven and then comes back to tempt men because of envy. This is the narrative that was mainly created by Origen and then preserved in that form.

from Job, Ezekiel, and Isaiah and argued that Lucifer, the Prince of Tyre, and the Dragon were all one and the same.

Another aspect of the early church was the influence of monasticism and the psychological penetration of sin and evil on the idea of Satan. The descriptions of the demonic temptations of the desert fathers, in particular Athanasius' *Life of Saint Anthony*, gave "the concept of the Devil colour, particularity, and immediate sensual reality."[69] Here, the battle with Satan was not fought as martyr in the arenas of Rome or as soldier on the battlefields against the armies of evil, but against the power of temptation and seduction in the individual's soul. The devil and his demons attack through both mind and body, and they evoke fantasies, images, and dreams. What was taken from the accounts of the desert fathers was the understanding that the devil is present in every moment and has a variety of weapons to attack the human body and mind.

By the fifth century, the main attributes of the satanic story were pride, rebellion against God, envy of humans, ever-present tempter, and eventual punisher in hell.[70] Augustine then synthesized the existing diabology and constructed a relatively coherent approach to the problem of evil and the devil. As Jeffrey Burton Russell notes, "The clarity, power, and sheer quantity of Augustine's work ensured that most of his ideas would be fixed in the diabology of the western church."[71] The principal narrative consequently reads as follows: Satan is created, and then falls through his own choice, through pride. He takes with him some angels and is now the chief of evil forces in the cosmos. Out of envy, he tempts Adam and Eve in the form of a serpent, provoking their fall as well. Through Christ's sacrifice (or ransom) on the cross, Satan is beaten, but still present. His power is restricted by Christ, but not totally broken.

The concept of Satan has been shaped by different myths and legends from various cultural backgrounds, biblical texts, and spiritual experiences. It was driven by the attempt to come to terms with the question of evil that caused a major difficulty in the theology of the early church—and possibly continues to do so. Satan functions as scapegoat, his figure needed to be elaborated to avoid laying the responsibility for evil on the good God. The concept of Satan is not entirely convincing, there are inconsistencies and contradictions, and later theologians either attempted to improve the system of explanations, or left Satan in the realm of myth and narrative. In the tradition of Augustine, the image of the devil gradually grew more

---

69. Russell, *Satan*, 185
70. See discussion on hell as Satan's dwelling place, Part Two, chapter 5.6.
71. Russell, *Satan*, 218.

sinister. Satan appears as serpent, lion, dragon, dog, or giant. He possesses extraordinary sexual powers and is generally portrayed in black. The blackness refers to the lack of light and his emptiness. He is portrayed with a trident, both an instrument of torture and a reference to this threefold lordship over sea, earth, and the underworld. Sometimes portrayed as an ancient river God, he was more often associated with fire, symbolizing torment and destruction. He is occasionally good-looking but generally ugly. The theriomorphic aspects of Satan refer to the manifestation of his spirit as a beast and link Satan with animals such as the pig, cat, toad, dog, and serpent. They derive, according to Russell, from India, Egypt, and Mesopotamia, where animal appearances were ascribed to spirits of evil.[72] The association of Satan with a goat derives from the image of Pan, the son of Hermes, who, depicted as hairy with horns and cloven hooves, was a phallic deity who represented sexual desire and fertility. Together with other pagan gods, the fertility deities were rejected by Christianity and demonized. The wings associated with Satan come from his former existence as an angel and represent his power over the (dangerous) sphere of storms and winds. These main attributes were more or less established by the fifth century.

Some of the satanic attributes were very popular in subsequent centuries, while others were less common. Nevertheless, the early church had established in its writings and practice the main storyline and characteristics of Satan that the traditions and legends of the next thousand years or so would draw on. It was also soon established that Satan was a shapeshifter, able to take on different forms, or indeed, none at all:

> The notion that he in fact had no proper shape of his own was growing common. Whereas earlier it was often believed that demons possessed gross material bodies, it became usual to regard them as pure—though purely corrupt—spirit.[73]

Stories of Satan appeared everywhere, but they had mostly the character of folk tales and legends and were not of theological nature. They were found in collections of sermons and in sermon-handbooks, which provided great numbers of exempla and anecdotes gathered alphabetically by subject.[74] It was, however, not before the fourth Council of the Lateran in 1215 that the story of Satan's nature was officially confirmed:

---

72. Russell, *The Devil*, 254.
73. Russell, *Satan*, 191.
74. Kelly, *Satan*, 242.

> The devil and the other demons were indeed created by God good by nature but they became bad through themselves; man, however, sinned at the suggestion of the devil.[75]

It was around the same time, during the heights of scholasticism, that Thomas Aquinas synthesized the thoughts of Augustine on the devil in his work *Summa Theologica*. For Thomas, the devil was pure spirit and had power over humankind, but only because he was given that power by God. Furthermore, human beings sinned at the suggestion of the devil, but it was ultimately human will that gave in to the suggestion.[76] The Middle Ages and the Reformation period primarily saw the application of the then traditional views.[77] It was the literary period of Romanticism, following the philosophical paradigm shifts of Enlightenment and secularization that saw the first challenge of the traditional theological picture of Satan.[78] After having established the "official" storyline of our character, it is time to move on to his presence in works of modern fiction, discussing some of his best known attributes and functions.

---

75. Fourth Council of the Lateran, Canon 1, in Schroeder, *Disciplinary Decrees of the General Councils*, 236–96.

76. Kelly, *Satan*, 248.

77. For a discussion of Satan during the Reformation, see Russell, *Lucifer, and Mephistopheles*.

78. See also Part One, chapter 4.

three

Satan in Story and Myth

The Myth of Evil

Satan is part of the myth of evil and if we assume that the story is one way to approach the reality of evil, we need to examine the myth in more detail. From a secular viewpoint, any metaphysical approach to the question of evil does not work. The responsibilities for all human actions lay, since Kant, in the agent's will and accordingly, so does the decision to commit an evil deed. Nevertheless, despite all efforts to explain human behavior with psychology, sociology, biology, and psychoanalysis, there seems to be an explanatory gap when it comes to actions that hurt and destroy others. This gap is still commonly bridged through referring to the concept of evil. The characterization of a certain person as evil is a consequence of a lack of understanding and of fear. But even through just scratching the surface of the term, it becomes clear that the concept of evil can never act as a satisfactory explanation for human behavior. The idea of evil can be used to describe someone's intentions, but this is ultimately a mere description of the individual's actions, not of his character. Even though we may describe a person as evil, we are no closer to understanding the concept of evil. The reason we still refer to the term "evil" is the fact that the use of psychology and social disciplines never fully explain why individuals decide to will evil, that is, deciding to do something that will hurt others in full knowledge of what they are doing. The attraction of the term "evil" lies in its promise to give an explanation of the unexplainable.

Satan in Story and Myth

In his book *The Myth of Evil* (2006), Phillip Cole claims that the concept of evil enables us to fill the gaps of our understanding. He gives certain political and sociological examples (e.g., witch hunts, vampire epidemics, the murder of James Bulger by two ten-year-old boys, the Holocaust, the war on terror after September 11, 2001) in order to demonstrate how the concept of evil has been used and even exploited to deal with the limits of understanding human behavior. He claims that the public's conception of evil bridges the gaps between understandable causes and inexplicable consequences.[1] Cole refers to Nietzsche and Freud in linking the concept of evil to human fear. We are not only scared of our own mortality and our connection with death, but also of ourselves:

> We recognise our own capacity for evil. What frightens us is not the fragility of the boundary between life and death, but of the boundary between our "civilised" self and our "evil" self. We may well project that capacity on to others and into fictional representatives, but it is profoundly our capacity, and this is why we find such projections and representations so disturbing—they threaten to destabilise our conception of our selves as human beings, indeed our conception of humanity itself.[2]

Phillip Cole claims that the use of the term "evil" works only on a mythological level. Myth and narrative provide the space for a concept of evil. Contrary to human reality, narratives do not require analysis of evil's psychology or social background, instead providing a plot to drive the story forward. Evil is therefore neither a philosophical nor a religious concept, but a mythological concept that appears in narratives:

> Evil itself is an idea that only makes sense in a narrative context, in a story we tell about people and about the world. When we describe someone as evil, we are not saying anything about their character or their motivations—we are instead making them a figure in a story in which they play a specific and prescribed role. And in making them such a figure we do away with any need to understand their history, motives, and psychology. Narrative characters have no such features, or rather they simply have the history, motives, and psychology ascribed to them by the narrative plot, those required to drive the story forward.[3]

---

1. Cole, *The Myth of Evil*, 126.
2. Ibid., 118.
3. Ibid., 236–37.

Warning against applying the monstrous concept on the real world, Cole suggests abandoning the concept of evil and restricting its use to the realm of myth. He sees the danger of using the language of myth in the context of politics, psychology, and sociology:

> But the fact is that this idea of evil—closest to the monstrous conception I described in Chapter 1—pervades popular culture, the media, and much political and legal culture too. It's all very well to "play" with such mythological characters in fiction, but this fiction has a devastating effect when it invades and dominates conceptions of reality. . . . "Evil" is a black-hole concept which gives the illusion of explanation, when what it actually represents is the failure to understand.[4]

While the concept of evil does not necessarily help us to understand human behavior, myth and narrative can nevertheless help to develop an understanding of what we experience as evil. It is different from understanding evil's nature; evil refers to an abstract concept and bridges an explanatory gap in human behavior. In its expression through narrative we might be able to approach evil on a non-ontological or non-empirical level. The causes for "evil" behavior might—what the secular worldview suggests—lay entirely within the individual: in our genetic makeup, social-political environment, and psychopathological personality. But the myth or the narrative has something to tell us that goes beyond simple explanations of human behavior as "monstrous" or "demonic." Narrative is the mirror of human behavior, not vice versa. We will subsequently see how narrative creates a different level of understanding that goes beyond empirical observations and that might help us to cope with the reality of human suffering caused by other humans.

The Role of Satan

We have now seen how myth can be relevant in approaching the question of evil. Looking at the figure of Satan, we find he is first and foremost a character in a narrative and he is best characterized through the role he plays in a myth or a story. The characters of evil in myth and narrative are legion. Here, we are primarily interested in the Christian Satan, but even with this restriction, we face several different characters in various narratives. As seen above, Christian theologians had to make sense of these separate tales in order to ascribe Satan his place in a coherent theological system:

4. Ibid., 236.

Satan in Story and Myth

In practice, then, theology is often a kind of narrative, even when disguised as hermeneutics. Conversely, the art of traditional narrative itself is always the interpretation and adaptation of previous stories.... So even when he is the subject of learned discourse, Satan remains a narrative character, and the effort to understand him produces a retelling of his story.[5]

In *The Old Enemy—Satan and the Combat Myth*, Neil Forsyth discusses the role of Satan in myth and narrative. He suggests that

> The complex cosmological systems of the fathers are in essence elaborations of that basic plot whose structure had been proved through countless transformations, the myth of combat with a supernatural adversary.... For the most part, Satan was conceived not as a context-free repository of various beliefs but as an active character in a drama that was still unfinished and in which everyone was an actor. Satan was an agent in a myth, and the object of the church fathers' intellectual efforts was to ensure that the myth made good narrative as well as theological sense.[6]

As we have seen, the Bible says very little about Satan—his role in different narratives is incoherent, and he appears in many functions. The story of Satan, as we tell it today, is the result of the attempt of theologians to make sense of his position in different biblical narratives. Essentially, his role in all narratives is to provide *opposition*. He exists to oppose God, humankind or God's Son. His functions are varied; he can appear as the cosmic rebel, the tempter, or liar, but he always fulfills the role of adversary:

> The separate devil-tales were all seen as cases of one basic opposition; that of Christ and Satan, and that opposition was conceived throughout the whole of the early Christian period in the terms provided by one of the most widespread of Near Eastern narrative patterns, the combat myth.... It defines a being who can only be contingent: as the adversary, he must always be a function of another, not an independent entity. As Augustine and Milton show, it is precisely when Satan imagines himself independent that he is most deluded. His character is, in this sense of the word, a fiction.[7]

---

5. Forsyth, *The Old Enemy*, 13.
6. Ibid., 13–14.
7. Ibid., 4–6.

Part One: The Dwelling Place of Satan

What is the ground then of this fictional character? He appears in the stories of human beings through centuries, shifts his shapes, changes his appearance and the setting of scenes and notoriously escapes any definition:

> The pattern persists because the tradition we are following is continuous, despite major historical and cultural shifts, and because the story of the adversary, whatever its local form, answers a basic human need—to cope with anxiety by telling ourselves stories in which the *archē* or origin of the anxiety may be located and defined and so controlled.[8]

As we have already seen above, fear is a powerful motive when it comes to understanding evil.

The Satanic character is one expression of evil, one approach to understand evil in the world by telling the story of the eternal adversary, the opponent of that which should be, the personification of what should not exist but still does:

> For Satan is a character about whom one is always tempted to tell stories, and one may best understand him not by examining his character or the beliefs about his nature according to some elaborate and rootless metaphysical system, but rather by putting him back into history, into the narrative contexts in which he begins and which he never really leaves.[9]

Satan fulfills a certain function in the narratives he appears in. He is easily recognizable through his physical features, behavioral patterns, and his most famous haunts. He is the stranger we are somehow familiar with, because we have encountered him in other stories. Like other characters of myth and folklore, he has a role to play in the narrative; he represents something abstract the storyteller or author wants to express, something challenging for the hero of the story, something that is in his way and needs to overcome. Satan is a tragic figure, because he cannot escape the role ascribed to him. He can play it with grandeur, pathos, or humor; but in the end, the stage belongs to someone else.

Please Allow Me to Introduce Myself

Robert Johnson reputedly sold his soul to the devil when he met him at a Mississippi crossroad. In return, he received the gift of the blues. The exact

---

8. Ibid., 12.
9. Ibid., 4.

Satan in Story and Myth

location of this fateful place is debated amongst blues fans, but it *was* probably a crossroad, for this is where a traveler is most likely to meet Satan. Where a traveler's path forks and a decision needs to be made, the devil appears. He uses the moment of uncertainty and hesitation to interlope. Satan is often encountered by travelers. Robert Wringham[10] meets Gil Martin while he is taking a walk: "As I thus wended my way, I beheld a young man of a mysterious appearance coming towards me."[11] The second encounter also takes place on a private path in the field and wood of Finnieston: "Near one of the stiles, I perceived a young man sitting in a devout posture, reading on a Bible."[12] The devil can also be met at particular places in nature, such as mountains, woods, and deserts. This does not, however, mean that one is secure in one's house and home. Mephisto appears to Faust in his study; the composer Adrian Leverkühn encounters Satan while he is reading Kierkegaard and listening to Mozart's *Don Giovanni*. Satan can be summoned in a number of ways, but most effectively by an incantation.

The devil is frequently a foreigner or speaks with a foreign accent. He is often not part of a community, but comes from outside. He is the stranger, the one outside the known, and the one in the shadows. He evokes interest and fear at the same time, but the curiosity is generally greater, especially when the encounter with him promises adventure and excitement:

> "Excuse me, please," said the stranger with a foreign accent, although in correct Russian, "for permitting myself, without an introduction . . . but the subject of your learned conversation was so interesting that . . ." Here he politely took off his beret and the two friends had no alternative but to rise and bow.[13]

> The stranger has been surveying the overly hot room. . . . Then he comes limping across the room.[14]

His manners are usually excellent and his outer appearance and his behavior sometimes classify him as an aristocrat.[15] During the first encounters,

---

10. Hogg, *The Confessions of a Justified Sinner*.
11. Ibid., 110.
12. Ibid., 116.
13. Bulgakov, *The Master and Margarita*, 11.
14. Heym, *The Wandering Jew*, 12.
15. "I am a bona-fide prince, believe me, and of such descent as none of your oldest families can boast, but my dominions are long since broken up and my former subjects dispersed among all nations,—anarchy, nihilism, disruption and political troubles generally, compel me to be rather reticent concerning my affairs. Money I fortunately have in plenty,—and with that I pave my way. Some day, when we are better acquainted, you shall know more of my private history. I have various other names and titles besides

Part One: The Dwelling Place of Satan

Satan usually impresses with knowledge, culture, and good taste. Generally, he is educated,[16] well-read (particularly in philosophy and theology),[17] and a good speaker. The physical appearance of the satanic figure regularly shows references to a hoof, a sulphurous or particular smell, and (sexual) attractiveness.[18] He can be handsome and well-dressed, like Gil Martin who Gideon meets in the gorge[19] or Judge Holden, whose crisp suits stand in sharp contrast to his harsh desert environment.[20] Often, the satanic character is strangely familiar[21] or has information no one could possible know. He creates interest, fascination, and sometimes even sympathy.[22] He is often linked with games of chance or appears as a trickster. When Paulus von Eitzen meets Leuchtentrager for the first time, he is impressed not only by his theological knowledge, but also by a card trick.[23] Judge Holden plays similar games with men, considering them to have no other purpose.[24]

---

that on my card—but I keep the simplest of them, because most people are such bunglers at the pronunciation of foreign names," (Corelli, *The Sorrows of Satan*, 32).

16. "'He is a prodigy', he said at last. 'He is an emissary of pity, and science, and progress, and devil knows what else,'" (Conrad, *Heart of Darkness*, 47).

17. "He has been all over the world. Him and the governor they sat up till breakfast and it was Paris this and London that in five languages, you'd have give something to of heard them. The governor's a learned man himself he is, but the judge," (McCarthy, *Blood Meridian*, 123).

18. "At last Woland began to speak, smiling, which made his sparkling eye as if to flare up, 'Greetings to you, Queen, and I beg you to excuse my homely attire.' . . . Woland placed his hand, heavy as if made from stone and at the same time hot as fire, on Margarita's shoulder, pulled her towards him, and sat her on the bed by his side" (MM, 254).

19. "For he was absurdly well dressed for his surroundings. He had on sharply creased black trousers and a black polo-shirt buttoned up to the throat, and a black jacket that looked like it was almost new," (Robertson, *The Testament of Gideon Mack*, 272).

20. "The judge arrived last of all, dressed in a well-cut suit of unbleached linen that had been made for him that very afternoon" (BM, 169).

21. "I seen him before, said the kid. In Nacogdoches. Tobin smiled. Every man in the company claims to have encountered that sootysouled rascal in some other place" (BM, 124).

22. "I felt a great comfort in his presence" (TGM, 296).

23. "He produces from his pocket a pack of cards such as are now artfully printed and are often called the devil's prayer book. . . . 'That is the one!', proclaims the stranger. 'The ace of hearts. Am I right, Studiosus?'" (WJ, 18–19).

24. "The judge smiled. Men are born for games. Nothing else. Every child knows that play is nobler than work. He knows too that the worth or merit of a game is not inherent in the game itself but rather in the value of that which is put at hazard. Games of chance require a wager to have meaning at all. Games of sport involve the skill and strength of the opponents and the humiliation of defeat and the pride of victory are in themselves sufficient stake because they inhere in the worth of the principals and define them. But trail of chance or trial of worth all games aspire to the condition of war for

Similarly, when Woland visits Moscow, he holds a show of black magic in the Variety Theatre that brings turmoil and chaos to the Muscovites.[25] Helmut Krausser's description of the Satanic figure of Nagy plays with common stereotypes of the literary embodiment of Satan: we learn of his "ice-cold jism,"[26] he appears in the disguise of a poodle, he grew up with his grandmother,[27] he likes to use games and tricks, and his power and influence on human beings is necessarily dependent on contracts. Generally, the initial introduction of the satanic character is in the form of an encounter between the character and an individual. This first encounter with Satan is a mixture of familiarity and strangeness; he appears as one of us, but there is some element of otherness to him that cannot be pinpointed. Satan changes his shape to fit his circumstances and the needs of the protagonists. The introduction is physical, leaving an impact on the protagonist and awakening curiosity, along with slight feelings of discomfort and suspicion.[28]

Hope You Guess My Name

Faust: What is your name?

Mephistopheles: Small, Sir, the questions seems From one who gives the Word its lowest rate, Who, far removed from semblances and dreams, Only the depths of life will contemplate.[29]

The devil is a rogue: while roaming like a roaring lion, he also sneaks around like vanishing thoughts and airy fog.[30]

---

here that which is wagered swallows up game, player, all" (BM, 249).

25. "Fagott snapped his fingers, and with a rollicking 'Three, four!' snatched a deck of cards from the air, shuffled it, and sent it in a long ribbon to the cat. The cat intercepted it and sent it back. The satiny snake whiffled, Fagott opened his mouth like a nestling and swallowed it all card by card. After which the cat bowed, scraping his right hind paw, winning himself unbelievable applause" (MM, 123).

26. Krausser, *The Great Bugarozy*, 113.

27. GB, 40.

28. "Young Eitzen casts a sidelong glance at his companion's common, everyday face with the little beard to it and the dark brows so strangely tipped, and for a moment it is to him as though he were seeing an appearance hovering about the other's humped shape, a mixture of fog and shadow, and since just then a cloud is moving across our dear sun, Eitzen shudders and sets the spurs to his animal" (WJ, 24).

29. Goethe, *Faust, Part One,* trans. Philip Wayne, 74–75.

30. "Der Teufel ist ein Schelm, und wenn er auch umhergeht wie ein brüllender Löwe, so schleicht er noch viel mehr herum in Gestalt von flüchtigen Gedanken, luftigen Nebeln gleich" (own translation from Gotthelf, *Geld und Geist,* 32).

Part One: The Dwelling Place of Satan

After the initial encounter, Satan makes himself known eventually; the moment where his true nature is revealed is usually connected with the revelation of his name.[31] The devil has a lot of names all over Europe.[32] Muchembled claims that the use of diminutives or nicknames brought the devil closer to humans and presumably made him less alarming. As a result of such naming rituals, the devil becomes fallible and consequently, the Evil One did not always have the last word and could be tricked, vanquished, and made fun of: "The motif of the devil mastered by humans was a powerful antidote to anxiety. It never wholly disappeared from European culture."[33]

In folk myth and tales, Satan is often portrayed as a baboon. This was built upon in the mystery plays of the Middle Ages, where Satan frequently played the role of the cheeky rogue who was outsmarted by the hero.[34] Various proverbial folklore expressed this view of the devil and offered advice on how to get rid of him and his temptations:

> Satan was always a hero in the theatre, in medieval mystery plays and in the baroque dramas of the seventeenth century; tragedies, tragic-comedies, pastorals and ballets regularly featured devilish goings-on of a frivolous nature, which primarily reveal a taste for metamorphoses. The revolutionary audiences,

---

31. "Ah, Brother Leuchtentrager, you're a true miracle man!' . . . Thus Eitzen has finally come to hear the stranger's name, and being quite learned after four years of Latin school in his hometown of Hamburg, he quickly associates its meaning—namely bearer of light—with the unholy angel Lucifer; but thanks to the goodness of God we are living in Germany where a light is a light, serving just one simple purpose, while those who carry it are mere night watchmen" (*WJ*, 19).

32. "Satan, Lucifer, Asmodeus, Belial, or Beelzebub originate in the Bible and in the apocalyptic literature; Old Horny, Black Bogey, Lusty Dick, Dickson, Dickens, Gentleman Jack, the Good Fellow, Old Nick in English, Charlot in French, Knecht Ruprecht, Federwisch, Hinkebein, Heinekin, Rumpelstiltskin, and Hämmerlin in German" (Muchembled, *A History of the Devil*, 15).

33. Muchembled, *A History of the Devil*, 16.

34. In this tradition also falls the story of the devil living with his grandmother, who combs his hair to put him to sleep at night. The German folk tale *Der Teufel mit den drei goldenen Haaren*, told by the Brother's Grimm, describes the adventures of a young man, who needs to bring three golden hairs of the devil and tricks him with the help of the devil's grandmother. Sometimes the devil is provided with a wife and their marriage is unhappy because the devil was deceived, fooled, and beaten by his wife. Other legends remember incidents of how the devil was tricked by a village or town: during the construction of the cathedral of Aachen, money ran short and the devil finished the building, demanding as payment the first soul to enter. Following the advice of a wise monk, the people brought a wolf and the animal entered the building and the church door was firmly shut after him. The devil got so angry that he rushed out and slammed the door behind him so hard that the cracks appeared that are still visible in the church door.

Satan in Story and Myth

too, liked plays including devils. The vein may date back to the familiar Beelzebub of popular culture who was portrayed in many tales and legends right up to the twentieth century as an imbecile easily duped by humans.[35]

The revelation of the name usually coincides with the temptation, or pact Satan has to offer. Generally, the pact between a person and Satan involves the exchange of the human soul for a satanic favor. The idea of the pact with the devil goes back to the fifth-century story of St. Basil, and the sixth-century story of Theophilus of Cilica, which eventually gave rise to the Faust legend. Theophilus, a clergyman from Asia Minor, swore his allegiance to Lucifer and signed a formal pact. The legend that spread across Europe contains "infernal reflections of both Christian baptism and feudal homage."[36] During scholasticism, the idea of the pact was further elaborated and eventually resulted in the belief that pacts with Satan could be explicitly or implicitly made.[37] The most famous pact between Satan and Dr. Faustus has been retold in countless stories throughout Europe.[38] Faust signs a pact with the devil and in return for knowledge, the ability to perform superhuman exploits, and the joys of sex, he abandons his soul. In different versions of the story, Faust is either saved by the innocent Gretchen or he fails to repent and is condemned to the torments of hell. Where the focus lays depends on the moral and religious perceptions of sin and punishment throughout the centuries. The pact with the devil emphasizes the power of an individual's will to resist demonic temptation. In the present novels, the pact plays an important role: Glanton seals his pact with the Judge without saying a word;[39] Gideon seals it by drinking and sleeping with Satan,[40]

---

35. Muchembled, *A History of the Devil*, 190–91.

36. Russell, *The Prince of Darkness*, 118.

37. Russell argues that scholastic theology and in particular the idea of the pact was one of the elements that supported the witch craze of the fourteenth till seventeenth century: "Aggravated by the religious and political tensions of the Reformation, witchcraft was both cause and result of the revival of the Devil, whose strength had been flagging but witchcraft provoked both judicial prosecution and popular persecution, and the victims numbered in the hundreds of thousands" (ibid., 166).

38. Johann Faust was a doctor and astrologer from Württemberg who died in 1540. The stories evolving around him, however, are much more important than the actual historic figure himself.

39. "Glanton just studied him. It was a day's work to even guess what he made of that figure on that ground. I don't know to this day. They've a secret commerce. Some terrible covenant" (BM, 126).

40. "He came and went through the night, if it was the night, just as he had before, but often when I woke, or half-woke, he was there against my back. Nothing happened between us, Bill, I swear it. Nothing sexual, I mean. We were like soldiers camping out

Eitzen by agreeing to accept Leuchtentrager's help in his exam[41] and throughout his career and personal life, Margarita by accepting Azazello's offer to join Woland,[42] and Marlow by deciding to follow Kurtz into the heart of darkness.

The knowing of the name and the true identity of the tempter is equally important since it suggests a voluntary and conscious decision to cooperate with Satan. The naming of Satan or the recognition of the true nature can be associated with a supernatural experience, such as the miraculous healing of Gideon's leg, or the apparition that young Eitzen sees while riding with Leuchtentrager. The name that Satan uses, however, does not always reveal his true nature, just as Faust tries to reassure Gretchen of his faith: "For me, I have no name to give it: feeling's surely all. Names are but noise and smoke, obscuring heavenly light."[43]

Gideon's satanic friend in the gorge shares this opinion. Satan can easily deceive by taking on another shape or name; however, recognizing the true name or nature of the satanic counterpart gives the protagonist power over Satan by providing a chance to unmask him.[44] Every encounter with Satan involves an element of initiation where any doubt of the true nature of the stranger is eliminated and where the protagonists take part in the satanic business: Margarita serves as royal hostess of the great spring ball in Moscow on Good Friday where the gates of hell are opened; Paulus von Eitzen is wedded by his friend Leuchtentrager in a ceremony that perverts the form of a Christian wedding ritual;[45] and the Glanton gang takes part in the Judge's process to create gun powder, which is described by Tobin as accessing the middle of the earth where the "this world touches the other."[46]

---

under the stars. Comrades. I felt a great comfort in his presence," (TGM, 296).

41. WJ, 65.

42. "'Oh, no!' exclaimed Margarita, shocking the passers-by. 'I agree to everything. I agree to perform this comedy of rubbing in this ointment, agree to go to the devil and beyond'" (MM, 229).

43. Goethe, *Faust I*, Vers 3456 f., 153.

44. "It's his name. Don't you understand? It's like Rumpelstiltskin. Call the devil by his real name and you'll tear him apart" (GB, 148).

45. "Master Eitzen knows the text well and he knows that Leuchtentrager is speaking it as it was written, and yet it is to him as though these words from the Scriptures, coming as they do from his friend, were pure mockery and derision, especially since his desire is not to his meagre bride but to the naked Margriet on whose hip the hand of the Jew is resting as though he owned her. . . . And Leuchtentrager bends down to untie his shoe, the one he wears on his misshapen foot, and places this shoe on the bedcover just above the bride's joypiece, saying: 'This is so you may know under whose boot you will live from now on and who your master is,'" (WJ, 161–62).

46. "I'd not go behind scripture, but it may be that there has been sinners so

In such contexts, Satan is always described as male:

> He has a powerful grandmother, probably an avatar of an ancient fertility Goddess; he also has a wife and seven daughters, representing the seven cardinal sins. He is the father of Antichrist, whom he begets on a Babylonian whore.... The Devil's impregnation of a mortal woman, particularly his fathering of Antichrist, is a parody of the divine Incarnation.... Most basic is the sexist assumption that any figure of such enormous power has to be male. Lucifer's mother, sometimes called Lilith, is proud of her son, the Devil. In a parody of Mary and the angels, she and the demons join in singing praises around her son's throne.[47]

That does not mean that women cannot be personifications of evil. But in the ever-evolving satanic myth, they are accomplices and are used by Satan to fulfill his purpose: according to Christian theology and folklore, Satan (or an evil spirit) can possess human beings and abuse them for sexual acts.[48] The witch craze in Europe at the beginning of the Early Modern period is one example of how powerful and destructive the myth of Satan can be.

The female figures of Margarita, Margarethe, or Gretchen appear occasionally in connection to satanic stories. In Goethe's *Faust*, Gretchen is an innocent victim of Faust's pact with Mephisto. Goethe was inspired by the true case of the maid Susanna Margaretha Brandt, who killed her newborn child in 1771 and was executed in Frankfurt in 1772.[49] Authors like Bulgakov and Heym have used the name to make reference to the tragedy of Gretchen, but changing the nature of the female character considerably: in the case of Bulgakov's novel, it is Margarita who enters into a pact with

---

notorious evil that the fires coughed em up again and I could well see in the long ago how it was little devils with their pitchforks had traversed that fiery vomit for to salvage back those souls that had by misadventure been spewed up from their damnation onto the outer shelves of the world," (BM, 130).

47. Russell, *The Prince of Darkness*, 116–17.

48. In contrast to Satan as a tempter, the seductive Satan approaches in an emotional, carnal, and sexual way. The female body in the Christian tradition was over centuries perceived as threatening and as a home for evil. "They were, according to numerous authors, quick-tempered, brazen, lying, superstitious, and lecherous by nature, motivated only by the impulse of their womb, from which proceeded all their sickness, in particular hysteria.... Women sinned shamelessly, committing first and foremost the sin of lust, most frequently illustrated, then those of envy, vanity, laziness, and pride," (Muchembled, *A History of the Devil*, 75).

49. The motif of infanticide played a prominent role in the literature and poetry of eighteenth-century Europe.

Satan in order to be reunited with her lover.[50] In the case of *The Wandering Jew*, Margarita is the demonic lover of Ahasver, tempting Eitzen and appearing to him in visions until her true nature is revealed.[51] Infanticide, especially when committed by the mother, has often been associated with demonic influences. Lilith, according to Jewish folklore[52] the first wife of Adam who refused to become subservient to him, is often depicted as a demon who kills newborn children. Lilith, originally a Sumerian goddess, has become a figure in Jewish and Christian myth and was probably the archetype for a legion of demonic and vampiric seductresses[53] who appear in the dreams of men.[54]

The Nature of my Game

Mephistopheles: This hour, my friend, shall stir your senses, more
Than any pleasures you have known before,
More than a year in tame existence spent. . . .

Faust: The other side weighs little on my mind;
Lay first this world in ruins, shattered, blind:
That done, the new may rise its place to fill.[55]

We can distinguish between two main aspects of the satanic character in narrative. The first aspect is generally more common and more elaborated in the story and can be described as the "satanic sidekick": the Satanic

---

50. In MM, we encounter the motif of infanticide in the fate of Frieda, who killed her illegitimate newborn with a handkerchief, because she had no way of feeding her. In hell, she wakes up every morning with the handkerchief on her bedside table (MM, 267).

51. "Later, as he opens his eyes to the general cry of horror, he sees lying before him what remains of the woman who lured and tempted him all his life: a wooden ball the size of a skull, with a feather duster stuck to it for hair, and with holes carved in it for eyes and nose and mouth, and next to it a bundle of straw with some rags tied around it, such as the peasants place on their fields to scare the crows. But in the end, aren't we all just ashes and dust, and vanity, and a devil's delusion?" (WJ, 244).

52. Alphabet of Ben Sira, eighth to tenth century.

53. Cf. Woland's servant Hella in MM.

54. "And he perceives that she must be embracing an incubus, and at the same time is growing aware that the woman he is riding, now in full gallop and then again at a slow, sensual pace, and who is holding him tight until he feels as though his very life were draining from him and nothing would remain of him but his shrivelled skin, must be the naked Margriet" (WJ, 162–63).

55. Goethe, *Faust* 1, 78, and 86.

figure appears in the context of an encounter with the protagonist of a story, generally in moments of personal crises, and his prime function is to tempt or test. Traditionally, the role of Satan is seen as tempting humans to commit sin, to act against God's will. But the attraction of Satan lies in the fact that he appeals to human needs and desires that are well known to everybody. The satanic figure in narrative is introduced to portray the personal dilemma of the protagonist or hero. He brings chaos into life—or appears in circumstances that are chaotic and out of the ordinary. He is a symbol of doubt, discontent, and ambition to change, or of greed and lust. In this "relational" role, Satan can fulfill various functions: he can entertain the reader by "spicing up" the story. In his role as tempter, Satan often appears in the story as a facilitator:

> *Mephistopheles:* Part of that Power that would
> Alone work evil, but engenders good.[56]

The figure of Satan, in all his disguises and literary incarnations, also has the intriguing quality of being strangely necessary wherever he appears. His persona functions often as the driving force for evolution and development of a character and story, and in this process becomes an indispensable transmitter of knowledge, consciousness, or self-awareness. The role of evil, as we will approach it here, is of a slightly paradoxical nature: it cannot appear to be necessary as such, for if it did, it would be deprived of its essence, which surely must consist of the drive to engulf its opposite, for that, and only that can provide the driving force behind an entity that can still bear the name evil. At the same time it is the influence of what can be considered "evil forces" that provide circumstances under which creative forces come into power. Hence what we ascribe to evil are two roles: the first one being essential to the nature of evil, namely that it should aim for the complete destruction of the good; and the other one being the creative process that comes about as a result of this struggle, creating something new altogether, a furthering of the human project. In the light of the latter, Satan can be viewed as the enabler of progress, creativity, art, and freedom. In the Medieval Mystery and Passion Plays, Satan was often the most important actor on stage, since without the satanic intrigue, the whole plot of humanity's fall and the salvation through Christ would fail. Regularly, Satan has been associated with creativity in art, music, and literature: Niccolo Paganini (1782–1840), a gifted violinist who played his compositions with new and unusual techniques, was said to be have made a pact with the devil. The tritonus, a triad in music that sounds dissonant, shrill, and full of suspense,

---

56. Goethe, *Faust* 1, 75.

was said to be created by Satan—the musical expression of urge, discontent, and incompleteness. The notion of imperfection, experienced in every human life, finds expression and projection in the idea of the devil, which inspires and awakens creative forces.

The second aspect of the satanic portrayal in the story is that of the tragic hero—Satan appears in the role of the rebel against the divine law. According to the traditions of theology, the fall of Satan was caused either by envy or by pride. The difference depends on whether the fall of Satan happened before or after the creation of humanity. The theologians of the early church connected Satan's fall to the creation of humanity; with Origen and later Augustine, the orthodox position would become that Satan fell as a result of pride.[57] The element of rebellion came into play and Satan was seen as the rebel angel, a creature refusing to accept the divine order of the cosmos. Milton, and later the Romantics, saw the tragic element of his character who represents the deviation from the order of things.[58]

Stefan Heym uses the early notion of the satanic envy as a motif for Lucifer's and Ahasver's rebellion against God in his novel *The Wandering Jew*.[59] The uprising ends tragically. As in the book of Revelation, the Son rides out on a white horse, with him the four horsemen of the Apocalypse, in order to "change the world in your image."[60] In Heym's version of the ultimate battle, it is the Son who raises the sword to kill God in the last act of rebellion:

---

57. See also Part One, chapter 2.

58. Romanticism revived Satan after he had nearly completely lost his significance in the aftermath of Enlightenment and secularization: "At the time, the discrediting of the witch craze helped to discredit the idea of the Devil as well, and in the eighteenth century the rationalist philosophies of the Enlightenment undermined the epistemological foundations of Christian tradition and further weakened diabology. By the end of the eighteenth century most educated people were ready to dismiss the idea altogether. Just at that time, however, Romanticism revived the Devil as a powerful and ambivalent symbol" (Russell, *Mephistopheles*, 12).

59. "But Lucifer, the head of the lower orders and lord of the depths, spoke to us: Do not bow down yourselves before him or praise him as do the angels! It is fitting for him that he bow before us who are of the essence of fire and of a spiritual nature, but not for us to bow down before something that is made of a speck of dust. Then there rose the voice of God and talked to me and said: And you, Wandering Jew, whose name means Beloved by God, will you not bow down before Adam whom I have made in my image and after my likeness? But I looked to Lucifer who stood before the Lord, upright and dark and huge like a mountain, and raised his fist so it pierced the firmament, and I answered God: Why do You turn on me, o Lord? I will not worship him who is younger than I and the lesser of us. I was there before he was created, he does not move the world but I do, toward Yea or Nay, he is dust, but I am spirit" (WJ, 9).

60. WJ, 296.

Satan in Story and Myth

> The old man began to grow of a sudden and grew and grew to the size of a giant and stood there with his feet planted on the destroyed earth and his head high in the clouds; and he raised his hand that was the hand in which he once had held all of creation, including his angels and the stars up above and the man Adam, and a voice rose which was stronger than the loudest thunder and at the same time like the whispering of the wind in the leaves, and spoke one word, one word only, namely his own name, the unutterable, secret, and hallowed name of God.[61]

We have seen now the figure of Satan and what makes the myth of him so fascinating: the concept of the opposition against what is created good; the will to turn against the other for personal gain, pleasure, or out of pride. In this context, Satan is evil.

---

61. WJ, 296–97.

four

Satan and the Written Word

In many ways, Satan is closely tied to the written word. Visitors to the Wartburg in Eisenach can still see the stain that is allegedly the result of Martin Luther throwing an inkpot at Satan while he worked to translate the Bible. The invention of the movable printing press by Johannes Gutenberg in Mainz contributed to the massive increase of printed books in Europe, and together with the efforts of the Reformation and the Counter-Reformation to educate the people, it created a literate society. Early modernity can be seen as the époque of the written word and Satan quickly became intrinsically linked to the new medium. The early modern period is a peak time of satanic interest. The book, and in particular the Bible, was used as a method to combat evil spirits. To read from the Bible would chase the evil spirits away and, occasionally, the holy book itself was used as a physical remedy and was placed on the possessed person.[1]

But Satan was also aware of the power of the written word and was known in many instances to inspire the readings of those he wanted to gain control of. Generally, these were frivolous books. In accounts of possession or witchcraft, the "Devil's Book" is frequently mentioned as the (un)holy scripture of those conspiring with Satan. Especially at the time of the Confessional Wars, the devil was used to discipline Catholics and Protestants: Satan was used as "enemy propaganda" by both sides to enforce moral values. The most obvious examples are the so-called "Teufelsbücher" (devil books), written by Lutheran pastors in simple language for the edification of the faithful between 1545 and 1607.[2] The sale of the books was

---

1. Cf. Cambers, "Demonic Possession, Literacy and Superstition in Early Modern England," 3–35.

2. It was the German Protestants who started publishing so-called "Teufelsbücher"

Satan and the Written Word

prohibited in the Catholic regions of Germany, but they produced works of their own on the same subject. A total of thirty-nine titles were published, and they were intended to denounce vices and sins and to warn men and women not to resort to superstition, magic, or witchcraft.

> They were part of a wider genre, illustrated by works of social criticism, often didactic or satirical, known by the name of Spiegel (that is, Mirrors).... They were original in that they each portrayed a specialized devil.[3]

There were amongst others the *Fluchteufel* (swear devil), the *Spielteufel* (gambling devil), the *Jagdteufel* (hunting devil) and the *Eheteufel* (wedding devil). They usually dealt with demonology, personal vices or sins and social life, and the family circle:

> Based on the idea of Christian perfection, the final moral of each work defined a positive attitude which ought to replace the deplorable behaviour described in the body of the text. Each reader was urged to wage a personal battle against the specific devil concerned, and given detailed advice as to how to set about doing so.[4]

The main purpose of these narratives was to enforce moral behavior by inflicting fear and horror of the devil.

In the context of Satan and the written word, it is impossible not to mention what are arguably the two greatest satanic figures of classic literature: Goethe's *Mephistopheles* and Milton's *Satan*. Shaped by writers who gave their own interpretation of religion and myth, both literary figures have somehow influenced every subsequent satanic narrative. Mephistopheles and Satan are fully developed characters, who shifted the focus from the role of the satanic figure in the Christian salvation story to the individual character. Milton set out to write a theology and created a powerful literary figure. Daniel Defoe, who is seen today as one of the earliest proponents of the novel, criticized *Paradise Lost* for being historically inaccurate and misinterpreting the scriptural account.[5] For the Romantics, who saw themselves in his tradition, it was precisely that attribute of Milton's rewriting of the Satanic myth that was so inspiring: *Paradise Lost* is a defining moment in the discussion of Satan as a literary figure, creating a new role for him that

---

during the sixteenth century. Heinrich Grimm (1959) counted 235,000 copies with roughly a million readers between 1500 and 1600 in Germany.

3. Muchembled, *A History of the Devil*, 113.
4. Ibid., 116.
5. Defoe, *The History of the Devil*.

67

differed from the description of the Middle Ages and Early Modern Period: "Milton's is the last convincing full-length portrait of the traditional lord of evil. In the eighteenth and nineteenth centuries, the concept would be worn down by rationalism and distorted by Romanticism."[6]

The Romantics interpreted Satan as a rebel against the system. He not only has the sympathy of the reader through his tragic role in the story, but is frequently painted in a positive light by writers of this period. For the first time in Christian history, the theological system is challenged.

The eighteenth century saw two very different streams of thought concerning the appearance of Satan: following the ideas of enlightened thought and secularism, the belief in Satan was dismissed as unempirical; yet simultaneously, in the course of modernity and the shift of attention towards the individual, the figure of Satan as person or personality becomes more prominent. This process started with the Reformation in Europe in the sixteenth and seventeenth centuries and continued throughout early modernity and the period of Enlightenment. The emphasis was not on the celestial combat myth, as in the Middle Ages, but on the lonely struggle of the individual against the powers of evil. Consequently, the Faust Legend is very characteristic of its time: "The story of Faust was a great watershed in the literature of the Devil."[7] The various accounts of Doctor Faustus circle around the conflict between the man and Satan. In fact, Satan in the Faust legend plays more of a literary role than a symbol of the evil forces around human beings. Mephistopheles in Goethe's *Faust* cannot be readily identified with the traditional Christian concept of Satan, even though Goethe relates in his prologue to the wager between God and *Hasatan* (the Satan) in the book of Job. The legend is anthropocentric and focuses on the inner dilemma of Faust more than on the celestial struggle between good and evil as in the Middle Ages. The individual fights a lonely struggle against the powers of evil. The Faust legend had an enormous influence on the shift from the devil as theological character to the devil as literary figure. Its popularity and literary development can also be seen as a consequence of the individualism of Protestant theology and spirituality.[8]

Satan flourished in the power of the spoken word, but gained even more power through the written word. Satan appears as the Master of Letters, he is the one who keeps the story alive. Woland, the satanic character

---

6. Russell, *Mephistopheles*, 127.

7. Russell, *The Prince of Darkness*, 177.

8. The Faust legend has undergone constant development and is, according to some scholars, a deeply German myth. Münkler, "Der Pakt mit dem Teufel: Doktor Johann Georg Faust," 109–47.

Satan and the Written Word

in *The Master and Margarita*, returns the burned novel to the Master, fulfilling the role of the preserver of the story:

> "Forgive me, but I don't believe you," Woland replied, "that cannot be: manuscripts don't burn."[9]

---

9. MM, 287.

Part Two

Satanic Characters

As we have seen in the discussion of his biography, Satan is a paradoxical figure, showing contradictory characteristics and constantly evading definition. In this section, I explore how different satanic characters in literature represent manifestations of evil, in conjunction with the theological concepts of theodicy and theological discussions of evil. I refer to it as a literary exploration of postmodern or contemporary thoughts on evil in philosophy and theology. We have seen now how Satan is a literary figure and finds his *raison d'être* through narrative. But what happens to Satan in late modern fiction? Is there room for talk of the devil outside proverbs and popular culture? It seems difficult for the figure of Satan to prevail in a post-secular world. The paradigm shift after the Enlightenment, the focus on empirical science, and the critique of metaphysics has reduced any reference of Satan to superstition or radical evangelicalism. There is little doubt that the historic realities of the twentieth century changed the face of evil, and together with the theological "death of God" discourse, this has given the Prince of Darkness a deep identity crisis. We experience evil in our socio-cultural context, but there is seemingly no metaphysical framework in place to ascribe any meaning to it. After the collapse of the metaphysical system that had been in place since scholasticism, humanity has been burdened with the responsibility for everything evil. Reason, empirical science, psychology, and sociology looked for the explanation for evil in the human condition. The human evil experienced in the twentieth century met a vacuum and left those who experienced it without mechanisms to cope. Despite the unspeakable horror of millions of deaths in just a few decades, the atrocities of the twentieth century are not the only dark period in the history of humankind. But the questions that have been asked afterwards could not be answered—and all that was left was a silent void. The death of God and, at the same time, the disillusion about the belief in human progress and the ability to find the key to human behavior were landmarks of the twentieth century. With no way to turn either towards a God or towards the reassuring rationality of empirical science, we were left to face two World Wars, the Holocaust, and the nuclear threat. The problem of evil in the twentieth and twenty-first centuries is therefore not new, but has raised new discussions, in particular in relation to the events of Capital Imperialism, the Third Reich, and the Holocaust: "The Shoah has, in other words, simultaneously justified our perennial concern with the question of evil, and by its enormity placed a question mark against all the previous answers."[1]

---

1. Lindsay, "Nothingness Revisited," 4.

Part Two: Satanic Characters

The image of Satan cannot be seen detached from the socio-historic realities and even though the changes to his portrayal in literature are not necessarily chronological, there is a certain development that stands in close connection with the history of thought in the Western world since roughly the Middle Ages.

The portrayal of Satan seems to offer different answers to the challenges of life; he appears to tell the story of humankind. He takes on the role of the rebel against the divine being, he tempts humans to destroy what is created and to become aware of their own identities, including their shadow sides, he acts as hero, fool, and seducer, he tries to challenge the system that is in place until the point where the system itself collapses and there is no up or down, heaven or hell; with all boundaries gone Satan is left to float in a vacuum of thoughts, and eventually realize that all is one.

The following chapter looks at models and attributes of satanic figures that have relevance in contemporary narratives. The underlying question is: how does the talk of Satan fit in the system of modern theology and how do the narratives of Satan contribute towards an understanding of evil? The Satan of the twenty-first century leaves behind the trademarks of his last big historical entrance during Romanticism: the heroic figure is lost, Milton's Satan has left the stage and the satanic figures are indifferent and nihilistic—they do not challenge a system because there is none in place anymore. The contemporary Satan is truly grey, banal even. It is Hannah Arendt's characterization of evil that comes to mind in the context of a postmodern Satan. The term "postmodernity" is overused and academically problematic. Postmodernity in our context means an approach to ideas and systems without the clear definition of discipline and structure. While modernism is characterized by rapid innovation and the belief in human power in body and mind, postmodernism recognizes the limits of any progressive and teleological understanding of the world and human behavior:

> Postmodernism is modernism stripped of teleology. It is chiefly characterized by the routinization of novelty. The modernist faith in progress has been undermined in the postmodern world. Yet the drive to innovate that fired the engines of progress has been intensified and accelerated. Innovation now constitutes an end in itself, unencumbered with the baggage of final purposes, ultimate goals, or cosmic designs for humankind.[2]

In the following, I will undertake a character study of the literary Satan, approaching him as a symbol or a mirror for some aspects of evil that

---

2. Thiele, "Postmodernity and the Routinization of Novelty: Heidegger on Boredom and Technology," 490.

humanity encounters today. I have chosen recent or contemporary novels from Western authors that feature satanic figures in one way or another[3] and I hope to reveal the complex nature of the satanic figure and its relationship to our understanding of evil in late modernity.

---

3. Generally, we can in our texts differentiate between the literary appearance of a metaphysical entity clearly associated with the Satan of Christian folklore (MM, WJ, GB) and the appearance of a character that shows Satanic attributes, but is *per definitionem* a human being (Judge Holden, Kurtz, Adolf Hitler).

five

The Restless Wanderer

> That he is more of a vagrant than a prisoner, that he is a wanderer in the wild unbounded waste. . . . So Satan and his innumerable legions rove about hic & ubique, pitching their camps (being beasts of prey) where they find the most spoil. . . . Satan being thus confined to a vagabond, wandering, unsettled condition, is without any certain abode.[1]

According to his biography, Satan was cast out of heaven and fell into the abyss. At the same time, he has been described as roaming the earth. His state, however, is most certainly one of exile and homelessness, though freely chosen. The following takes a closer look at the notion of evil as alienation and elimination and explores the literary character of Satan as a wanderer between the worlds.

A Place of Its Own

> The Word became flesh and made his dwelling among us.[2]

I start with a linguistic analysis of two terms that characterize a state of being—to dwell and to roam. Dwelling means to live and to reside, it expresses steadiness and security, but at the same time permits mobility and flexibility. It conveys feeling at rest, being at home. The Greek word σκηνοῦν means to set up a tent, to live in a tent or to settle. The word recalls the

---

1. *The History of the Devil*, chapter VI, 1, 63.
2. John 1:14.

Part Two: Satanic Characters

Hebrew שכן, which means "to dwell." The word "dwelling" is used in the Old Testament to describe the dwelling of God with Israel.[3] In the early Jewish tradition, the tent played an important role: for a nomadic tribe, the pitching of a tent was to create a (temporary) home. The tent was also a home for God in the desert, his presence inhabited the tent. Rudolf Bultmann suggests that the expression was chosen as a play on the common use in the Orient of the dwelling of the Godhead, referring to its salutary presence among humanity in a town or in a temple.[4] In classical Greek, the verb σκηνοῦν was used to describe the setting up of a stage for a drama. In John's Gospel, these two meanings are combined: The Word pitched a tent among us; it finds a place to live among human beings, becomes one of them, but is ready to move again and to be somewhere else. The Word creates a scene for the drama to begin. The notion of dwelling might be one aspect of the incarnation that cannot be applied to the idea of an incarnation of evil. We will see in the following how Satan surprises us again with a paradox: without a place of its own, Satan is condemned to wander, but finds a temporary dwelling place in literature.

The idea of dwelling plays an important role in the philosophy of Martin Heidegger. With the term "dwelling,"[5] Heidegger refers to the way humans *are* on earth.[6] "Building Dwelling Thinking" has been frequently used in connection with architectural philosophy and approaches to building and constructing. We will concentrate on Heidegger's thoughts of dwelling and try to relate it to the idea that the enfleshed word dwelled among us.[7]

3. E.g., Exod 25:8; 29:46; Zech 2:14.

4. Johnson, *The Origins of Demythologizing*, 96. Note the parallels in the Wisdom myth: *Eth. En.* 42:2: "Wisdom went out to seek a dwelling among the children of men"; Sir 24:4: "I established my dwelling in the height"; 24:8, "And he who made me, set up my tabernacle and said to me: In Jacob shalt thou dwell and take possession of Israel."

5. In German, Heidegger uses the word *wohnen*.

6. Heidegger, *Poetry, Language, Thought*, 148. In the 1971 edition, Albert Hofstadter edited seven writings by Martin Heidegger that are concerned with art and creation. In the following, I discuss two of Heidegger's writings from this: "Building Dwelling Thinking" ("*Bauen Wohnen Denken*"), a lecture Heidegger gave in August 1951 in the course of the Darmstadt Colloquium II, and "Poetically Man Dwell" ("*dichterisch wohnet der Mensch*"), a lecture from October 1951, given at "Bühlerhöhle." Both works concern dwelling as a form of existence and being.

7. Heidegger claims that dwelling (*wohnen*) and building (*bauen*) are essentially the same. He uses references to linguistics to support his arguments: "The Old English and High German word for building, *buan*, means to dwell. This signifies: to remain, to stay in a place. The real meaning of the verb *bauen*, namely, to dwell, has been lost to us. But a covert trace of it has been preserved in the German word *Nachbar*, neighbor. The neighbor is in Old English the *neahgebur*; *neahm*, near and *gebur*, dweller. The *Nachbar*

Dwelling relates to the sense of how a person *is*, to be situated in a place:

> Where the word *bauen* still speaks in its original sense it also says how far the nature of dwelling reaches. . . . I dwell, you dwell. The way in which you are and I am, the manner in which we humans are on the earth, is *Buan*, dwelling. To be a human being means to be on the earth as a mortal. It means to dwell.[8]

Dwelling is not something human beings *do*; in Heidegger's philosophy "dwelling" is not so much used as a verb, but rather as an adjective. Dwelling means to set something free into its own presence, to practice the essence of human existence.[9]

For Heidegger, dwelling and poetry are closely connected—they depend on each other and are descriptive of human nature. Again, Heidegger tries to capture the full meaning of dwelling:

> When Hölderlin speaks of dwelling, he has before his eyes the basic character of human existence. He sees the "poetic," moreover, by way of its relation to this dwelling, thus understood essentially. . . . Thus we confront a double demand: for one thing, we are to think of what is called man's existence by way of the nature of dwelling; for another, we are to think of the nature of poetry as a letting-dwell, as a—perhaps even the—distinctive kind of building.[10]

Following Hölderlin, Heidegger suggests that poetry first causes dwelling to be dwelling. If we look at the origins of the word poetry, it becomes clear what Heidegger means: poetry comes from the Greek word ποιήσις, a making or creating. So it is in creation that human beings dwell. Dwelling is thus not a passive but a very active way of existence.

Heidegger then asks the question where we humans get our information about the nature of dwelling and poetry. He sees the answer in language, but not language as a mere medium for the printed word. It is the response to the appeal of language that speaks in the element of poetry:

---

is the *Nachgebur*, the *Nachgebauer*, the near-dweller, he who dwells nearby" (Heidegger, *Poetry, Language, Thought*, 147).

8. Ibid.

9. Heidegger refers to language development to come closer to the understanding of human existence on earth: "The Old Saxon *wuon*, the Gothic *wunian*, like the old word *bauen*, means to remain, to stay in a place. But the Gothic *wunian* says more distinctly how this remaining is experienced. *Wunian* means: to be at peace, to be brought to peace, to remain in peace" (ibid., 149).

10. Ibid., 215.

> The more poetic a poet is—the freer (that is, the more open and ready for the unforeseen) his saying—the greater is the purity with which he submits what he says to an ever more painstaking listening.[11]

Humankind exists through dwelling and this dwelling is poetic, because it responds to language that "poetry does not fly above and surmount the earth in order to escape it and hover over it. Poetry is what first brings man onto the earth, making him belong to it, and thus brings him into dwelling."[12] Poetry for Heidegger is the primal form of building and therefore the original admission of dwelling. Human beings dwell in this world, finding a place through the creative power of language. If we use Heidegger's definition of dwelling as an existential form of humanity's being on earth, the words of John 1:14 acknowledge that God exists in some form among us. Created in the image of God, humanity is home to God's word through creative endeavors, and therefore a true resting place for it. Dwelling then refers to the aspect of divine incarnation and the idea that God finds a home in the midst of human beings and human beings find a home in God.

No Place of Its Own

> Be alert and of sober mind. Your enemy the devil prowls around like a roaring lion looking for someone to devour.[13]

Satan, however, does not find his home on earth. The book of Job shows that Satan also moves about, but that his moving is restless, with neither goal nor aim:

> On another day the angels came to present themselves before the LORD, and Satan also came with them to present himself before him. And the LORD said to Satan, "Where have you come from?" Satan answered the LORD, "From roaming through the earth and going back and forth in it."[14]

According to Christian theology, Satan was never able to find a permanent place among human beings. He only lodges temporarily, but does not have a being in the flesh. While the incarnation of the Word is described by the verb "dwelling," the most appropriate term for any attempt of the incarnation

---

11. Ibid., 216.
12. Ibid., 218.
13. 1 Pet 5:8.
14. Job 2:1–2.

of evil would be "to roam" or "to wander." Both dwelling and wandering/roaming imply motion, but while dwelling means actually being somewhere and with someone, roaming and wandering express being homeless and unsettled. Satan does not have a place of his own; he roams the earth. Even though we have seen that the idea of dwelling is somehow dynamic, it still involves a feeling of being at home, of being able to rest somewhere. Roaming or wandering is the opposite of dwelling. Satan's wanderings are generally characterized by restlessness. The Scripture refers to our world as the kingdom of Satan, but Satan does not find his home in human beings. Having to wander can be a liberating experience, and Jesus himself asks his followers to leave the restrictions and routines of their everyday lives behind in order to be open to the truth of the good message. In fact, Jesus describes himself as having "no place to lay his head."[15] But this wandering involves freedom and the certainty of having an eternal home outside of this world. According to Christian legend, Satan's wandering is the tragic consequence of his turning away from God, and there is nowhere for him to return. The gate is shut, so to speak, leaving him to roam the earth in search for a temporary home. The archetypal motif of the eternal wanderer has been popular in narrative and legend, and is reflected in satanic imagery. It is no coincidence that one of the strongest literary representations of Satan can be found in Romanticism—a literary genre that was also preoccupied with the notion of wandering. The feeling of homelessness is also a characteristic notion of the postmodern human, dislocated and *entwurzelt*[16] after the processes of pulling down the foundations of a theocentric worldview. Two wandering figures who are closely related to Satan are Cain and Ahasver (or the Wandering Jew). Both find—like Satan—their roots in biblical narratives.[17] Through looking at some of their characteristics we approach the implications of being without a dwelling place.

A Restless Wanderer on Earth: The Story of Cain

In the Bible, we first hear of the eternal wandering in Genesis 4. After killing his brother Abel, Cain is condemned to wander the earth:

> The LORD said, "What have you done? Listen! Your brother's blood cries out to me from the ground. Now you are under a curse and driven from the ground, which opened its mouth to receive your brother's blood from your hand. When you work

15. Matt 8:20; Luke 9:58.
16. Meaning "without roots" or "uprooted."
17. According to Midrashic literature, Cain was the son of Satan and Eve.

> the ground, it will no longer yield its crops for you. You will be a restless wanderer on the earth." Cain said to the LORD, "My punishment is more than I can bear. Today you are driving me from the land, and I will be hidden from your presence; I will be a restless wanderer on the earth, and whoever finds me will kill me." But the LORD said to him, "Not so; if anyone kills Cain, he will suffer vengeance seven times over." Then the LORD put a mark on Cain so that no one who found him would kill him. So Cain went out from the LORD's presence and lived in the land of Nod, east of Eden.[18]

The Land of Nod denotes wandering. Cain is condemned to wander the earth; he has to leave his community because he has violated the social order by committing the crime of fratricide.

We hear of Cain's mark; the prohibition from killing him is God's second punishment: "If no one may kill Cain, he must live forever. Here we see the parallel to Ahasver, the cursed one, whose restlessness like Cain's, is eternal; he can neither die nor be killed."[19]

The idea of life without death, of living without the promise of fulfillment is daunting—being trapped in the physical body, in a world full of suffering and pain. Romanticism knew the idea of eternal life in a young body. The reality of death is threatening, the idea of not being able to die unbearable.

Cain's punishment refers to the first crime of humanity, and reveals a lot about the nature of human evil. His story also emphasizes that the human condition is one of exile and alienation.[20] Cain, like Satan, was a popular figure of Romanticism, another rebel against the laws of God and therefore a divinely imposed ignorance; Eden and the state of innocence came to its final and necessary end through the murder of Abel. In his work *Cain*, Byron brings together the two biblical figures of disobedience and transgression in order to investigate the origin of human evil. Byron, like other Romantics, was concerned with the question of why a man, who is naturally good, can commit evil deeds. Cain's punishment for the murder of his brother was to wander eternally. The punishment is severe, particularly for a member of a community that relies strongly on the protection of his family and tribe and for whom exile is a certain death sentence. Cain knew this, as becomes clear in his reaction. But God does not want Cain dead; he put a mark on Cain, so that no one could kill him:[21] "The rest of us, like

---

18. Gen 4:10–16.
19. Isaac-Edersheim, "Ahasver—A Mythic Image of the Jew," 201.
20. Cantor, "Byron's Cain," 50–71.
21. The nature and meaning of the mark are unclear, but it suggests parallels to

Cain in his tragic as opposed to his jealous mode, simply exist, as Springsteen says, 'from the dark heart of a dream,' permanently marked, wandering helpless in our private wilderness."[22]

No Harbor and No Shore: The Myth of Ahasver

> Once we understand the story of Cain, then we will also understand more about Ahasver's offence and punishment.[23]

The inability to die is the greatest curse that can befall a human being. Apart from Cain, it is the figure of Ahasver who has been most prominently referred to on the subject eternal wandering. The legend of the Wandering Jew spread in Europe in the thirteenth century as part of Christian folklore. The story goes that a Jew taunted Jesus on his way to Golgotha and was then cursed to wander the earth till the second coming of Christ. The legend exists in various forms and contexts and the identity of the Wandering Jew is not always the same. Sometimes he is described as a shoemaker, in other traditions he is the doorman of Pontius Pilate's estate or the attendant Malchus, whose ear Peter cut off during the arrest of Jesus in Gethsemane. The Wandering Jew is often connected with the name Ahashver or Ahasverus/Ahasuerus, most likely referring to the Persian king Ahasuerus or Xerxes I in the book of Esther.[24] Scholars also see parallels to other archaic religions and belief systems, for example the Germanic myth of Odin or Wodan, the Spirit of the Universe that wanders the earth, and the tale of the Wild Huntsman. The legend is referred to in two passages from the New Testament:

> I tell you the truth, some who are standing here will not taste death before they see the Son of Man coming in his kingdom.[25]

> Peter turned and saw that the disciple whom Jesus loved was following them. (This was the one who had leaned back against

---

Ricoeur's interpretation of the primary symbols for evil, cf. Part Two, chapter 2, § "The Symbolism of Evil."

22. Dorris, "The Mark of Cain," 11.
23. Isaac-Edersheim, "Ahasver—A Mythic Image of the Jew," 200.
24. The origin of that name is not entirely clear, but might refer to medieval Jewish legends that portray Ahasuerus as stupid and a fool. David Daube points out that in the traditional plays acted by Jews on the Feast of Esther, Esther and Mordechai are the heroine and the hero, Haman the villain, and Ahasuerus the fool (Daube, "Ahasver"). Werner Zirus also mentions a relation to the Oriental mythological tradition of the Godhead Chidhead or Chadhir (*Der ewige Jude in der Dichtung*).
25. Matt 16:28.

> Jesus at the supper and had said, "Lord, who is going to betray you?") When Peter saw him, he asked, "Lord, what about him?" Jesus answered, "If I want him to remain alive until I return, what is that to you? You must follow me." Because of this, the rumor spread among the brothers that this disciple would not die. But Jesus did not say that he would not die; he only said, "If I want him to remain alive until I return, what is that to you?"[26]

The idea of waiting for the Lord merges with the motif of the curse through the story of Christ's torturer who hits Jesus in the face before his crucifixion:

> When Jesus said this, one of the officials nearby struck him in the face. "Is this the way you answer the high priest?" he demanded.[27]

Unlike Judas, whose death is reported by the Gospels, the figure of the Wandering Jew is punished for his mockery with the curse of eternal wandering and restlessness.

The biblical sources are poor and the actual origin of the legend lies in medieval Christian folklore. Werner Zirus collected the image of the Wandering Jew in German and English literature and tradition[28] and showed the mutual influence the variations of the legend in both countries had on each other. The legend has experienced very different interpretations throughout the centuries, one of which was the particularly anti-Semitic use of the expression "eternal Jew" (Der Ewige Jude) by German National Socialist propaganda:

> Within the Wandering Jew wanders the father-God rejected by the young generation, the symbol of the intergenerational struggle, who continues to remain alive, yet had to be humiliated in the attempt to dominate him, to forget him.[29]

Through the curse placed upon him by Jesus, God, or the Archangel Michael (depending on the tradition), the Wandering Jew is damned to eternal wandering. He experiences the death of his children and grandchildren, he witnesses the downfall of nations, he survives wars and natural disasters, and he experiences unendurable pain but is not allowed to die. This notion of wandering has little in common with the romantic tradition

26. John 21:21–23.
27. John 18:22.
28. Zirus, *Der ewige Jude in der Dichtung. Vornehmlich in der englischen und deutschen*.
29. Issac-Edersheim, "Ahasver—A Mythic Image of the Jew," 205.

The Restless Wanderer

of wandering, but focuses on the unbearable feeling of eternal restlessness and the experience of endless repetition without any other wish than to be able to die and rest.

The rhapsody *Ahasver* by Christian Friedrich Daniel Schubart[30] creates one of the darkest images of the Wandering Jew in the tradition of that legend. The tragedy of having to see the centuries going by, trapped in the human body that wants to die but is not allowed to, is an image of hell on earth.

> Den Staubleib tragen!
> Mit seiner Totenfarbe—und seinem Siechtum!
> Seinem Grabesgeruch!
> Sehen müssen durch Jahrtausende
> Das gähnende Ungeheuer Einerlei
> Und die geile, hungrige Zeit.[31]

Schubart's work influenced Percy Bysshe Shelley's later work on Ahasver.[32] In Shelley's poems, we find a connection between the image of the Wandering Jew and Milton's Satan in *Paradise Lost*: both figures share the restlessness, homelessness, and the tragic fate that awaits those who deny the acceptance of order. And, as we shall now see, Shelley was not alone in seeing parallels between Ahasver and Satan.

Ahasver and Satan

Stefan Heym's novel *The Wandering Jew* (1984; German original *Ahasver*, 1981) sees Lucifer[33] and Ahasver as brothers in spirit. They are both fallen angels, both creatures "made out of fire and the essence of the infinite, in nobody's image or likeness"[34] who could not accept God's order to worship

---

30. Written in 1783, published in 1786.

31. "*To bear this body of dust*
    With its deadly color—and its lingering illness!
    Its tomb exhalation!
    Forced to see through the centuries
    The yawning monster monotony
    And the horny hungry time" (own translation).

32. The motif of the Wandering Jew can be found in his writings "Ghasta or the Avenging Demon," "The Wandering Jew, or the Victim of the Eternal Avenger," "St. Irvyne" and "The Wandering Jew's Soliloquy" (1810), "Queen Mab" (1811), "Alastor" (1816), "Prometheus Unbound" (1820), and "Hellas" (1822).

33. Heym plays with the name Lucifer: Paulus Eitzen's mysterious friend and benefactor is called "Leuchtentrager" and so is the Professor in Jerusalem who is corresponding in with Professor Beifuss in Berlin in the GDR of the 1980s.

34. WJ, 7.

Adam, the creature made from dust at the sixth day. Both are expelled from heaven at the end of the sixth day of creation, because they refused to worship Adam:

> We are falling. Through the endlessness of the upper heavens that are made of light, the same light of which our raiment was made whose glory was taken from us, and I see Lucifer in all his nakedness, and how ugly he is, and I tremble. Do you regret it? Says he. No, I do not.[35]

After being cast out from heaven, Ahasver and Lucifer are wandering the earth together. Their opposition to God's order continues throughout the time. But while Satan follows his old and familiar roles of rebellion and temptation, Ahasver is motivated by another reason, and is concerned with his deep love for God and the Reb Joshua.

The novel has three different narrative strands or storylines and the structure of the novel is reminiscent of Bulgakov's *Master and Margarita*.[36] The first storyline is based on the mythological-biblical background of the story, with its main sources in Jewish and Christian mythology: Ahasver and Lucifer are expelled from heaven for not worshipping the newest creation of God—man. Throughout the novel, both Ahasver and Lucifer meet occasionally in the realm of nothingness, in the world of myth. It is in this storyline that Ahasver recalls his encounters with Reb Joshua and his disciples. The second storyline is set during the German reformation in the sixteenth century with its main sources in folk legends and Hans Christian Andersen's *Ahasuerus*. The story follows the life of Paul von Eitzen, superintendent and later bishop in the Lutheran church in the north of Germany, who made a pact with Lucifer to be successful in his church career and private life.[37] The third storyline is set in the GDR between December 1979 and January 1981 and follows an exchange of letters between a scholar from the GDR and a Hebrew scholar from Tel Aviv on the topic of the Wandering Jew. Heym's novel was published in the last decade of the GDR and is regarded as a criticism of the political system. It is agreed upon in the academic world that *Ahasver* marks a change in Stefan Heym's work. The three storylines can be read as three different approaches to the satanic character in general. The encounters between Lucifer, Ahasver, and

---

35. Ibid.

36. Some scholars suggest four or more narrative lines. I follow Marc Temme's suggestion of three main story plots. For the discussion, please see Temme, *Mythos als Gesellschaftkritik*.

37. Paul von Eitzen (1521–98) is a historic figure. In 1602, an anonymous pamphlet claims that Paul von Eitzen met Ahasver. This piece of writing is considered the first appearance of Ahasver in German literature.

the Reb Joshua refer to the Scriptures and are generally located in the realm of myth. Eitzen's story relates to the folkloric element of Satan, using the popular attributes of the satanic appearance. The dialogue between Jochanaan Leuchtentrager from the Hebrew University in Jerusalem and Professor Siegfried Beifuss from the Berlin Institute for Scientific Atheism can be read as a parody of the discourse between science and religion/myth (or reality and fiction) in modernity.

Heym's Ahasver is a revolutionary, somebody who does not give up on the human race and who firmly believes that change is possible. This is what differentiates him from Lucifer who is cynical about the future of the existence of the world and does not believe in any form of redemption. But both are wandering: Ahasver is cursed to roam the earth till the second coming of the Lord and Lucifer is his eternal companion. There is no home for him among the humans and even though he himself chose the distance from God, there is still a great love in him for the Creator and a deep feeling of belonging. During the last supper before Reb Joshua's death, it is Ahasver who rests by him: "And I leaned my head on his bosom as though I were the disciple he loved most, and talked to him."[38]

Stefan Heym follows in his interpretation of rebellion against obedience the Romantic writers who saw Satan as the true rebel. But the novel nevertheless acknowledges the tragedy of restlessness and being without roots. Ahasver's allegiance to Lucifer and his decision to challenge God makes him the eternal wanderer. It is exactly in this homelessness that Ahasver sees his chance of bringing change to the world, and in Heym's novel he succeeds in persuading the Rabbi to give up his passiveness: "And I know that his thought is reverting to the cross on which he died, and to my sending him away from my door because he refused to stand up and fight; but now he did fight."[39] The rebellion against God fails, one word from whom silences all, "And spoke one word, one word only, namely his own name, the unutterable, secret, and hallowed name of God."[40] And then, from Ahasver:

> We are falling, the Rabbi and I. My eternal brother, says he, do not you leave me. And I leaned my head on his breast, as I had done at his last supper, and he kissed my brow and put his arm about me and said that I was like flesh of his flesh and like a shadow which belonged to him, and like his other self. And we united in love and became one.[41]

38. WJ, 77.
39. WJ, 295.
40. WJ, 297.
41. Ibid.

Part Two: Satanic Characters

Hell as the Place of Exile

Hell is other people (Jean-Paul Sartre)

Hell is the absence of the other (Jean-Luc Marion)

If we suppose Satan does not have a home, that he roams the earth and wanders the centuries, never able to find a true dwelling place, what do we do with the image of hell? Is it possible to locate Satan's dwelling place in the fiery inferno that has occupied the imagination of many writers and artists? Even more so than the image of Satan, the image of hell finds its origins in narrative.[42] Originally, hell in the Christian concept was not necessarily connected with the figure of Satan. Again, the Scriptures give no clear idea of hell, and certainly do not define it as the realm of Satan. Most accounts of hell in early Christian writings and the early Middle Ages would portray several devils, demons, or beasts that torture souls, but no Lord of Hell. Christian theology was reluctant to place Satan in hell, since he was seen as wandering the earth, and could therefore not be bound in hell. It seems difficult to precisely decide the time and context in which Satan was put into hell and eventually in charge of it: by the fourth century, the doctrine of the harrowing of hell had been established.[43] Between his death and his resurrection, Christ descended *ad infernos* in order to rescue the souls of the righteous, but in the writings of the early church, Satan was not his opponent there, he is actually one of the condemned souls. One of the first very detailed descriptions of Satan in hell is given in *Tundale's Vision*,[44] the best known probably in Dante's *Inferno*.[45] Satan is sitting in the ninth and last circle of hell, the place for the worst sinners—those who betrayed their lords or benefactors. Dante's Satan is a grotesque figure with three heads that are constantly devouring the sinners Brutus, Cassius, and Judas.[46] Satan

---

42. Especially in the Mystery Plays of the Middle Ages, hell and the mouth of hell was a popular and widely used theatrical element.

43. "He descended into hell; on the third day he rose again from the dead," (Apostles' Creed, Roman Rite, 2011); see also John Norman Davidson Kelly, *Early Christian Creeds*, 368.

44. Tundale's vision, or Latin Visio Tnugdali, is the account of the Irish knight Tnugdalus from the twelfth century. The text was very popular in the Europe of the Middle Ages and was translated into several languages. The account, written down in Regensburg, tells the story of Tundale's experience of afterlife, both heaven and hell, during a three-day-long out-of-body experience (Palmer, *Visio Tnugdali*).

45. *Inferno* is the first part of Dante Alighieri's *Divine Comedy* (fourteenth century). It describes Dante's allegorical journey through hell, guided by the Roman poet Virgil.

46. Judas, here suffering in hell, is like Satan a popular figure in literature. He plays a role in two of the novels discussed here (*The Master and Margarita* and *The Wandering*

is frozen fast in the icy lake that surrounds him and he is weeping. He has wings, but no feathers, and is moving them as if he was trying to escape.[47]

Dante's Satan, however, is not the Lord of Hell, but more its prisoner. Again, it was Milton who manifested the idea of Satan as the Lord of Hell in his epic *Paradise Lost*:

> Here at least we shall be free; the Almighty hath not built
> Here for his envy, will not drive us hence:
> Here we may reign secure, and in my choice
> to reign is worth ambition though in Hell:
> **Better to reign in Hell, than serve in Heaven.**[48]

At the same time, however, Milton formulated another aspect that is essential for the Christian understanding of hell:

> Me miserable! Which way shall I fly
> Infinite wrath and infinite despair?
> **Which way I fly is hell; myself am hell;**
> And in the lowest deep a lower deep,
> Still threat'ning to devour me, opens wide,
> To which the hell I suffer seems a heaven.[49]

Milton seems thus to equate the inner, bottomless depths of the modern self with hell, it is in damnation that we truly know ourselves.[50]

Jew) and has traditionally been seen as an ally of Satan, even though his role stays ambivalent in the interpretation of the biblical narrative. Luke sees Satan acting through Judas: "Then Satan entered in to Judas called Iscariot, who was of the number of the twelve" (Luke 22:3–6). John also sees Satan acting through Judas; he specifies the time of Satan entering Judas during the Last Supper: "As soon as Judas took the bread, Satan entered into him" (John 13:27). John's account of the events leaves open whether only Jesus knew who was going to commit the necessary act of betrayal, or whether he appointed Judas beforehand to fulfill the plan of the father (John 13:26). The Gnostic tradition sees Judas as an instrument of the Sophia (Divine Wisdom) and his betrayal of Jesus was a victory over the carnal world. The Gnostic idea was that Judas helped Jesus on his way to the cross, knowing that Jesus had to return to his non-fleshly, heavenly home. According to Irenaeus, Judas had "exact knowledge of these things, and since he alone knew the truth better than the other apostles, he accomplished the mystery of the betrayal" (Irenaeus, *Against the Heresies*, 31). The *Gospel of Judas* that was mentioned by Irenaeus, was found in Egypt near Beni Masar and was partly reconstructed in 2006. The text has a strong focus on Judas Iscariot and there is an ongoing academic discussion around its presentation of Judas in his relationship to Jesus.

47. Alighieri, *Inferno*, Canto 34.
48. Milton, *Paradise Lost*, I.258–63 (emphasis added).
49. Milton, *Paradise Lost*, IV.73–78 (emphasis added).
50. Forsyth, *The Satanic Epic*, 149.

Part Two: Satanic Characters

The topic of hell is theologically controversial.[51] Modern and contemporary Christian theology generally has defined hell more as a state of loss or exile than a place.[52] *Poena damni* has since Innocent III been used to describe the punishment of the loss of vision of God.[53] According to the catechism of the Catholic Church from 1992, hell is self-exclusion from communion with God,[54] but it can also be understood in a more immanent context as the self-alienation from others through sin. Hell can be the absence of the other, as Jean-Luc Marion sees it,[55] or it can be other people, as Jean-Paul Sartre's character Garcin defines it in *Huis Clos*.[56] Though contradictory at first, both sentences understand hell as a state created through the self-inflicted absence of love and relationship between persons. In that context, Satan's dwelling place is hell, since he freely turned away from God. Hell, then, is as a state of freely chosen renunciation of God.

The question remains whether anybody could turn away from God's love. Theologians like Origen, and more recently Karl Rahner and Hans Urs von Balthasar have affirmed that hell must exist as an option, but that it is in fact empty.[57] Stefan Heym's Satan roams the earth, but at the same time is restricted to hell, defined as a state outside God and his creation:

> In the depths of the space which is called Sheol and which extends outside the limits of creation, without light or darkness, in every direction, in an endless curve. Here we may talk, says Lucifer; there is no God here and none of his creatures, be they spiritual or corporal; this is the absolute nothing, and the nothing has no ears.... I've been looking for you, Brother Ahasverus, he says. Where are the others? Says I. Where are your dark hosts

---

51. For an overview of literature on hell, see, Vorgrimler, *Geschichte der Hölle*.

52. "The images of hell that Sacred Scripture presents to us must be correctly interpreted. They show the complete frustration and emptiness of life without God. Rather than a place, hell indicates the state of those who freely and definitively separate themselves from God, the source of all life and joy. This is how the *Catechism of the Catholic Church* summarizes the truths of faith on this subject: 'To die in mortal sin without repenting and accepting God's merciful love means remaining separated from him for ever by our own free choice. This state of definitive self-exclusion from communion with God and the blessed is called "hell" (n. 1033)" (John Paul II, "GENERAL Audience").

53. Ratzinger, Joseph: "Hölle." The other component is *poena sensus*, meaning sensory pain of some sort.

54. *Catechism of the Catholic Church*, n. 1033.

55. Marion, "Evil in Person," in *Prolegomena to Charity*, 1–30.

56. Sartre, *Huis Clos*, 182.

57. Vorgrimler, *Geschichte der Hölle*, 339. This question has also been discussed in theology with the term *apokatastasis* or universal reconciliation.

that were cast out from heaven along with you and me when we refused before God to worship man whom He made in His image out of a speck of dust and a droplet of water and a breath of wind and a spark of fire. Where are they? Everything seems to be losing itself here, he says. And I see him trembling in the great cold which is all around us, and I begin to perceive why he was looking for me, for harder to bear than the thought of the vastness of the nothing is the thought of its lasting forever.[58]

Summary

We have seen how the motif of the restless wanderer has played a significant role in Western literature and how Cain and Ahasver have been identified as Satan's spiritual brothers in the situation of *Gottferne*. The distance is self-inflicted, the restless wandering a result of disobedience, pride, and envy. In the context of the Christian theological narrative, Satan is God's creation and he fell from him and is since damned to wander the earth, without the possibility to return to where he was meant to be. He lost his place in heaven, but cannot find it amongst humans either. Just like Cain and Ahasver, Satan is a tragic figure, thrown out into exile, roaming the earth and still always wearing the mark that bears the possibility of forgiveness, of eventually finding peace:

> The image of wandering and murderous Cain can be potent. It is a tragedy that for centuries many Christians, following the lead of Ambrose and Augustine, applied it to Jews, as though the misguided desire on the part of some to have Jesus crucified could appropriately characterize all, as though the crucifixion of Jesus were closely comparable to the murder of Abel, and as though continuing devotion to the God of their fathers should count for nothing. If the image is to be of value today it would surely better be applied to those restless and ever-discontented people who, resentful of the hand they have been dealt in life, allow themselves to become enslaved to urges that are expressed in behaviour that is destructive towards others, and often also towards themselves; a type of person sadly as common today, *mutatis mutandis*, as in antiquity.[59]

We have now tried to explore the experience of homelessness and restlessness, referring to parallels between the narrative figures of Cain,

58. WJ, 164–65.
59. Moberly, "The Mark of Cain," 27.

Part Two: Satanic Characters

the Wandering Jew, and Satan. The same motif can be found in the myths of the Ancient Mariner, Flying Dutchmen, the Wild Huntsman, and many other cursed wanderers and sailors in Christian and Pagan legends and in Romantic narratives. All these narratives share the same symbolic of wandering and roaming. The individual is damned to wander the earth or the oceans as punishment for a sin. The wandering is usually eternal and can only be ended through either the breaking of the spell by another person or the final salvation through the coming of the Savior. The figures in all these myths are condemned to repetition and there is no teleology in their actions. Even though they are finite in their being, they are caught in a never-ending circle of aimless wandering. The greatest human fear is thus not the leaving of this earth through death, but the eternal existence on this planet, without the ability to rest. The (often disproportionately cruel) punishment of eternal wandering is in most legends accepted as fate and accompanied by intense feelings of regret. It is only during the Romantic period that the possibility of revolt against the divine judgement comes into play. We have seen in this chapter that Satan does not have a dwelling place; he cannot have a permanent home in people, because the human is made in God's image and thus cannot incarnate evil. We could not locate him in the systematic approach of Christian theology, because he is notoriously subversive and escapes any attempt to satisfactorily incorporate him in a system that is based on a single omnipotent and good deity. And finally he seems to prove French existentialists right in leaving hell empty. We conclude here that Satan's dwelling place is the narrative, it is through myth and stories that he has been created and is kept alive. Theologically, there is the experience of evil and suffering, which human beings are left with—the question of theodicy, of how a good and omnipotent God can accept evil. Psychologically, there is the need for embodiment: Satan has to be created, we keep creating him. Satan dwells in literature by wandering through literature, as the ever newly-created character, bound to a life of constant re-creation.

six

The Tormented Shadow

Joseph Conrad's character Kurtz is a restless wanderer,[1] dying in utter isolation and self-inflicted exile:

> He cried in a whisper at some image, at some vision,—he cried out twice, a cry that was no more than a breath—"*The horror! The horror!*" I blew the candle out and left the cabin. . . . Suddenly the manager's boy put his insolent black head in the doorway, and said in a tone of scathing contempt—"Mistha Kurtz—he dead."[2]

Literary critics have offered different interpretations of Kurtz's last words, but it is the ambivalence of them that make Joseph Conrad's novel, published in 1902, a vision of the twentieth century. Whether Kurtz speaks the words to describe his actions, the condition of humankind, or the entire existence of universe, Marlow is unsure and so is the reader. We are left with the experience of absolute horror in the face of death, with no interpretation, no reconciliation, and no hope:

> Conrad's *Heart of Darkness* (1899) is a text that has consistently resisted analytic closure. That is to say that its relevance to the twentieth century (and now the twenty-first century) is apparent through the allusions to the story in our media and culture. As each new "horror" of the post-modern world emerges, *Heart*

---

1. "As to me, I seemed to see Kurtz for the first time. It was a distinct glimpse: the dug-out, four paddling savages, and the lone white man turning his back suddenly on the headquarters, on relief, on thoughts of home—perhaps; setting his face towards the depths of the wilderness, towards his empty and desolate station" (HD, 57).

2. Ibid., 112.

Part Two: Satanic Characters

of Darkness acquires new meanings that extend its relevance beyond the imperial boundaries of the Belgian Congo of the 1880s and '90s, and bring to Conrad's vision a shockingly contemporary pertinence.[3]

Kurtz is certainly a personification of evil; he resembles the evil genius and there are quite a few observations during Marlow's journey that can be read as references to a satanic figure. However, Kurtz is not Satan; he is a human being, a "wandering and tormented thing."[4] Joseph Conrad anticipated many other "real" figures of the twentieth century with his character Kurtz, and recognized the dilemma of categorizing human evil.

Kurtz—A Satanic Figure?

He had taken a high seat amongst the devils of the land—I mean literally.[5]

Kurtz symbolizes the spirit of evil, but at the same time must keep his identity as a man. The reader knows his history: from a cosmopolitan background,[6] he was partly educated in England, worked as a journalist, and eventually joined a Belgian ivory-trading company to earn some money, so as to marry his fiancée (his "Intended") in spite of her higher social status. During his employment as chief of the inner station, some 200 miles away from Kinshasa, Kurtz increasingly distances himself from the company and gradually isolates himself. Despite having sent back the biggest amount of ivory of all outposts to the outer station, the trading company wants to stop him, aware of rumors of his growing insanity and his controversial techniques of raiding one area of the river which may make future trade difficult. Marlow, a river steam boat captain assigned by the ivory company to find Kurtz, discovers this story in the course of his journey, but the man nevertheless exerts a strange fascination on both Marlow and the majority of people he meets. His personality impacts upon anyone who gets to know him; however, no one seems able to define or explain their fascination. The brick-maker of the Central Station calls him "a prodigy, an emissary of pity, and science,

---

3. Dryden, "To Boldly Go," 500.
4. HD, 143.
5. Ibid., 81.
6. His mother was half-English and his father half-French (ibid., 83). We know from previous observations that Satan himself is often an educated cosmopolitan or even foreigner.

and progress, and devil knows what else."[7] The Harlequin assures Marlow that Kurtz made him "see things."[8] Kurtz's Intended agrees with Marlow that "it was impossible to know him and not to admire him."[9] The reader learns with Marlow that Kurtz was educated in many aspects and had talents as an artist—he was known as a painter, a musician, and a poet. In Marlow's opinion, he was a universal genius.[10]

The jungle, the place of impenetrable darkness, turned Kurtz's genius into madness, or rather, as Marlow puts it, "his nerves went wrong."[11] Marlow of course knows that Kurtz's behavior is far beyond irritable nerves, in fact, he refuses to listen to the Harlequin when he refers to the cult of Kurtz, fearing to hear things that would be more disturbing than the skulls on poles. At a later point, Marlow observes that Kurtz's "intelligence was perfectly clear" but "his soul was mad. Being alone in the wilderness, it had looked within itself, and, by heavens! I tell you, it had gone mad."[12] There is a developmental aspect to Kurtz's behavior; he changes during his time in the jungle from an idealist to a mad and violent bully, in particular when he demands to "exterminate all the brutes."[13] He does not have an originally degenerated character, but the circumstances transform his idealism into brutal madness:

> However, the effects of loneliness, isolation, and sickness are affecting him. "Idealism" gives way to egotism: power, greed, loneliness and sickness combine to disorientate him, and trading gives way to armed raiding, the toleration of bloody tribal rites becomes an encouragement of them.[14]

This image of Kurtz reflects the ideas of the nineteenth century, which felt the explanation for evil lay largely in the social and psychological circumstances of the individual.

But we have conflicting explanations for Kurtz's madness: following Sigmund Freud and his pleasure principle, Conrad portrays civilization as a protection against the nature of humanity, a means to control the beast. Kurtz is a lustful creature, full of desire, with no morality. He illustrates the

---

7. Ibid., 47.
8. Ibid., 91.
9. Ibid., 119.
10. Ibid., 116.
11. Ibid., 83.
12. Ibid., 107.
13. Ibid., 84.
14. Stephens, "*Heart of Darkness*," 275.

possible irrelevance and inadequacy of morality to human beings. In the nine years he spends in the jungle, he rids himself of the restrictions of the laws of human interaction and acts upon motives that are not entirely clear but certainly involve greed, sexual desire, and megalomania.[15] In Freudian terms, he leaves behind the reality principle and succumbs to the uncoordinated instinctual trends of the *id*.[16] Evil in the *The Heart of Darkness* is lack of restraint that arises from an inner hollowness and the lack of belief in something: "I saw the inconceivable mystery of a soul that knew no restraint, no faith, and no fear, yet struggling blindly with itself."[17] In the conditions in which Kurtz and Marlow live, the constant temptation of the wilderness can only be resisted with faith in *someone* or *something*. Kurtz is a satanic character through his conscious rebellion against the moral framework and through his tragic denial of his own and others' personhood. The character of Kurtz is caught between reality and fantasy, eternity and evanescence, light and dark, plenitude and hollowness. Conrad portrays a figure who is torn and tormented, succumbing to the dark temptations of power and violence, and who is eventually destroyed by his internal struggle.[18]

Marlow, the Disciple

Kurtz is a gifted speaker[19] and it is the voice of Kurtz that calls Marlow into the darkness. Marlow's quest for Kurtz does not give him the answers

15. "I've seen the devil of violence, and the devil of greed, and the devil of hot desire; but, by all the stars! these were strong, lusty, red-eyed devils, that swayed and drove men—men, I tell you. But as I stood on this hillside, I foresaw that in the blinding sunshine of that land I would become acquainted with a flabby, pretending, weak-eyed devil of a rapacious and pitiless folly. How insidious he could be, too, I was only to find out several months later and a thousand miles farther" (HD, 34).

16. "But the wilderness had found him out early, and had taken on him with a terrible vengeance for the fantastic vision. I think it had whispered to him things about himself which he did not know, things of which he had no conception till he took counsel with this great solitude—and the whisper had proved irresistibly fascinating. It echoed loudly within him because he was hollow at the core" (ibid., 95).

17. Ibid., 108.

18. This Manichaean struggle is expressed in the figures of the two women in Kurtz's life that Marlow encounters; the native woman who dances on the shore when Kurtz is taken back and who was presumably his lover and the Intended, who Marlow visits after Kurtz's death. The criminal hero discovers in the ultimacy of evil redemptive possibilities and some sort of belief (Knowles, "Who's Afraid of Arthur Schopenhauer?" 92).

19. "The point was in his being a gifted creature, and that of all his gifts the one that stood out pre-eminently, that carried with it a sense of real presence, was his ability to talk, his words—the gift of expression, the bewildering, the illuminating, the most

he was looking for. Even though he gets to talk to him—something he eagerly anticipated—Marlow does not find the real Kurtz, but just his shadow. Kurtz is described as "unsteady, long, pale, indistinct, like a vapour exhaled by the earth [which] swayed slightly, misty and silent."[20] His actions "only showed that Mr. Kurtz lacked restraint in the gratification of his various lusts, that there was something wanting in him—some small matter which, when the pressing need arose, could not be found under his magnificent eloquence."[21] The fascination with the unspeakable horror that is associated with Kurtz—the "fascination of the abomination"[22]—drives Marlow into discipleship.

Marlow, in his fascination for Kurtz, is an equally interesting figure in *Heart of Darkness*. Marlow calls the Harlequin "Kurtz's last disciple,"[23] but this role really belongs to Marlow himself. He defends Kurtz's writings against the agents of the Company and he brings Kurtz's personal belongings to his Intended. He is not entirely clear about his own motives, but she is the last connection to Kurtz and therefore provides a last point of contact with the phantom Marlow has been chasing:

> All that had been Kurtz's had passed out of my hands: his soul, his body, his station, his plans, his ivory, his career. There remained only his memory and his Intended—and I wanted to give that up too to the past, in a way,—to surrender personally all that remained of him with me to that oblivion which is the last word of our common fate.[24]

In the course of Marlow's journey deeper and deeper into the heart of darkness, he begins to question moral frameworks, he becomes fascinated with the man he is searching for, and increasingly more vulnerable to the darkness that surrounds Kurtz. The actual evidence of evil is fragmentary, and impossible to describe.[25] Marlow presents the figure of Kurtz as absolute evil: "I did not betray Kurtz—it was ordered I should never betray

---

exalted and the most contemptible, the pulsating stream of light, or the deceitful flow from the heart of an impenetrable darkness" (HD, 79).

20. Ibid., 105.
21. Ibid., 95.
22. Ibid., 50.
23. Ibid., 96.
24. Ibid., 117.
25. "What were we who had strayed in here? Could we handle that dumb thing, or would it handle us? I felt how big, how confoundedly big, was that thing that couldn't talk, and perhaps was deaf as well. What was in there?" (ibid., 49).

Part Two: Satanic Characters

him—it was written that I should be loyal to the nightmare of my choice."[26] Marlow admires Kurtz, the more he learns about him the more he is drawn to him:

> He won't be forgotten. Whatever he was, he was not common. He had the power to charm or frighten rudimentary souls into an aggravated witch-dance in his honour; he could also fill the small souls of the pilgrims with bitter misgivings: he had one devoted friend at least, and he had conquered one soul in the world that was neither rudimentary nor tainted with self-seeking.[27]

The journey along the river is a journey into the center of things (Africa, Kurtz, Marlow, human existence), but a journey without an aim.[28] At the center we encounter darkness, as Owen Knowles notes:

> The world of *Heart of Darkness* does not turn upon structured relations between historically distant myths and the present: more disturbingly, the tale posits a monistic and originating source for contemporary myths in the form of a freshly dead father-figure whose dying brings to birth an unwillingly loyal disciple.[29]

The fascination of Marlow is expressed in his own analysis after Kurtz's death:

> It is his extremity that I seem to have lived through. True, he had made that last stride, he had stepped over the edge, while I had been permitted to draw back my hesitating foot. And perhaps in this is the whole difference; perhaps all the wisdom, and all truth, and all sincerity, are just compressed into that inappreciable moment of time in which we step over the threshold of the invisible.[30]

There is a strange kinship between Kurtz and Marlow, between the protagonist and his shadow, a connection similar to the one between Jekyll and Hyde in R. L. Stevenson's novel. Kurtz is Marlow's alter ego, his darker self, the part of him that is untamed by society and unleashed in the wilderness of the jungle:

26. Ibid., 104.
27. Ibid., 84.
28. The classic interpretation by Albert J. Guerard sees the novel as a journey within the self ("The Journey Within").
29. Knowles, "Who's Afraid of Arthur Schopenhauer?" 81.
30. HD, 114.

Marlow is thus making of Kurtz a mirror-image of his own disordered imagination, the "proof" that he requires of the existence of inscrutable and unknowable "powers of darkness." So while Marlow torments himself with "the fascination of the abomination," the real Kurtz and the reality he represents is obscured under a fog of evasive words and evasive actions, and a constant invoking of Dark Powers.[31]

Evil as the Shadow

I had to beat this Shadow—this wandering and tormented thing.[32]

This brings us to the Jungian interpretation of *Heart of Darkness*. The term shadow or shadow aspect of a personality was introduced to analytical psychology by Swiss psychiatrist Carl Gustav Jung, a former student and colleague of Sigmund Freud, who defined the shadow as a part of the unconscious mind. He developed this thought in the context of his work on archetypes, first used as a term 1919 in an essay titled "Instinct and the Unconscious."[33] Archetypes describe innate universal dispositions in the human psyche that reflect the basic themes of human life. The shadow refers to rejected aspects of the human personality. It is part of the human psyche and consists of repressed weaknesses, instincts, and shortcomings.

Jung's theory of psychoanalysis was influenced by the literature and philosophy of the Romantic movement in Europe, particularly Germany. One of the leitmotifs of Romantic literature is the *doppelganger* and Jung developed his idea of the shadow on the basis of this motif.[34] One of the Romantic novels that influenced Jung's theory on the shadow was *The Devil's Elixirs* by E. T. A. Hoffmann.[35] The main focus of the novel, dealing with guilty love, incest, temptation, and supernatural phenomena, is the struggle of the monk Medardus with his dark side, personified in the mad monk, his half-brother and rival, whom he encounters in different situations. The reader only gradually discovers that he is in fact the illegitimate

---

31. Stephens, "Heart of Darkness," 279.
32. HD, 106.
33. Jung, "Instinct and the Unconscious."
34. Kerr, "*The Devil's Elixirs*, Jung's 'Theology' and the Dissolution of Freud's 'Poisoning Complex.'"
35. Hoffmann, *Die Elixiere des Teufels*.

brother of Medardus, begotten through incestuous relationships.[36] The brother Viktorin haunts Medardus in reality and in his dreams. Before he is even aware of his identity, Medardus nearly kills his *doppelganger*, and takes on his role. The role change is not definite, but fluent. Throughout the whole story, Medardus and his brother change identities, so that the reader is not always sure who he is dealing with. After the failed fratricide, Viktorin appears in different situations to rescue Medardus and even accepts the blame for Medardus's crimes. Medardus' brother appears as the evil twin, the wholly other who is related through blood, but brings corruption and damnation. The brothers do not meet each other in real life after their first encounter, but each dreams of the other's existence, and Medardus feels his brother's haunting presence in his feverish dreams. For Medardus, Viktorin is the personification of the damnation from which he cannot flee, because it is part of his own personality. The only other physical encounter between the two brothers occurs after Medardus' attempt to kill his bride and half sister Aurelien. He flees into the dark woods where someone attacks him and wrestles with him till the hours of dawn:

---

36. The incestuous ancestry of Medardus is regarded as fateful preposition: "A destiny you could not escape gave Satan power over you and in evil-doing, you were merely his tool. But do not hope that you thus are less guilty in the eyes of the Lord, because you were given the power to overcome Satan in the battle. In every human's heart, the Evil storms and contradicts Good, but without that fight there would not be any virtue. Because virtue is only the victory of the good principle over the evil, just as the opposite outcome is the source of sin" (Hoffman, *Die Elixiere des Teufels*, 268, own translation). Satan sees potential in the offspring of incestuous relationships. The idea that incestuous relationships are inspired by or allow access to evil are a recurrent motif in literature: nearly two hundred years after ETA Hoffmann's novel, Norman Mailer describes a similar setting in his last novel *The Castle in the Forest* (2007). Dieter, a member of Special Section IV-2a, is narrator in Norman Mailer's *The Castle in the Forest*, and also assistant to Satan. After observing potential in young Adolf, Satan gives order to watch him closely. The allegedly incestuous relationship of Hitler's parents serves as one explanation for his evilness. "I did, and eventually was selected to oversee the work of a number of minor demons who were keeping watch on an Austrian family whose developed potentialities might yet prove astounding. Insignificant at present was this embryo, and his parents equally so, but he had ancestral fault-lines full of intoxicating stink of our old friend blood-scandal. So I was to stay close to him after his birth. I did not dare to ask, but at this point, the Maestro chose to speak directly to my curiosity. He said: 'Why have I been so interested in this creature not yet born? Can it be that he will yet possess a mighty ambition? I may propose that you take him on full-time. At present, however, it is no more than a project. It could certainly fail. In time, if he develops the greater part of his promise, he could, as I say, become our own client. Must I say more?'" (*The Castle in the Forest*, 77–78). Incest is a social taboo in most societies, and it is mostly not so much the sexual aspect of the incestuous relationship but the violation of the social order and the transgression of kinship rules.

The Tormented Shadow

> In vain, I tried to shake him off—I threw myself down, pressed my back against the trees, all in vain. The man chuckled and laughed viciously; then the moon came out, bright through the dark fir trees and I saw the pale and horrible face of the monk, the alleged Medardus, the Doppelganger. He starred at me with the same horrible glance that I saw from up the wagon.— "Hihihi, little brother, brother, always, always, I am with you, I never, never let you. . . . Cannot walk, you need to carry me, come from the gallows, they wanted to break me on the wheel, hihihi." So the ghost laughed and howled, while I jumped up with horror like a tiger, embraced by a constrictor. I rushed against trees and stones in order to kill or at least hurt him badly, so that he would have to let me go. He only laughed louder and I felt the sudden pain.[37]

It is his own self that Medardus is wrestling with, the burden of guilt and sin, the personified failure of human existence.

For Jung, the novel quintessentially underlined his theory of the dark counterpart in every human soul:

> But alas! It fares with us all as with Brother Medardus in Hoffmann's tale *The Devil's Elixiers*: somewhere we have a sinister and frightful brother, our own flesh-and-blood counterpart, who holds and maliciously hoards everything that we would so willingly hide under the table.[38]

The brother myth repeats itself—Cain and Abel, Romulus and Remus, Isaac and Jacob.

---

37. Vergebens versuchte ich, ihn abzuschütteln—ich warf mich nieder, ich drückte mich hinterrücks an die Bäume, alles umsonst. Der Mensch kicherte und lachte höhnisch; da brach der Mond hellleuchtend durch die schwarzen Tannen, und das totenbleiche, grässliche Gesicht des Mönchs—des vermeintlichen Medardus, des Doppelgänger, starrte mich an mit dem grässlichen Blick, wie von dem Wagen herauf.— "Hi . . . hi. . . . hi, Brüderlein. . . . Brüderlein, immer, immer bin ich bei dir. . . . lasse dich nicht. . . . lasse. . . . dich. . . . nicht. . . . Kann nicht lau. . . . laufen . . . wie du. . . . musst mich tra. . . . tragen. . . . Komme vom Galgen. . . . haben mich rä. . . . rädern wollen. . . . hi hi. . . ." So lachte und heulte das grause Gespenst, indem ich, von wildem Entsetzen gekräftigt, hoch emporsprang wie ein von der Riesenschlage eingeschnürter Tiger!—Ich raste gegen Baum- und Felsstücke, um ihn, wo nicht zu töten, doch wenigstens hart zu verwunden, dass er mich zu lassen genötigt sein sollte. Dann lachte er stärker, und mich nur traf jäher Schmerz (Hoffman, *Die Elixiere des Teufels*, 247–48, own translation).

38. Jung, *On the Psychology of the Unconscious*, 39.

Part Two: Satanic Characters

It is a common theme of literature, as Ricardo Quinones has shown in his book *The Changes of Cain*.[39] The importance of the Cain-Abel myth lies in the fact that it is not only concerned with the self, but also with relationships. While other great myths like *Faust* and the *Odyssey* are concerned with the development of one character, the brother myth focuses on the dynamic of relationships. If we understand evil as relational, it can only be characterized in differentiation from the other.[40] The brother myth and its concern with relationships and failed relationships therefore play an important role in the understanding of evil:

> Brothers suggest the possibility of failed prospects (what I call the shadowy other) that remind us of what was left behind, of the loss intimately connected with any success, of the deaths required by existence. [The theme's] moral force is derived from this essential encounter with another, which means that its fuller expression is dualistic.[41]

Medardus' fight with his own brother echoes the wrestling between Jacob and God,[42] and also the showdown which happens between Marlow and Kurtz on the shore. Marlow discovers that Kurtz's cabin is empty and he follows the crawling Kurtz through the grass—the ultimate confrontation has to happen in solitude, away from the safe ship, in unfamiliar and threatening territory: "I was anxious to deal with this shadow by myself

---

39. Quinones, *The Changes of Cain*.

40. The killing of Abel through Cain is the first murder of humankind, but it is not the first sin. The first sin of humankind is envy and envy requires a relationship and physical proximity. While envy first comes into the story of humanity through Cain, there is an earlier account of envy in Christian tradition: Lucifer's envy made him turn away from God and destroy God's creation, because he felt that human beings had taken his position.

41. Ibid., 7.

42. "That night Jacob got up and took his two wives, his two maidservants and his eleven sons and crossed the ford of the Jabbok. After he had sent them across the stream, he sent over all his possessions. So Jacob was left alone, and a man wrestled with him till daybreak. When the man saw that he could not overpower him, he touched the socket of Jacob's hip so that his hip was wrenched as he wrestled with the man. Then the man said, Let me go, for it is daybreak. But Jacob replied, 'I will not let you go unless you bless me.' The man asked him, 'What is your name?' 'Jacob,' he answered. Then the man said, 'Your name will no longer be Jacob, but Israel, because you have struggled with God and with men and have overcome.' Jacob said, 'Please tell me your name.' But he replied, 'Why do you ask my name?' Then he blessed him there. So Jacob called the place Peniel, saying, 'It is because I saw God face to face, and yet my life was spared.' The sun rose above him as he passed Peniel, and he was limping because of his hip" (Gen 32:22–31).

The Tormented Shadow

alone—and to this day I don't know why I was so jealous of sharing with anyone the peculiar blackness of that experience."[43]

Jung himself traveled to Africa, and in his autobiography, *Memories, Dreams, Reflections*, he describes his African experience as dreamlike.[44] Colleen Burke sees in *Heart of Darkness* a metaphor of Jungian psychology:

> Jung's reflexive entries on his African travels in *Memories, Dreams, Reflections* repeatedly echo Marlow's narrative on topics from the reason for setting forth in the first place to the expectations of inner change, from the experience of primordial time to the encounter with wildness and the recognition of personified shadow.[45]

The shadow of Kurtz *tempts* Marlow, he lures him deeper into the darkness, but unlike the traditional Satan, he does not have to offer much; it is a vague idea that drives Marlow, a voice, but with a distorted message. In the quest for a shadow, all Marlow has is a voice to follow. The man Marlow is seeking is without substance: "the whisper of the wilderness echoed loudly within him because he was hollow at the core."[46] Kurtz is a word, an idea—Marlow's attempts to discover a meaning beyond the word failed and so do the reader's.

Marlow's journey is one of self-discovery, the narrative explores

> something truer, more fundamental, and distinctly less material: the night journey into the unconscious, and confrontation of an entity within the self.... It little matters what, in terms of psychological symbolism, we call this double or say he represents: whether the Freudian id or the Jungian shadow, or more vaguely the outlaw.[47]

The Jungian shadow does not only refer to the personal unconscious, but Jung also regarded it as a trait shared by all humans individually, as well as collective phenomenon, expressed through cultural and religious concepts, such as Satan:

> For over two thousand years the figure of Satan, both as a theme of poetico-religious thinking and artistic creation, and

---

43. HD, 104–5.
44. "He was just a word for me. I did not see the man in the name any more than you do. Do you see him? Do you see the story? Do you see anything? It seems to me I am trying to tell you a dream" (HD, 50).
45. Burke, "Joseph Conrad's *Heart of Darkness*," 2.
46. HD, 95.
47. Guerard, "The Journey Within," 329–30.

Part Two: Satanic Characters

> as a mythologem, has been a constant psychological expression, having its source in the unconscious evolution of "metaphysical" images.... All the old ideas of God, indeed thought itself, and particularly numinous thought, have their origin in *experience*.[48]

While we have observed earlier that Kurtz and Marlow's identities and moral frameworks were shifted and corrupted by their surroundings and circumstances, it is also important to note that through the concept of the shadow, *Heart of Darkness* expresses the belief in the dark side of the person and therefore in an innate human capacity to *do* or indeed to *be* evil: "The mind of man is capable of anything, because everything is in it, all the past as well as all the future."[49]

The beginning of modern times had changed the perception of Satan in society and literature. Following the ideas of Enlightenment, the discoveries in medicine, psychology, and biology influenced the picture of Satan dramatically: the devil was humankind itself. Satan lost his face and figure, and transformed into the darker part of the human personality. The prototype for this new face of Satan was Mary Shelley's *Frankenstein* (1818). The relation between Professor Frankenstein and the monster is a symbol of the relation between God and the fallen angel:

> Like Adam, I was apparently united by no link to any other being in existence; but his state was far different from mine in every other respect. He had come forth from the hands of God a perfect creature, happy and prosperous but I was wretched, helpless, and alone. Many times I considered Satan as the fitter emblem of my condition, for often, like him, when I viewed the bliss of my protectors, the bitter gall of envy rose within me.[50]

Robert Louis Stevenson's *Dr. Jekyll and Mr. Hyde* (1886) takes the idea a step further: the novel develops an internalized conception of evil. Satan does not appear as a figure or monster, but is one part of a human psyche. The Freudian psychoanalysis emerging on Vienna also supported the rise of a syndrome of the split personality. For Sigmund Freud (1856–1939), the devil was no more than a collective illusion, but he saw the human personally determined by drives that are neither good nor bad, yet that are demonized by our moral conscience. The internalization of the devil influenced art and literature, and developed further in figures like Bram Stoker's *Dracula* (1897) and Murnau's *Nosferatu* (1922). The disembodied Satan did not,

---

48. Werblowsky, *Lucifer and Prometheus*, ix.
49. HD, 63.
50. Shelley, *Frankenstein Or The Modern Prometheus*, 91.

The Tormented Shadow

however, lose his power and got perhaps even more terrifying: intangible and omnipresent in the human world, he survived his disembodiment and grew even stronger as part of the human personality.

Back to the shadow aspect in *Heart of Darkness*, several commentaries have noticed parallels between the novel and Vergil's *Aeneid*, in particular the imagery and symbolism of the descent into hell:

> The epic descent is always a journey to find someone who knows the truth. Marlow realizes long before he has penetrated the Congo that the real purpose of his journey is to meet Kurtz and talk with him. When he discovers Kurtz, he finds, on one level, a man who has committed unspeakable crimes against his fellows. But on another and more important level, he finds a man who has allowed himself to sink to the lowest possible depths of evil, and by observing Kurtz, Marlow realizes that in all people there is this possibility. In other words, he discovers the potential hell in the heart of every person.[51]

The jungle into which Marlow ventures deeper and deeper "has sealed [Kurtz's] soul to its own by the inconceivable ceremonies of some devilish initiation,"[52] thereby equating it with hell.

Marlow discovers the potential for evil in the heart of every person, expressed in the words of the dying Kurtz. It is a frightening realization of a human's ability to sin, seen in the mirror of the self:

> The mind of man is capable of anything—because everything is in it, all the past as well as all the future. What was there after all? Joy, fear, sorrow, devotion, valour, rage—who can tell?—but truth—truth stripped of its cloak of time.[53]

From his journey into Hell and the encounter with his shadow, Marlow comes back a changed man. The darkness, however, has no meaning; it is in fact the absence of any meaning:

> I suggest, then, that the horror that assails Marlow has to do with the impossibility of disclosing a central core, an essence, even a ground to what Kurtz has done and what he is. There is no central thread in the weave of the evidences that constitute his character, much less no deep center to his existence as a surface of signs.[54]

---

51. Feder, "Marlow's Descent into Hell," 291.
52. HD, 81.
53. Ibid., 63.
54. Meisel, "Decentering *Heart of Darkness*," 25.

Part Two: Satanic Characters

The Symbolism of Evil

If we are looking at the myth of evil and the question of Satan as a symbol, we need to refer to the work of Paul Ricoeur,[55] who suggests that fault and evil are an absurdity that can be confronted only in the language of symbol and myth. Ricoeur's ideas on symbol and myth put narrative in the focus of the academic debate. Not only human ability, but also the human need to tell the stories become the starting point of philosophical and theological anthropology. This approach is truly phenomenological in its focus on the primal symbols and experiences of humanity: "Ricoeur's anthropology is in no case a description of the radical origin of evil but only the description of the locus of evil, the place where it appears and can be seen."[56] Ricoeur wanted to incorporate symbolic expressions into philosophical discourse. Since symbols only suggest a meaning and can never be analyzed, it seems probable that they can never be objects of philosophical thought. Ricoeur suggests that a *propaedeutic* is needed, a purely descriptive phenomenology of symbols, in which philosophers provisionally adopt a neutral mode of thought and accepts the symbols as if they were true.[57] The philosopher should describe and clarify the symbols and myths, before philosophically reflecting on them. The symbols are therefore not constructed, but are already there, as cultural deposits. Ricoeur is aware that these symbols can only be acknowledged through the philosopher's own cultural contingency:

> Since man's confession of his brokenness is always couched in symbolic language, phenomenological ontology must face the problem of interpreting the symbols of evil so they can be incorporated into philosophic thought—if this is indeed possible.[58]

Using original sin as an explanation for the existence of evil is insufficient for Ricoeur. His starting point is somewhere else: behind the myth of evil, there is an abundance of evil in primary symbols, such as stain, guilt, and sin. Ricoeur refers to them as symbols of the fault. For him, such symbols have a primitive and spontaneous meaning, whereas myth and speculative doctrines add a second or third level of meaning. The three functions of myth are identified by Ricoeur as concrete universality, temporal orientation, and ontological exploration:

---

55. Ricoeur, *The Symbolism of Evil*.
56. Stewart, "Paul Ricoeur's Phenomenology of Evil," 94.
57. Ibid., 134.
58. Ibid., 35.

> First, they place the whole of mankind and its drama under the sign of an exemplary man, an Anthropos, an Adam, who symbolically stands for the concrete universal of human experience. Secondly, they give to this history an élan, an allure, an orientation, by unfolding it between a beginning and an end; they thus introduce an historical tension into human experience, starting from the double horizon of a genesis and an apocalypse. Finally, and more fundamentally, they explore the cleavage in human reality represented by the passage or leap from innocence to guilt; they recount how man, originally good, has become what he is in the present. That is why myth can exercise its symbolic function only through the specific means of narrative: what it wants to say is already drama.[59]

Through narrative, myth uncovers a new level of experience and this adds to the revealing power of primary symbols.[60]

Narrative acts as a verbal enclosure for a form of life felt and experienced:

> Going up that river was like travelling back to the earliest beginnings of the world, when vegetation rioted on the earth and the big trees were kings. . . . The broadening waters flowed through a mob of wooded islands; you lost your way on that river as you would in a desert, and butted all day long against shoals, trying to find the channel, till you thought yourself bewitched and cut off for ever from everything you had known once—somewhere—far away—in another existence perhaps.[61]

The man of the myth is already the man of the fault, because he is the man who recognizes his separation from the fullness of being—the transition period from the pre-narrative consciousness to the mythical narrative itself is important. Ricoeur introduces a typology of principles of the myth of evil in order to move from the static categories (defilement, sin, guilt) to an analysis of the dynamic interaction of the basic schemes. He argues that a philosophy starts from symbols and promotes their meaning by creative interpretation: "All the symbols of guilt—deviation, wandering, captivity,—all the myths—chaos, blinding, mixture, fall,—speak of the situation of the being of man in the being of the world."[62]

---

59. Ricoeur, "The Hermeneutics of Symbols and Philosophical Reflection," 197.
60. Stewart, "Paul Ricoeur's Phenomenology of Evil," 157.
61. HD, 59.
62. Ricoeur, *The Symbolism of Evil*, 356.

Part Two: Satanic Characters

Summary: A High Seat amongst the Devils of the Land

The language of *Heart of Darkness* is full of symbolism: the long river, the greyness of the world, and the looming threat of Kurtz's presence create an atmosphere where evil exists in the nature of human beings and the land. The symbolism of *Heart of Darkness* raises two particular aspects that are relevant for our purpose: first, evil lies ungoverned in human nature, only suppressed by social and moral rules of conduct, and can be easily unleashed in circumstances that challenge the system in place. The idea that human beings carry the capacity to sin in their nature is theologically expressed in the dogma of the original sin. The state of sin, however, is seen as a direct result of the fall of humankind, which according to Christian theology was caused by Satan and the dilemma of free will. Kurtz's voyage into the heart of darkness can thus be read as sinful, even satanic, in the denial of the traditional world order:

> Kurtz's degradation is not the traditional result of a moral failure; it is exalted and incredible, perhaps God-like: it is the effect of his setting himself apart from the earth and the morality of the earth—apart, even, from the language of the earth with which he had such magnificent facility.[63]

Following Ricoeur and his thoughts on symbolism, the image of the shadow could thus be read as a further symbol of the fault and the immediacy and physicality of evil.

Second, and in relation to the first observation, evil appears as the shadow or the dark side of the self, referring to an internal struggle between aspects that influence human behavior. Since the rise of modern psychology and especially psychoanalysis, the aspect of the "dark side" of the human soul is often categorized with clinical diagnosis such as depression, personality disorders, and schizophrenia. As we have seen above, Jung and others have interpreted the shadow as a powerful symbol of the experience of self-alienation and destruction. In theological terms, Satan is that shadow: the encounter with Satan usually occurs in private; consequently, satanic temptation represents an internal struggle. Kurtz's "The Horror, the Horror" essentially foreshadowed the experiences of the twentieth century with its experience of megalomania, human destructiveness, and the various attempts to create new world orders through oppression, violence, and death:

---

63. Guetti, *The Limits of Metaphor*, 491.

There was nothing either above and below him, and I knew it. He had kicked himself loose of the earth. Confound the man! He had kicked the very earth to pieces.[64]

---

64. HD, 107.

seven

The Zeroing Zero

Nothing. That is precisely the miracle. After the death of God, Nothingness was at the door, and Hitler was its only born son. In a certain sense he never existed; he was, as it were the *Hitler Lie* made flesh. The absolute, logical Antichrist.[1]

The Case of Hitler

Carl Gustav Jung was witness to another shadow that came over Europe during his lifetime: Adolf Hitler. In his essay *Wotan* (1936), Jung described Germany as "infected by one man who is obviously possessed" in addition to "rolling towards perdition."[2] Jung's analysis of Hitler, however, is just one of many attempts to understand the most notorious satanic figure of twentieth-century history. In his *Anatomy of Human Destructiveness*, philosopher and psychoanalyst Erich Fromm diagnosed Adolf Hitler as a clinical case of necrophilia.[3] Fromm analyzes Hitler's childhood, his main source being the biography by B. F. Smith (1967), to which author Norman Mailer also refers to in his novel *The Castle in the Forest* (2007).[4] According to Fromm, necrophilia is not merely a phenomenon, but a character-rooted passion. He bases his thesis on clinical observations, influenced by

---

1. Mulisch, *Siegfried*, 149.
2. Jung, *Civilisation in Transition*, 185
3. Fromm, *The Anatomy of Human Destructiveness*, 369.
4. He also draws on the memoirs of Albert Speer, referring to Maser, *Adolf Hitler: Legende—Mythos—Wirklichkeit*.

the theories of Sigmund Freud, on the life and death instincts, stating that "I had been deeply impressed by his concept that the striving for life and the striving for destruction were the two most fundamental forces within man."[5] Fromm names a few character traits of a necrophilous personality, such as interest in sickness and death, narcissism, the conviction that the only way to resolve a conflict is by force and a particular attitude toward the past and property:

> For the necrophilous character, only the past is experienced as quite real, not the present or the future. What has been, i.e., what is dead, rules his life: institutions, laws, property, traditions, and possessions. Briefly, things rule man; having rules being: the dead rule the living. In the necrophile's thinking—personal, philosophical, and political—the past is sacred, nothing new is valuable, drastic change is a crime against the natural order.[6]

The fascination with death and destruction does not, however, exclude a fascination for creation and particularly technique: "His approach to the whole world around him—and to himself—is intellectual; he wants to know what things are, how they function and how they can be constructed or manipulated."[7] Fromm draws his conclusion from clinical case studies and the most popular one is his character analysis of Adolf Hitler. Fromm characterizes Hitler as a destructive personality, referring to the Holocaust as well as to Hitler's warfare and his ambivalent attitude towards building and destroying cities. He had a fear of dirt, poison, and contamination, which according to Fromm are the typical neuroses of the necrophiliac.

Norman Mailer's analysis of Adolf Hitler resembles that of Erich Fromm—they both refer to Hitler's childhood and young adult years using the same resources. However, while Fromm tries to explain Hitler's action with a clinical diagnosis, Norman Mailer's novel looks for another explanation: Satan himself becomes aware of the potential in young Adolf and sends his agent to keep a close eye on him and to guide him in the right direction. The idea behind these two very different interpretations is the same: how can human beings commit evil deeds? Not just evil in the way that Erich Fromm describes "benign aggression" (in relation to defense or attainment of what one wants), but the wish to destroy for the sake of destruction:

> The fallacy lies in the belief that a thoroughly destructive and evil man must be a devil—and look his part; that he must be

---

5. Fromm, *The Anatomy of Human Destructiveness*, 331.
6. Ibid., 339.
7. Ibid., 352.

devoid of any positive quality; that he must bear the sign of Cain so visibly that everyone can recognize his destructiveness from afar. Such devils exist, but they are very rare. As I indicated earlier, much more often the intensely destructive person will show a front of kindliness; courtesy; love of family, of children, of animals; he will speak of his ideals and good intentions. But not only this. There is hardly a man who is utterly devoid of any kindness, of any good intention. . . . Hence, as long as one believes that the evil man wears horns, one will not discover an evil man.[8]

The psychoanalytical approach to Hitler's personality, indeed to any personality, can only play a small part in the understanding of human behavior. Even in forensic psychiatry, the limits of any psychoanalytical attempt to explain evil are acknowledged. A direct relationship between a psychological condition and a specific action is still not established and the mental condition of a person only explains their behavior to a certain extent. Hans-Ludwig Kröber, director of the Institute for Forensic Psychiatry at the Berlin Charité Hospital, claims in an interview with the newspaper ZEIT in 2009 that "evil lives in the deed."[9] For Kröber, evil is more than a result of personal circumstances or biological determinism. He asserts that evil is the deliberate will to destroy, best expressed through unmediated and direct *experience.*

Hitler and the Story

Dutch author Harry Mulisch (b. 1927) approaches the subject form a literary angle, taking account of previous psychoanalysis of Hitler. His novel *Siegfried*, published in 2001,[10] tells the story of the Dutch writer Rudolf Herter, who is Mulisch's alter ego. Herter is a successful writer in his seventies who visits Vienna to read from his work. In an interview, he asserts that it may be only through fiction that the unique evil of Adolf Hitler can be truly expressed and comprehended. After a public reading, Herter is approached by an old couple, the Falks, who tell him the incredible story of how they witnessed the birth of Hitler's son by Eva Braun. They took on the child, Siegfried, and raised him as their son, until they were ordered to kill

---

8. Ibid., 432.

9. *"Das Böse lebt in der Tat."* Ein Gespräch mit Hans-Ludwig Kröber, Charité Berlin.

10. 2003 in English, translated by Paul Vincent.

the boy towards the end of the War. Rudolf Herter is fascinated by the story and begins his own thought experiment on Hitler and the nature of evil.

Gradually, he becomes obsessed with the idea that Hitler was in fact the personification of evil. Confronted with the inexplicability of Hitler's character through the story he hears from the Falks, he takes the "metaphysical route out":

> Hitler was a singularity in human form—surrounded by the black hole of his retinue! If you ask me, no one has yet come up with that idea. Right. I am not going to give this all devouring Nothingness a psychological foundation, as is always attempted in vain, but a philosophical one, since it is first and foremost a logical problem: a cluster of predicates without a subject. This makes it the exact opposite of the God in the negative theology of Pseudo-Dionysius Areopagita, from the fifth century: in that God is a subject without predicates, since he is too big for us to be able to say anything about him. So you could assert that, in the framework of negative theology, Hitler is the devil—but not in the official, positive theology of Augustine and Aquinas. Anyway, enough.[11]

For Herter, in his seventies and with his own memories of the reality of war, the thought experiment becomes more than the research for a new literary project, but an obsession with finding the right and final approach to explain the phenomenon of Hitler. What he records is the culmination of modern and postmodern thought in the *Gestalt* of Hitler. He sees in him the logical conclusion and, even more, the rebirth of Friedrich Nietzsche. He regards him as the personification of Nothingness, as the incarnation of the Totally Other.

What started out as a literary attempt to approach Hitler soon becomes Herter's personal theology of evil. Herter claims that Hitler's essence was the absence of any personhood and best expressed by the image of a hollow statue:

> "Of course this isn't an explanation—the secret remains a secret—but perhaps it says something about the nature of the secret. That is, that he was actually nobody. A hollow statue, as you say. And the fascination he exerted and exerts to this day, and the power given him by the German people, was not *despite* the fact of his being soulless, but *because of* that fact." Herter sighed. "We must of course be careful that we don't deify him, even if it is with a negative sign. But if that one God (as history seems to indicate) does not exist, Hitler's deification perhaps

---

11. Mulisch, *Siegfried*, 133–34.

Part Two: Satanic Characters

> touches the heart of the matter. In that case he is the deification of something that doesn't exist."[12]

After a meeting with the Dutch conductor Constant Ernst in the Dutch embassy, Herter develops this idea further:

> If Hitler were the adored and cursed personification of nothingness, in whom there was nothing to restrain him from anything at all, his true face could not be revealed in a literary mirror, as Herter had suggested yesterday to Constant Ernst, since there *was* no face. In that case he was more comparable with Count Dracula, a vampire feeding on human blood: one of the "undead," with no reflection. Hence he was different not in degree but in essence from other despots, like Nero, Napoleon, or Stalin. They were demonic figures, but even demons are still something positive, whereas Hitler's essence was its absence. In a paradoxical way, precisely the lack of a "true face" was his true nature. Did that imply that Herter himself would have succeeded only if he did not manage to write his revelatory phantasm? In that case Hitler would have escaped for the umpteenth time, but he wouldn't get the chance this time.[13]

But as the plot continues and Herter hears the Falks' whole story, he realizes that no fiction could ever really capture the essence of Hitler, and he remarks "reality bats imagination."[14]

As Mulisch/Herter develop the idea further, it becomes clear that Hitler was the only absolute logical Antichrist.[15] The answer to the mysterium of Hitler does not lie in psychology, Herter observes, but in philosophy and eventually in theology. Mulisch retells the history of postmodern thought in his novel, as his protagonist Herter establishes a logical line from Plato to Kant, to Hegel, Schopenhauer, and Nietzsche, and finally Hitler. He draws a connection to the negative theology of the mystics and eventually refers to German Protestant theologian Rudolf Otto (1869–1937) and his idea of the *mysterium tremendum ac fascinans*,[16] the simultaneously horrific and fascinating secret. Herter himself explains the theological concept as follows:

12. Ibid., 75.
13. Ibid., 76.
14. Ibid., 131.

15. Cf. ibid., 149. The Antichrist is generally understood as a single human person opposing Christ or true Christians. The biblical references are from the Johannine Epistles, the book of Revelation, and the Pauline Epistles. Despite his common association with Satan, the Antichrist is not a demonic figure and not the incarnated Satan. Mulisch uses both terms, devil and Antichrist, to describe Hitler.

16. Rudolf Otto uses the term *fearful mystery* to describe the central character of

Rudolf Otto had pointed to the core of all religion: the terrifying "Totally Other," the absolutely foreign, the denial of everything that exists and can be thought, the mystical Nothingness, the stupor, the sense of being "knocked out cold" that both attracts and repels. That was a different tune from the Christians' benign "dear Lord." He was an asthmatic descendant of the authentic, wild heavenly men and women—who, by the way, did not shrink from sacrificing his own son, an act he had once forbidden Abraham from committing. No, only Hitler was the epiphany of that chilling tradition.[17]

The connection between Adolf Hitler and Friedrich Nietzsche has been made before, even though the philosopher has been regularly misinterpreted in the light of National Socialism and the Third Reich.[18] In *Siegfried*, Herter takes this connection one step further into the absurd: he sees not only Nietzsche's thoughts realized in Hitler's absolute will for destruction, but also interprets Hitler as the *physical* reincarnation of the philosopher.[19]

Hitler, a Satanic Figure?

In Mulisch's novel, we encounter Ullrich Falk, who worked as Hitler's personal servant before he was asked to take care of Siegfried, and who tells Herter how he once saw Hitler, woken up by a nightmare and shaken in horror:

> I tore the door open and saw him standing bewildered in the middle of the room in his nightshirt, pouring with sweat; he looked at me with blue lips, his hair disheveled, his face contorted with fear. I shall never forget what he said: *he . . . he . . . he . . . was here.*[20]

It might have been the devil Hitler saw in that nightmare, it might also have been his personal shadow, the awareness of the horror that he was responsible for.

God, the numinous dread, in *The Idea of the Holy*.

17. Mulisch, *Siegfried*, 136.

18. Contemporary scholars on Nietzsche in Germany agree that his philosophy was abused for National Socialist propaganda. See Aschheim, *Nietzsche und die Deutschen*, and Kirchhoff, *Nietzsche, Hitler und die Deutschen*.

19. Mulisch, *Siegfried*, 146. Nietzsche's thoughts will feature more in the next chapter.

20. Ibid., 82.

Part Two: Satanic Characters

Portraying Hitler as either the devil, the ultimate personification of evil, or being begotten by Satan is not original to Harry Mulisch. Apart from Mulisch's novel, Norman Mailer's last work *The Castle in the Forest* (2007) deals with the unholy connection between Satan and Hitler as his agent. Both novels can be seen in a long tradition of identifying historic personalities as agents of Satan, collaborating with Satan, or even being the Lord of Darkness himself. In the same way as men with absolute power often assume a divine status, they are equally likely to be vilified up to the point of being identified with the Antichrist or Satan. There are of course countless examples of that association, including Judas Iscariot, Pilate, Herod, Nero, Napoleon, Pol Pot, and Stalin—probably most despotic leaders of several centuries—most antipopes, several heretics, the reformers and counter-reformers, and psychotic mass murderers. What lies behind the need to explain human evil with possession or satanic pacts—apart from politically motivated defamation and instrumentalizations—is the inability of the human mind to comprehend the extent of the "evil nature" of certain humans and the need to find explanations. What characterizes a person as evil is extremely difficult to say and depends almost entirely on the methodology of the debate. It is not only the obvious criteria of committing evil, that is, causing somebody else pain and suffering, but there are underlying issues of conscience, morals, motions such as envy and jealousy, and malevolence. It is difficult to understand the complexity of an evil character entirely and this leaves us all the more speechless when faced with evil:

> In the course of time, he continued, countless experts had racked their brains over the question of when Adolf became Hitler. First he was an innocent infant, then a delightful toddler, then a growing child, then a young man eager to learn—where, when, how, as a result of what had he changed into absolute terror? No one had yet given a satisfactory answer. Why not? Perhaps because the psychologists were not philosophers, and especially not theologians. And perhaps in turn the monotheistic theologians gave Hitler a wide berth and became caught up in theodicy: how could the one God allow Auschwitz? Yes, he was suddenly sure of it. None of the theologians dared go to the ultimate extreme, like Hitler himself. Fear of the Totally Other had paralyzed them, too. Hitler had knocked them out cold, too—some even regarded it as immoral to try to understand him. But now Hitler found him, Herter, on his path.[21]

21. Mulisch, *Siegfried*, 137.

The Zeroing Zero

What is left is the attempt to approach the evil character through narrative, to tell his story, to make him or her the center of attention and to create a space for them. For those who have not witnessed the terror themselves, the Holocaust and therefore the personality of Hitler come alive through narrative. This is Herter's intention in Mulisch's novel: to try to understand Hitler through fiction.

When it comes to explaining the phenomenon of Adolf Hitler, the reference to Satan has been made frequently. The danger of associating Hitler with Satan lies in denying Hitler his humanity and therefore taking away the full responsibility for his actions. Such comparisons are nevertheless made due to the notion that evil cannot be explained by one academic or scientific discipline, but needs a second level, a meta-level:

> When the ambassador had finished, Herter said that Hitler, precisely because of his enigmatic nature, was the dominant twentieth-century figure. Stalin and Mao were also mass murderers, but they were not enigmatic; that was why so much less had been written about them. There had been countless people like them in history, and there still were and would always be, but there had been only one Hitler. Perhaps he was the most enigmatic human being of all time. . . . Wouldn't it be nice if as the conclusion of the twentieth century the last world could be said about him, as a kind of Final Solution to the Hitler Question?[22]

The reception of Harry Mulisch's *Siegfried* by German and Austrian critics was not very positive. This may be due to a translation issue, but is more likely related to the skepticism that contemporary Germans (and possibly Austrians) display in the context of any fictionalized account of Adolf Hitler:

> What is most annoying about this book is that despite its success in the Netherlands, it claims to have solved the "mystery" of Hitler. Much more worrying is the de-realization of the dictator through a mixture of terminology from theology and existential philosophy that the author uses to relate to Hitler.[23]

---

22. Ibid., 29–30.

23. "Was wirklich ärgerlich ist an diesem in den Niederlanden außerordentlich erfolgreichen Buch, das sich übrigens, dies sei zugegeben, durchaus spannend liest, ist nicht so sehr die Selbstermächtigung eines Schriftstellers, der vorgibt, das 'Rätsel Hitler' gelöst zu haben. Viel bedenklicher ist die Entwirklichung des Diktators durch das Begriffsbrimborium aus Theologie und Existentialphilosophie, mit dem der Autor seinen Hitler ausstaffiert," (own translation); Krause, Tilman: Rezension zu Harry Mulischs Siegfried. *Die Welt* (die literarische Welt), Ausgabe 42, Belletristik. Samstag, 3. November 2001, 4.

Part Two: Satanic Characters

The crucial word here is *Entwirklichung*, translated as "De-realization." Instead of bringing a literary character to life through words, a historic character is dematerialized through the same process. A similar reaction met Norman Mailer's *The Castle in the Forest*. Published in German in 2007, the book's launch coincided with a heated debate about the portrayal of Hitler in fiction, initiated by Dani Levy's comedy film *Mein Führer—die wirklich wahrste Wahrheit über Adolf Hitler*.[24] Salomon Korn, Vice-President of Germany's Central Council of Jews commented on *The Castle in the Forest* in conversation with the ARD (German Public TV station):

> One cannot forbid artists from dealing with Hitler but art will never achieve an understanding of the phenomenon— it will rather serve as a distraction. Anyone tackling [this subject] artistically should carefully consider what their real intentions are.[25]

What has been missed in the German discussion is that narrative does not replace history, but that it can add an important new level to the understanding of a phenomenon that will never be fully explained by any methodology or thought model. The person of Hitler and the consequences of the will of one man can be approached through many different methodological possibilities: the historic approach, the sociological approach, the psychological approach. If all fail, like Herter suggests in *Siegfried*, it is the artist who can make one last attempt to solve the mystery:

> But it will continue for centuries. By now a hundred thousand studies have been devoted to him, if not more: political, historical, economic, psychological, sociological, theological, occult, and so on ad infinitum. He's been examined from all sides, a line of books has been written about him that would reach from here to the Stefansdom, more than about anyone else, but it hasn't gotten us anywhere. I haven't read everything—one lifetime is too short for that—but if anyone had explained him satisfactorily, I would know. He has remained the enigma that he was to everyone from the beginning—or no, he has simply become more incomprehensible. All those so-called explanations have simply made him more invisible. If you ask me, he is sitting in hell laughing himself silly. It's time that was changed. Perhaps fiction is the net that he can be caught in.[26]

---

24. A summary on the reception of the film is given in Wikipedia, "Mein Führer— Die wirklich wahrste Wahrheit über Adolf Hitler."

25. Smee: Mailer's young Hitler novel angers Germans.

26. Mulisch, *Siegfried*, 15.

In the case of *Siegfried,* the critics might also have overlooked the fact that Herter writes himself into destruction. The author's experiment to approach the subject of Hitler through story fails. Reality beats fiction, and the attempt to explain brings nothing but horror and death. Mulisch's referral to metaphysics does not really contribute anything to the discussion about Hitler's personality and psyche and does not bring us any nearer to an understanding of the Holocaust. But it shows one thing: the attempt to explain the reality of evil fails; what is left is the experience of it, tangible in the account of the Falks and through Herter's imagination, made possible through the human ability to empathize.

Adolf Hitler has served as a face for the atrocities of the Holocaust and has been demonized in many aspects. The horrors of the Third Reich have left Jewish and Christian theologians speechless; the problem summarized by Herter's simple question: "How could the one God allow Auschwitz?"[27] The question is *not* whether the fictive connection between Hitler and a satanic figure makes more sense of the horrific realities of the Third Reich, but whether fiction can provide access to the underlying concept of evil. Adolf Hitler in *Siegfried* is not to be understood as a real historic figure, but rather as a symbol for something that threatens humanity in general. The strict separation between "reality" and "imagination" does not contribute to the understanding of evil. Reality and fiction merge; our understanding of the Holocaust is shaped by our imagination. In 1995, Bernhard Schlink, German law professor and crime author, published his novel *The Reader.* In it, the protagonist Michael Berg comments on reality and fiction:

> When I think today about those years, I realize how little direct observation there actually was, how few photographs that made life and murder in the camps real. We knew the gate of Auschwitz with its inscription, the stacked wooden bunks, the piles of hair and glasses and suitcases; we knew the building that formed the entrance to Birkenau with the tower, the two wings, and the entrance for the trains; and from Bergen-Belsen the mountains of corpses found and photographed by the Allies at the liberation. We were familiar with some of the testimony of prisoners, but many of them were published soon after the war and not reissued until the 1980s, and in the intervening years they were out of print. Today there are so many books and films that the world of the camps is part of our collective imagination and completes our ordinary everyday one. Our imagination knows its way around it, and since the television series Holocaust and movies like *Sophie's Choice* and especially

27. Ibid., 136.

Schindler's List, actually moves in it, not just registering, but supplementing and embellishing it. Back then, the imagination was almost static: the shattering fact of the world of the camps seemed properly beyond its operations. The few images derived from Allied photographs and the testimony of survivors flashed on the mind again and again, until they froze into clichés.[28]

Evil as Nothingness

The thought of evil as nothingness plays an important role in Mulisch's novel and has been a widespread approach in the tradition of Christian theology. The most popular explanation for the existence of evil in traditional Christian theology is the idea that evil is the absence of good. That approach tries to reconcile the real experience of evil and suffering with the existence of a benevolent and omnipotent deity through the definition of evil as the lack of good. The idea of evil as privation does not mean that evil *is* nothing. It might be nothing in substance, but its effect of deprivation is positive in so far as it has an effect on reality. This theology goes back to St. Augustine of Hippo who was a follower of Manichaeism before he converted to Christianity, and whose theology was directed against the Manichaean idea of the dual nature of good and evil. The Augustinian theology on evil is also closely connected with the idea of original sin and the fall of humankind as a result of the misuse of human freedom. Augustine's thoughts on evil have influenced Christian theology strongly and, as we have seen earlier, the Christian concept of Satan also owes a debt to his teachings. Augustine's idea that evil is no entity of its own, but an absence of good, comes from Neo-Platonism, mainly from the teachings of Plotinus. Augustine believed, like the Neo-Platonists, in a God who is both perfectly good and eternal. But for Augustine, God's whole creation is good and expresses the perfect goodness and beauty of God. It is the complexity of creation that reflects God's perfectness and goodness. This *principle of plenitude* is also Augustinian: the perfect universe is one exemplifying every possible kind of existence, from beautiful to ugly, from perfect to imperfect. Augustine laid "the foundation for a Christian naturalism that rejoices in this world, and instead of fleeing from it as a snare to the soul, it seeks to use it and share it in gratitude to God for His bountiful goodness."[29]

---

28. Schlink, *The Reader*, 146–47.
29. Hick, *Evil and the God of Love*, 45.

Evil for Augustine is not a positive force or substance, but the malfunctioning of something that is essentially good, the "corruption of a mutable good."[30] This thought is generally described with the expression *privatio boni*. Augustine compares evil to a wound or a defect:

> What, after all, is anything we call evil except the privation of good? In animal bodies, for instance, sickness and wounds are nothing but the privation of health. When a cure is effected, the evils which were present (i.e., the sickness and the wounds) do not retreat and go elsewhere. Rather, they simply do not exist any more. For such evil is not a substance: the wound or the disease is a defect of the bodily substance which, as a substance, is good.[31]

Augustine believes in privation of good; there can be no evil without good:

> Evils, therefore, have their source in the good, and unless they are parasitic on something good, they are not anything at all. There is no other source whence an evil thing can come to be. If this is the case, then, in so far as a thing is an entity, it is unquestionably good. If it is an incorruptible entity, it is a great good. But even if it is a corruptible entity, it still has no mode of existence except as an aspect of something that is good. Only by corrupting something good can corruption inflict injury.[32]

But how does this corruption occur? Augustine believes that because creation is mutable, everything created is capable of turning away from God. This is generally referred to as the *free will defense*, something that, for Augustine, explains both the moral evil of sin and human suffering in its many forms. The privative definition of evil together with the free will defense explain within this Christian theology how there can be evil in a good creation: evil is not created, but consists of the free and voluntary turning away from good:

> The evil will as an experienced and experiencing reality is not negative. It can be a terrifyingly positive force in the world. Cruelty is not merely an extreme absence of kindness, but is something with a demonic power of its own. Hatred is merely lack of love, or malevolence merely a minimum degree of goodwill.[33]

---

30. Ibid., 46.
31. Augustine of Hippo, *Confessions and Enchiridion*, Enchiridion, III, 11.
32. Ibid., Enchiridion, IV, 14.
33. Hick, *Evil and the God of Love*, 57.

Part Two: Satanic Characters

Augustine's approach to evil can be characterized as follows: evil exists, but has no entity of its own; it is merely the absence of good (*privatio boni*). The origin of evil lies in the free will of the creation to turn away from the creator (free will defense). The existence of metaphysical evil (e.g., imperfection in creation, finitude of every life, illnesses, etc.) is explained by Augustine with the idea that the perfect universe has to contain every possible form of existence (principle of plenitude). All three aspects of Augustine's thought model suggest an aesthetic theme—that Augustine believed that in the sight of God all things form a perfect harmony:

> To thee there is no such thing as evil, and even in thy whole creation taken as a whole, there is not; because there is nothing from beyond it that can burst in and destroy the order which though hast appointed for it.[34]

Augustine's thoughts on evil have influenced orthodox theology throughout the centuries. For our purpose, I focus more on evil as the absence of good or, as other thinkers have put it, the idea of evil as nothingness. I cannot provide more than a summary of the Augustinian theodicy and its perceptions and, equally, this is not the place to critique it. Nevertheless, it seems important to mention the most problematic aspects of Augustine's thought system when it comes to the existence of evil, in particular, why does the human, who is created spiritually and morally good, decide with free will to sin? And why did God create a being that could sin freely? The aesthetic approach of Augustine's theology also does not concern the *ethical* aspect of the debate. It generally focuses on the causes of the problem, instead of looking for the solution to it. The emphasis lies on the aspect of metaphysical evil and not on moral or ethical aspects. For the contemporary debate of evil, this approach leaves too many questions unanswered and demands an approach that shifts the focus from the *origins* of evil to the *images* of evil.

The idea of evil as nothingness, however, has been one of the most widely discussed approaches in Christian theology. In particular the Christian mystics of the fourteenth to the sixteenth century understood evil and Satan ultimately as nothingness:

> The contemplative's desire to avoid definitions and their hesitation to press for rational explanations deterred them from dwelling on the Devil intellectually. Yet in practise they felt his presence more often and more immediate than most.[35]

---

34. Augustine of Hippo, *Confessions and Enchiridion*, Confessions VII, 13.
35. Russell, *The Prince of Darkness*, 161.

The Zeroing Zero

Swiss theologian Karl Barth gave one of the most complex explanations of the nothingness of evil in recent thought:[36]

> There is no doubt that Barth's doctrine of *das Nichtige* as the non-willed reality on the margins of God's creation and providence, represents of the most remarkable attempts in theological history to comprehend the problem of evil.[37]

In short, Barth's doctrine of the nothingness of evil assumes a third factor (next to God and his creation) that exists in the form of opposition and resistance. This factor takes the form of nothingness, in the shape of sin, pain, suffering, and death.[38] In ontological terms, only God and his creature really and properly exist.[39] But nothingness still has a real existence that is experienced; it is not just that *which is not*. Barth explains *das Nichtige* as that which God did not elect to create; that which is non-willed and therefore rejected. Nothingness, outside God's creation and therefore outside his grace, constantly threatens the creation through evil and death, causing "affliction and misery."[40]

For Barth, evil can have a substance, despite its ontological nothingness: "Nothingness is falsehood. It exists as such, having a kind of substance and person, vitality and spontaneity, form and power and movement."[41]

In his tractate on creation in *Church Dogmatics*, he talks about the devil as the father of all lies, whose origins we find in nothingness and who poses a threat to God's creation: "In Biblical terms we can also describe it as chaos, or darkness, or evil. . . . Or we might call it the being which denies all true being and is denied by it."[42]

The biggest criticism of Karl Barth's concept of evil as nothingness is ontological: it seems difficult to understand how nothingness can have existence and why God would create a world with the third factor of nothingness.[43] In his thoughts on Karl Barth and the Holocaust, Mark Lindsay suggests the approach of evil as nothingness that can contribute to an understanding of the phenomenon of evil that is historically applicable: nothingness is a universal threat to every creature and one that makes of us both

---

36. Barth, "God and Nothingness," §50 in *The Doctrine of Creation*, 289–368.
37. Lindsay, "Nothingness Revisited," 6.
38. Hick, *Evil and the God of Love*, 138.
39. Barth, *The Doctrine of Creation*, 289 90.
40. Ibid., 354.
41. Ibid., 527.
42. Ibid., 523.
43. Hick, *Evil and the God of Love*, 142–43, 192–93.

Part Two: Satanic Characters

potential victim and agent.[44] This is a constant possibility in any personal or historic concept. Mulisch's interpretation of evil as nothingness also creates another line of argument: his literary figure of Adolf Hitler is empty of everything that constitutes personhood. Evil looks at us from a human face, but the essence of the person is absent—void of anything that characterizes it as created in the image of God.

The Body of Satan

In the context of Mulisch's novel, I now examine the portrayal of Satan's physical forms. Is Satan the incarnation of evil? Does nothingness have a physical form or even a body? Can Satan be incarnated in a human form? Or is evil best understood in the term "possession"? The mutual reference point of the terms "incarnation" and "possession" is the body. If we speak of the body in a theological context, we mean more than just flesh or our appearance and bodily functions. It is through the body that we act; it is through our body that we harm or heal others. The occasional feeling of not being in control of one's body is frightening and leaves us with a feeling of weakness and powerlessness. It is probably exactly that feeling of a lack of control that lies at the ground of every idea of external governing of the human body. Patients who suffer from mental illnesses such as schizophrenia and panic attacks experience the feeling of being guided by someone or something in the most powerful and destructive way. Most cultures and religions practice rituals and traditions that recognize the body as a mediator for non-physical experiences and as an instrument to enact certain tasks. Some members of charismatic and evangelical Christian groups experience God or the Holy Spirit talking through them. The acting of an external entity through the human body does not leave it unaffected. The experience of not being in control of the physical self is disturbing and generally changes the awareness of oneself. There is, however, a difference in the concepts of the transformation of the body.

Being in the Flesh

Incarnation means *enfleshment*. Something without a physical body takes on the form of a physical being to become visible and perceptible. The word "incarnation" however implies more than just that. It is different from other words that describe the same idea, for example, embodiment,

---

44. Lindsay, "Nothingness Revisited," 16.

personification, or possession. Incarnation refers to something more substantial. It involves the process of an essentially immaterial entity taking on a material manifestation. Incarnation is more than possession, where something takes control of a being, and it is more than embodiment, which is defined as a physical entity typifying an abstraction. Incarnation implies that the immaterial entity becomes real in its material manifestation and finds its true form. Incarnation is irreversible and unique and implies voluntariness. It is not a process of overtaking, but one of completion. Even though incarnation happens in a specific person and in a specific time, it is endless in its existence. It is continued as a phenomenon. In Christian theology, incarnation is the process of the λόγος becoming flesh. The second person in the Christian Trinity becomes human, being conceived by the Virgin Mary through the Holy Spirit. The terminology comes from John 1:14— καί ὁ λόγος σάρξ ἐγένετο ("and the Word became/was made flesh"). The nature of the incarnation was defined by the First Council of Nicaea in 325 CE. The Greek term ὁμοούσιος (of one essence) was agreed upon against the Arian idea of ὁμοιούσιος (alike in essence). This subsequently became the Christian understanding of incarnation: to be truly God and truly man simultaneously. God needs us to substantiate his being—he reacts to us. Incarnation is proof of his pure love, which happens without necessity and aims for completion, not destruction. According to Christian theology, God became incarnate in a human being because humanity is his creation and therefore good. It is incompatible with the concept of the Christian body being evil. This became clear very early in the history of Christian dogma: Christian theology sees the human creation as essentially good and that is necessary for the concept of incarnation. God only finds a place in a being that is in its nature good:

> If Christianity can reinterpret its concept of incarnation along these lines, so that incarnation (metaphorically understood) becomes a matter of degree, and is no longer confined to the one instance of Jesus of Nazareth, we shall have a doctrine which points clearly to Jesus as a supreme revealer of God's love, and as one in who God was manifestly at work, but a doctrine which does not claim an exclusive revelation that undermines the validity of the other great world religions.[45]

---

45. Hick, "Evil and Incarnation," 84.

Part Two: Satanic Characters

Possession of the Body

Other than the concept of incarnation, the act of possession does not involve an essential and lasting transformation of the body, but a temporary and purposeful intrusion of a spirit into a body.

> Although the relationship between spirit and host has been described in many ways, most indigenous descriptions suggest the spirit's entrance, intrusion, or incorporation into the host. The relationship is one of container to contained.... The spirit is said to mount the host (who is likened to a horse or some other beast of burden), to enter, to take possession of, to have a proprietary interest in, to haunt, to inhabit, to besiege, to be a guest of, to strike or slap, to seduce, to marry, or to have sexual relations with the host. In part, this variety reflects changes in the spirit-host relationship, a relationship that should not be regarded as static, well-defined, and permanent but rather as dynamic, ill-defined, and transitory.[46]

Possession is not necessarily a negative experience; the term is also used to relate to communication with the spiritual world or in the context of healing. In some societies, possessions are valued because they support the community's religious, moral, or political order. The result of possession is usually described as an altered state of consciousness.

In the Christian belief system, though, possession is traditionally connected with demons and witchcraft. An evil spirit gains control over a mortal's body and uses it for destructive or evil purposes. For the authors of the New Testament, the demons ($\delta\alpha\iota\mu\omega\nu$) are subject to the devil; in the hierarchy, they stand between God and humans:

> They attack people and take possession of them. They cause illnesses (Mark 1:32–34 and par.; Matt. 9:32–35; 12:22–24 and par.) or destroy the self, so that it is finally they who speak through those possessed by them (Luke 4:33–37 and par.).[47]

> It is in the New Testament literature that the notion of indwelling possession begins to dominate the perception of humanity's interaction with demonic and divine spiritual forces. Although demons are occasionally portrayed as exterior persecutors in the synoptic gospels, they most often appear as interior inhabitants of the human body, and it is as indwelling possessors

---

46. Crapanzano, "Spirit Possession," 8689.
47. Röhl, "Demons," 795.

who adversely affect human physiology that they are subject to exorcism.[48]

Possession is considered reversible, but generally, it needs an outer influence to break the connection between the possessor and the possessed. This act is generally referred to as exorcism, the practice of evicting demons or other spirits from persons or places:

> Exorcisms serve as visible signs that accompany the spoken word of the eschatological overthrow of the kingdom of Satan. . . . The New Testament stories of exorcism individualize this warfare to make the body of the possessed a battleground within which the demonic and divine forces engage.[49]

The exorcism of a demon or evil spirit from a person, place, or thing has been part of the belief system of several religions. It is through the Catholic Church that the rituals of exorcism are most known today, but the exorcism of demons has been part of the Christian tradition since the time of Jesus. It is traditionally through the naming of the demon that the exorcist can gain power over it. The knowledge of the name, that is, the demon's identity, gives power and authority over it. In the Synoptic Gospels and Acts, there are about fifty references to exorcism:

> The passages range from brief references to stories that provide enough detail to identify the person possessed, the form of possession, the exorcist, and the manner of exorcism. . . . In the New Testament demonic afflictions are described as physiological ailments or as self-destructive and isolating behaviors that often appear as the subjects of medical treatment in the Greco-Roman world.[50]

Thomas Aquinas observed that only God can inhabit the soul or mind. Since the devil's suggestions are external to it, he inhabits it only by his effects. The devil can only inhabit the body in forms of possession.[51] Today, any form of exorcism is regarded with great suspicion, since most symptoms of possession are now recognized as the result of neurological or psychological illnesses. I will not discuss the process of exorcism in the pastoral and liturgical practice of Christian churches. For our purposes, the idea of possession helps to illustrate the concept of Satan in literature:

---

48. Sorensen, *Possession and Exorcism in the New Testament and Early Christianity*, 119.
49. Ibid., 128–29.
50. Ibid., 122–24.
51. Aquinas, *On Evil*, 441–536.

Part Two: Satanic Characters

Satan can never be incarnated in a human form, can never fully transform or complete a person—he can only take on the human form temporarily. He needs a host, a vehicle, a story, in order to become alive.

The Parasitic Nature of Evil

One attribute of possession is the idea of a *host* governed by an evil spirit or demon. A human being or animal is no longer in control of themselves and is guided by something other than their own will. To describe the essential difference between the incarnation of God in a human being and any personification of evil it is necessary to refer to the parasitic nature of evil. Evil takes control of human beings, lives in them, and then leaves them emptied and injured, if not dead. In metaphorical terms, evil feeds on humans, but just as any parasitic life form, the parasite cannot live without its host. Satan, in essence pure nothingness, takes on a form through possession.[52] The idea of evil as a virus is old: the Hellenistic world of the Gospel writers was very aware of demons and their power over the human body and mind. The idea of evil as a virus requires the victim to be alive. Evil is destructive and in the long run self-destructive; but at the same time, it has no interest in preserving what it is exploiting.

Personhood

In the context of the discussion of evil as nothingness and the related aspects of incarnation and personification of evil, I would like to introduce a phenomenological approach[53] to evil, with an emphasis on the personal and

---

52. In fiction, the idea of evil forces using human bodies to its benefit is well known. The idea of a parasitic life form feeding on the human body has been especially popular in the science fiction and horror genres of the twentieth century. *Invasion of the Bodysnatchers* (1956 and several remakes), the *Alien* series (1979 till 2004), *The Thing* (1982), and most recently Lord Voldemort in *Harry Potter and the Philosopher's Stone* (2001), to name just a few of the most successful films, evolved around the idea of an evil life form that feeds on human bodies and/or brains to eventually gain control over humanity.

53. "The thing-out-there, the thing-in-itself, cannot be grasped. All that we can grasp is the phenomenon, the concept that we create of the thing. We can be certain of our knowledge of phenomena. Though we do not create nature, we construct it by organizing it into meaningful patterns, and since we are the organizers, we can fully know what we have organized" (Hegel, *Logic*, 240). If we want to approach the problem of evil through its expression rather than through its being, we need to turn towards phenomenology. As a philosophical method, it was first introduced by Edmund Husserl in the early twentieth century. The term itself had been used by Hegel, but it was

relational aspect. It is through this aspect that I hope to show how the figure of Satan can symbolize crucial aspects of evil. The argument will focus on Marion's phenomenology of evil as he portrays it in the first essay of his work *Prolegomena to Charity*.[54]

Satan or the Almost Defeat of the Person

Jean-Luc Marion establishes a phenomenology of evil that focuses on the relational aspect of human nature.[55] Marion's phenomenology takes the experience of pain and suffering as its starting point. The fact that evil hurts requires no proof or argument. The only reasonable response is to attempt to free oneself from that experience. Marion refers to what he calls the *logic of evil*, "to destroy the cause of the evil that is destroying me, to return to the evil its hurt, and to attack the attack."[56] Even though the cause of the suffering might be unknown, the first reaction to the experience is to plead one's own cause. This is where the desire for vengeance begins. In this context, Marion refers to Nietzsche: "Where there was suffering, one always wanted

---

Husserl's use of the term that established phenomenology as a philosophical discourse, referring to the study of phenomena. The study of that which appears and is perceived with our consciousness is conducted from a first-person point of view and therefore is the experience of or about some object. Phenomenology needs to be seen in the context of the Kantian and Hegelian history of thought. During the eighteenth and nineteenth century, phenomena had become increasingly important for scientific and rational research. Phenomena were seen as starting points in building knowledge, be it in an empirical way (sensory data or facts) or in a rational way (ideas that appear in our minds). For Husserl, influenced by the thoughts of his teachers Franz Brentano and Carl Stumpf (both philosophers and psychologists), reality is revealed through phenomena that are perceived through consciousness in their immediacy.

54. "Evil in Person," in *Prolegomena to Charity*, 1–30.

55. Influenced by the tradition of Husserl and Hegel, Catholic philosopher and phenomenologist Jean-Luc Marion (b. 1946) understands phenomenology as a *rescue* for theology. He connects God's role in the twentieth century with the destiny of metaphysics. He sees the death of God in philosophy (and also theology) as essentially belonging to the end of metaphysics: the overcoming of onto-theology becomes the condition for surpassing the naming of God in philosophy as efficient ground. For Marion, phenomenology is the natural and right way of practicing theology. It speaks of the return to the things themselves and is thus not a restoration of metaphysics, but—according to Marion—does not exclude the existence of a meta-physical being, of God: the things themselves just do not appear according to the figure of ground, but according to that of donation; no longer according to efficiency (*causa sui*) but according to the being-given. Marion credits to Emmanuel Levinas (1906–95) the understanding that ontology was not able to reach the ground because that ground did not belong to the domain of theoretical philosophy, but to that of *ethics*.

56. Marion, *Prolegomena to Charity*, 2.

Part Two: Satanic Characters

punishment, too."[57] In order to rid ourselves of evil, we must first make this evil a not-us, we must distance ourselves from it. Evil is perpetuated, universalized, and eventually personalized:

> To put a face to the cause of one's suffering is to be able, at one, to plead one's cause efficiently. I can only accuse a face, and the worst of sufferings consists precisely in not having any face to accuse.[58]

For Marion, the understanding of original sin lies exactly in that claim for innocence and the attempt to rid oneself of all evil by projecting it on someone else. Therefore, original sin takes the form of a series of self-justifying accusations. In the Garden of Eden, God asks for the sinner:

> And he said, "Who told you that you were naked? Have you eaten from the tree that I commanded you not to eat from?" The man said, "The woman you put here with me—she gave me some fruit from the tree, and I ate it." Then the LORD God said to the woman, "What is this you have done?" The woman said, "The serpent deceived me, and I ate."[59]

Adam transmits the responsibility to Eve, who then transmits it to the serpent:

> Sin enters the world replete with the entire logic of evil: transmit evil to the other so as to rid one's self of it and in this way lay claim to innocence.[60]

For Marion, in blaming the other for one's own suffering, the cycle of revenge and counter-evil begins.

Consequently, the only way to prevent the perpetuation of evil would be to acknowledge one's responsibility for it. According to Marion, there are two possibilities: either one endures evil and admits a total loss (no value and no compensation), or one attempts to pass it on (assure equity for myself by bringing iniquity for someone else). The resultant spiral of experiencing suffering and transferring it accordingly can only be interrupted by the death of Jesus Christ:

> Christ vanquishes evil only by refusing to transmit it, enduring it to the point of running the risk, in "blocking" it, of dying; the

---

57. Nietzsche, *Thus Spoke Zarathustra*, 20.
58. Marion, *Prolegomena to Charity*, 4.
59. Gen 3:11–13.
60. Marion, *Prolegomena to Charity*, 9.

just man is precisely he who endures evil without rendering it, suffers without claiming the right to make others suffer, suffers as if he were guilty.[61]

In this context, Marion believes the death of God is the only way to break the eternal transmission of sin and suffering, and that this is only possible if God is absolutely guilty, absolutely punished, and absolutely dead.[62]

"Evil is its essence, a lonely thing, a passion of the solitary individual soul."[63] Following the Augustinian definition of evil as the *privatio boni*, evil can be characterized most appropriately through absence. Evil is separation, not relation: "Such is hell. . . . comprehending that hell is the absence of every other."[64] The logic of evil betrays. As a result of revenge, the other is excluded from the world. Hell is the moment when the soul finds itself finally alone.[65] Evil forbids every relation with others or with oneself; evil creates emotional isolation from other people and from oneself. Evil is a condition, not an action. Grammatically, "evil" is used as an adjective or noun, but never as a verb and therefore does not create a relation. If hell is betrayal without betrayer, how then is Satan's existence necessary or possible? The soul is not deceived but it deceives itself—are we therefore not exempt from introducing the person of Satan? For Marion, the existence of Satan follows the *logic of evil*: "Satan tempts, deceives, and kills insofar as he dissimulates and slips away."[66] The absence of Satan constitutes his sole mode of action and he adds to revenge by manifesting its intention and its essence. Hell is the absence of every other, even of Satan. Ultimately, Satan acts evasively, as opposed to decisively, because he can do nothing else:

> We must give up imagining Satan as all-powerful: he is capable of nothing, or more exactly, only of what can become nothing, through possession; he is capable of nothing to counter the filial distance he has lost.[67]

---

61. Ibid.
62. Ibid., 10.
63. Machen, "The White People," 115.
64. Marion, *Prolegomena to Charity*, 19.
65. This is why suicide is considered as sin: in order to avenge myself from the world, I commit suicide and by doing so, I bar myself from every reconciliation with the other.
66. Marion, *Prolegomena to Charity*, 23.
67. Ibid., 24.

Part Two: Satanic Characters

> Satan only prospers from a diminished existence, a defeated personality, illiterate in charity:

> > In inflicting temptation, Satan tries to disfigure the person in man, to fill the distance within him, to erase his *similitude Dei*, temptation consist in the confrontation between a negative personality and a person who doubts his own personality: in temptation, a person fights to empty a personality of his person.[68]

Marion refers to Dante's picture of Satan in the *Inferno*: in hell, any access to the other is denied, and Satan has deprived himself of inhabiting the distance in which God gives himself: "Satan cries and slobbers at no longer being able to inhabit distance, that is to say at no longer being a person."[69] Marion characterizes Satan as the absolute negative of the person—the perfect idiot:

> More than every other soul, Satan suffers from hell, the ultimate circle of which binds him in a solitude so absolute, an identity so perfect, a consciousness so lucid and a sincerity so transparent to itself, that he becomes there the absolute negative of the person—the perfect idiot. Absolute idiot, enclosure from distance, personality empty of any living person: Satan does not let us prove his existence easily, for in fact his existence is as good as wholly annihilated. Satan or the almost defeat of the person.[70]

The definition of evil includes the absence of freedom. Evil depersonalizes the human being by taking away the free will. True freedom may be defined as "the human ability to satisfy personal claims and desires while concurrently satisfying the claims and desires of others."[71] For Marion, goodness and true freedom are inextricably intertwined, so the definition of evil includes the absence of true freedom.

Satan tries to destroy the person in the human being, to take from them all that makes them human. He kills by rendering an individual as solitary as himself: "Evil is the destruction of freedom because evil is the intentional destruction of reciprocity. To destroy reciprocity is to destroy the source of freedom."[72]

---

68. Ibid., 28.
69. Ibid., 25.
70. Ibid.
71. Dickson, "The Phenomenology of Evil," 5.
72. Ibid., 6.

Satan does not have the means to modify the human personality; he tries to delude us into believing that we already have no free will, so that eventually, we ourselves willfully annihilate our will:

> In temptation . . . Satan appears to us as such: evil in person, but paradoxically a personality empty of what makes the person (the free will to love), a personality who, in the mode of depersonalization, works indirectly to undo our person, so as to imprison us in the idiocy of hell.[73]

Evil destroys—it literally creates non-existence. The evildoer destroys not only the life of another person, but also his own personhood. By trying to achieve absolute freedom through alienating himself from any other, the evildoer puts himself in a position that is irreversible. But evil cannot exist in a vacuum; evil needs the person to achieve the aim: the human being, emptied of all personhood and without any relationship to the other, imprisoned in the idiocy of hell.

Summary: Satan—Personne or Person?

We have now touched upon another tension in the debate: is Satan a person or is he characterized through the absence of personhood? Marion's phenomenology of evil has a strong focus on the personal and relational aspect of evil. For him, there also lies the answer to the question of the existence of Satan:

> Does Satan exist? But really what does to exist mean here? Evil aims only to universalize what its reality—on the extreme fringe of nothingness—amounts to: a person bereft of all personality, an eternal absence inhabited only by this minimum of consciousness, which allows him to hate his inexistence; the person of Satan amounts to a nothingness that personalizes his despair.[74]

Marion uses a linguistic play on words in his native language French to express his understanding of the existence of Satan: "Satan can be called 'nobody' (*personne*): a person who hides only an absence of person; and thus the only indisputable proof of his 'existence' comes to us from the abyss, the vertigo of which, often, pushes us to suicide."[75]

---

73. Marion, *Prolegomena to Charity*, 29.
74. Ibid.
75. Ibid., 29–30.

Part Two: Satanic Characters

Following Marion's thoughts, it seems that we have discovered another paradoxical aspect of Satan's character: his existence is relational; he is defined in the relation to either God or human, his function of adversary always implies an *other*. But at the same time, his presence destroys relation and denies unity. Satan is portrayed as a character with personal features, but he simultaneously tries to destroy the personalities of people and to alienate them from themselves and the Creator. Marion's understanding of evil starts with the human experience of pain and suffering, acknowledges the attempt to get rid of these emotions by claiming one's own innocence and searching for retribution and revenge, and ends with the observation that true evil lies in the loss of personhood and the absence of the other. Satan is described as a person because he comes with the attributes of one. But in his tragic existence, he is the one who de-personalizes, who destroys relation, who takes away what truly characterizes a person.[76]

We have seen in this chapter that evil is often interpreted as nothingness or absence. However, the physical and personal experience of evil is an important aspect of the discussion. The personification of the abstract concept of evil can be approached in different ways. There is the idea that evil finds its manifestation in actual historic persons, often related to the idea of the Antichrist. There is also the attempt to find a body for evil in fictional characters. The important questions in both cases is whether evil finds its true home in a person, or whether evil can only have a physical form through parasitic methods, that is, possession. The figure of Satan is one possible personification of evil, and the paradox of this character serves as a very adequate interpretation of evil: according to Christian theology and folklore, Satan needs the human soul to compensate for his own soullessness. Satan appears as a person, but his aim is to destroy the personality.

---

76. This thought also appears in Karl Barth's discussion of evil in his *Church Dogmatics*, for example Part Three, chapter 3.

eight

The Creative Eliminator

> His courage will destroy his happiness on earth, he must be an enemy to the men he loves and the institutions in which he grew up, he must spare neither person nor thing, however it may hurt him.[1]

Blood Meridian or The Evening Redness in the West was published in 1985 and is today considered Cormac McCarthy's masterpiece. After publication, the novel received only lukewarm critical reception, but is now generally regarded as part of the American canon of literature, and is compared to Hermann Melville's great American myth *Moby Dick*. The narrative's protagonist is a nameless youth, referred to as Kid, who leaves home at fourteen and joins a gang of scalp hunters under the leadership of Captain John Joel Glanton. The gang is paid by Mexican governors to kill Indians, in particular Comanche warriors who regularly invade settlements like Chihuahua City. The story follows the bloody trail of the scalp hunters as they cross the American Southwest in the 1850s, murdering, raping, and looting indiscriminately. The novel is based on historic record, and is—as meticulously researched by McCarthy scholars and fans—geographically and socio-culturally correct.[2] The most enigmatic character of the novel is Judge Holden, who rides with the Glanton gang and is as intelligent as he is cruel. He breaks every taboo in the lawless environment of the unmapped landscape by raping and killing children. The gang eventually takes the

---

1. Nietzsche, "Schopenhauer as Educator," 143.
2. Two of the leading figures of the novel, John Joel Glanton and Judge Holden, are based on historical figures: see Smith, "John Joel Glanton, Lord of the Scalp Range," and Sepich, "What Kind of Indians Was Them?"

Part Two: Satanic Characters

Yuma ferry under their control and most of them are killed during an early morning attack by the Indians. The showdown of McCarthy's Western takes place between the Judge, who escapes the attack, and the Kid. Despite the chance to shoot the Judge, the Kid does not kill him, and both manage to escape the desert, the only two survivors of the Glanton gang. The novel then jumps forward twenty-five years and the Kid, now the "Man," faces the Judge for the final time, leaving the Kid dead in the jakes in the town of Fort Griffin and the Judge triumphantly laughing and dancing.

Blood Meridian is an unsettling account of violence and death and leaves the reader equally disturbed and fascinated by the descriptions of torture and murder that dominate the largest parts of the narrative. The episodes of war and destruction have no meta-narrative; the only connection is the presence of mindless violence. The reader is forced to follow the restless journey of the Glanton gang, hoping to find redemption in at least one of the characters, but is left without hope when the final scene describes the brutal murder of the Kid and the eternal dance of the Judge. Apart from short stays in towns and settlements that are usually concluded with drunken violence and looting, the gang members do not find any peace and are reminiscent of the ghostly cowboys, riding in the sky, forever damned to "catch the Devil's herd across these endless skies,"[3]

> Above all else they appeared wholly at venture, primal, provisional, devoid of order. Like beings provoked out of the absolute rock and set nameless and at no remove from their own loomings to wander ravenous and doomed and mute as gorgons shambling the brutal wastes of Gondwanaland in a time before nomenclature was and each was all.[4]

The motif of the restless journey is prevalent in many of McCarthy's works, most obvious in the journey of father and son in his 2006 novel *The Road*, but also in the travels of John Grady Cole in *The Border's Trilogy*:

> Most of McCarthy's novels, despite their apparent episodic organization, involve both metaphoric and literal journeys which bring their voyagers inevitably into a series of conflicts and confrontations with themselves as well as with the various communities intersected by their wandering. And, in most of

---

3. "(Ghost) Riders in the Sky: A Cowboy Legend," written by Stan Jones in 1948, is a country song, inspired by the Nordic myth of the Wild Hunt. Over fifty performers have recorded versions of the song that tells the folk tale of a Cowboy who is warned in a vision to change his ways, otherwise he would ride forever, chasing red-eyed, steel-hoofed cows across the sky.

4. BM, 172.

these novels, the central characters' journeys, however random in time and place they may be, are apparently rooted in dysfunctional families and troubled filial relationships.[5]

The aimless journey of destruction through a hostile country in *Blood Meridian* is only interrupted by dreamlike episodes and parables that circle around the Judge. The language of *Blood Meridian* is archaic and even biblical, the style pre-modern and epic. The writing of Cormac McCarthy has been compared to paintings by Hieronymus Bosch in their visions of hell and demons, and to the writings of William Faulkner and Herman Melville. It is difficult to decide where to start interpreting the symbolism of *Blood Meridian*. The language of Cormac McCarthy eludes interpretation, it seems impossible to decipher or analyze the images of the novel. This is precisely why *Blood Meridian* is such a gripping example of the destructive power of narrative. In Cormac McCarthy's novels, darkness is not a metaphysical possibility, embodied in evil or insane characters, but the reality of existence—present not just in the human existence, but in nature in general. In *Heart of Darkness*, Kurtz sees the horror, but it is seen as something that can be avoided. In *Blood Meridian*, the characters are entirely submerged in the horror. There is no possibility of salvation; the churches are ruins; there are only ex-priests and only natural history left, with no symbolism either in humanity or nature.

The protagonist of the novel is the Kid but only insofar as that he is in the reader's focus from beginning to end. There is no self-reflection or self-consciousness in the characters of Blood Meridian, neither the Kid nor any of the other gang members reveal any form of inner life. Cormac McCarthy observes and describes more than he narrates, and thus leaves the reader without an overarching structure or a meta-narrative that would explain the senseless violence through the psychology of the characters. Evil in *Blood Meridian* is approached through phenomena: in the lawless landscape of the borderland there is no room for *why*. The reader is confronted with a purely phenomenal world, with no first principles. The term "evil" seems inadequate to describe the actions or characters in the novel—there is no framework in place that would allow distinction between good and evil:

> *Blood Meridian* makes it clear all along that Mr. McCarthy has asked us to witness evil not in order to understand it but to affirm its inexplicable reality; his elaborate language invents a world hinged between the real and surreal, jolting us out of complacency.[6]

5. Sepich, "What Kind of Indians Was Them?" 176–77.
6. James, "Is Everybody Dead around Here?" 31.

Part Two: Satanic Characters

Blood Meridian has been described as an antinomian novel: it eludes fixed meaning or universal applicability of moral law. In precisely this nihilistic and amoral setting, devoid of moral framework, we encounter the Judge, without a doubt one of the most enigmatic characters of evil in twentieth-century literature.[7] In the context of this work, I will attempt to analyze Judge Holden as a satanic figure, and how he reflects the understanding of evil portrayed in *Blood Meridian*.

Judge Holden

Out of nowhere appears the Judge; the Kid asks "What's he a judge of?"[8] but does not get an answer. The Kid first encounters the Judge in the town of Nacogdoches, in a tent where Reverend Green, a preacher falsely accused of child abuse and bestiality by the Judge, seems to recognize his true nature: "This is him, cried the reverend, sobbing. This is him. The devil. There he stands."[9] But the reverend's statement does not make any impression on the crowd he is addressing; he gets lynched right away, because the trust of the masses belongs to the Judge. He is charismatic and authoritative and determines the fate of everybody in his surroundings. Furthermore, after this initial encounter, the reader follows the journey taken by the Kid who, together with the Glanton gang, has fallen under the jurisdiction of the Judge. The Kid and the reader encounter the Judge in a country without law; many of the scenes are set in the desert, far removed from civilization, exposed to the unregulated cruelty of the land. As we have previously observed, Satan is regularly encountered in the middle of nowhere, on a crossroad or in a situation that requires a decision. Everybody in Glanton's party claims to have seen the Judge before but he appears out of nowhere, leaving traces that cannot be followed. In the course of the novel, the Judge shows remarkable knowledge in areas of history, geology, philosophy, and jurisprudence. In the Christian tradition and in literature and myth, Satan has been associated with intellect and knowledge. Holden also speaks different languages and shows the dress code and the urbane behavior of a cosmopolitan. He is a magnificent dancer and a talented fiddler, again reinforcing the link with Satan, who "was said in the Middle Ages to own a violin with which he could set whole cities, grandparents and grandchil-

---

7. In 2002, *Book* magazine rated Holden, as appearing in *Blood Meridian*, as the 43rd greatest character in fiction since 1900 (National Public Radio, "100 Best Characters in Fiction Since 1900").

8. BM, 135.

9. Ibid., 7.

dren, men and women, girls and boys, to dancing, dancing until they fell dead from sheer exhaustion."[10]

McCarthy describes the Judge in a similar way:

> He never sleeps, he says. He says he'll never die. He bows to the fiddlers and sashays backwards and throws back his head and laughs deep in his throat and he is a great favorite, the judge. He wafts his hat and the lunar dome of his skull passes palely under the lamps and he swings about and takes possession of one of the fiddlers and he pirouettes and makes a pass, two passes, dancing and fiddling at once. His feet are light and nimble. He never sleeps. He says that he will never die. He dances in light and in shadow, he is a great favorite. He never sleeps, the judge. He is dancing, dancing. He says that he will never die.[11]

With Judge Holden we also reencounter the image of the wanderer. With the Glanton Gang, he roams the borderlands with neither aim nor place to rest. He shows super-human attributes, both in his appearance and his physical abilities: he is tall, massive in frame, and very strong; he is hairless like a child with no eyebrows or eyelashes and very pale, possibly Albino. He seems immune to sleep and aging and manages to survive many attacks without a scar on his body.

> He was among every kind of man, herder and bullhawker and drover and freighter and miner and hunter and soldier and pedlar and gambler and drifter and drunkard and thief and he was among the dregs of the earth in beggary a thousand years and he was among the scapegrace scions of eastern dynasties and in all that motley assemblage he sat by them and yet alone as if he were some other sort of man entire and he seemed little changed or none in all these years.[12]

The Judge is a satanic figure, but in the boundary-less world of *Blood Meridian*, he transcends the recognized portrayals of the devil and stands for something that lies beyond the Judeo-Christian concept of Satan. Judge Holden does not rebel against the divine order, he *is* the divine order—in his notebook, he rewrites the world as he sees it. Despite the attributes that might reveal his true nature, Judge Holden cannot be Satan in the sense of the Christian narrative. To his story, there is no tragic element, no sympathy,

---

10. Rudwin, *Devil Stories*, 256.
11. BM, 335.
12. Ibid., 325.

Part Two: Satanic Characters

and no redemption. Judge Holden goes beyond the categories of the Christian Satan.

The Judge as Fool

In the town of Corralitos, the gang is approached by a family of itinerant magicians seeking safe passage through the country to the city of Janos. At night around the fire, Glanton asks the man to tell their fortune. Three cards appear that night: the Kid picks the Four of Cups and Black John Jackson picks the Fool, the most powerful of all Tarot Trumps. Glanton picks the third card, but nobody sees it for it is taken away by the wind. But the blindfolded woman senses the card:[13] it is the Chariot, "card of war, card of vengeance,"[14] embodying the cyclic repetition in the turning of the wheels. John Emil Sepich[15] has given a detailed reading of *Blood Meridian*'s Tarot references,[16] claiming that Tarot symbolism can be found throughout the novel.[17] He also suggests that the Tarot scene links the character of the Judge to the archetype of the Fool:

> As the Fool is associated with eternal dancing, dancing which connects the end with the beginning, both in the Tarot and the novel, Judge Holden is defined by this card, the animating force of the Tarot. He stands both as judge of the dance that was the scalp hunters' war and as a personification of those universal energies, both super rational and mad folly, that are war itself.[18]

Sepich, also referring to Sallie Nichol's reading of the Tarot[19] in association with Jung, mentions the characterization of the Fool as giant, super-rational and mad, as a wanderer, energetic, ubiquitous and

---

13. McCarthy only gives the Spanish version, but the Cormac McCarthy Society provides a .pdf file with translations of the Spanish text fragments: "A Translation of the Spanish in *Blood Meridian*."

14. BM, 96.

15. John Sepich, an artist and scholar based in Illinois who exchanged letters and phone calls with Cormac McCarthy since 1988. He also wrote *Notes On "Blood Meridian."*

16. Sepich, "The Dance of History in Cormac McCarthy's Blood Meridian," 16–31.

17. Tarot cards have been used in Europe since the fifteenth century to play card games. Since around the eighteenth century, Tarot cards have been employed for divination and have been associated with mystics and occultists (ibid., 78).

18. Ibid., 24.

19. Nichols, *Jung and Tarot: An Archetypal Journey*.

immortal, free to travel of his own will.[20] Towards the end of the novel, Holden is accompanied by his mirror image, the Fool—an imbecile called James Robert who is kept by his brother in a cage to amuse paying spectators. *Blood Meridian* frequently alludes to carnival and circus, both of them references to "a continuous thread of allusion, both to bloody spectacle and to cyclic repetition."[21] Thus, "[t]he immense power of the sun, bound to the harshness of the country itself, drives men mad. Judge Holden is linked to the tarot Fool. And war requires an abundance of the willing."[22]

Judge Holden sees himself as the God of war, the dance as worship, as authoritative expression: "He dances in light and shadow and he is a great favorite. He never sleeps, the judge. He is dancing, dancing. He says that he will never die."[23] And,

> The dance is the thing with which we are concerned and contains complete within itself its own arrangement and history and finale there is no necessity that the dancers contain these things within themselves as well.[24]

In a similar context, Judge Holden is described as a gambler.[25] When asked his thoughts on child raising by Tobin, he gives the following statement:

> If God meant to interfere in the degeneracy of mankind would he not have done so by now? Wolves cull themselves, man. What other creature could? And is the race of man not more predacious yet? . . . He loves games? Let him play for stakes.[26]

Here, Judge Holden bears resemblance to Anton Chigurh in *No Country for Old Men*,[27] who tosses a coin to decide between dealing life or death.

The Judge as a Poet

The Judge creates and destroys simultaneously through writing and naming. The gang witnesses how in various circumstances, Holden writes and draws

---

20. Sepich, "Dance of History," 23.
21. Sepich, *Notes On "Blood Meridian,"* 169.
22. Ibid., 159.
23. BM, 335
24. Ibid., 329
25. "Men are born for games" (BM, 249).
26. BM, 146–47.
27. McCarthy, *No Country for Old Men*.

in his ledger, carefully recording artifacts and occurrences of the natural word, even though he seems to have distrust in books: "Books lie,"[28] he tells the gang. The only book that has value for him is his own. The Judge desires control; everything and everyone needs to submit to his will. William Dean Clement observes that "for the frontiersmen forging out during westward expansion, functional power lay in possessing the names of things."[29] We will see later how the namelessness of the Kid and thus his refusal to become part of the Judge's sketchbook is interpreted by Holden as a sign of rebellion and a refusal to submit to his order.[30] Glanton's men are aware of the Judge's power to create. He appears as the master over language; he creates through words. Amongst the gang, he is certainly the only one who is literate. He establishes his role in the group through his knowledge and through his use of language, with which he controls and governs the gang: "Books lie, he said. God dont lie. No, said the judge. He does not, and these are his words. He held up a chunk of rock. He speaks in stones and threes, the bones of things."[31]

The Judge is simultaneously creator and destroyer—he draws sketches of natural artifacts and destroys the original afterwards:

> Whatever exists, he said. Whatever in creation exists without my knowledge exists without my consent. . . . Only nature can enslave man and only when the existence of each last entity is routed out and made to stand naked before him will he be properly suzerain of the earth. . . . In order for it to be mine nothing must be permitted to occur upon it save by my dispensation.[32]

The Judge never sleeps, his eyes are always open, his senses right awake. This is in contrast to the other figures of *Blood Meridian* who are—often literally, most certainly metaphorical—deaf and blind and in the case of the Kid nearly mute. For the Judge, seeing is believing and most importantly, knowing. The Judge knows only what he sees, and everything that he sees or witnesses ceases to exist. The Judge is the logical consequence of modern thought: "The noon of his [man's] expression signals the onset of night. His

28. BM, 116.

29. Clement, *The Last of the True: The Kid's Place in Cormac McCarthy's* Blood Meridian, 34.

30. The Judge himself tells the Glanton group the story of an old Hueco whose portrait he had drawn. The man was subsequently terrified because he felt chained to his likeness and he feared that an enemy might get hold of it and deface it. Together with the man, the Judge then buries the portrait in a cave that only the Judge knew (BM, 141).

31. BM, 116.

32. Ibid., 198–99.

spirit is exhausted at the peak of its achievement. His meridian is at once his darkening and the evening of his day."[33]

The Judge as Mercurius

Blood Meridian can be read as a Gnostic novel. John Sepich and Leo Daugherty[34] interpret the characters of the Judge and the Kid as representatives of a dualist worldview in a Gnostic tragedy, following in its structure and content the Manichaean dualism. The Judge is the sovereign of this world; he is the master who lives without any awareness of good and evil. The Gnostics saw the world as evil, with only parts of the spirit imprisoned here. The landscape of *Blood Meridian* is the world created by the archons—the fallen aeons—and Glanton's scalp hunters are the human beings created by them: driven by envy, vanity, and lust for destruction, they are caught in their bodies as though in tombs. Only the spirit within is not from the archons, but comes from the original God of the *Pleromena*, imprisoned in the humans by the archons. This spirit is capable of learning and, in the Gnostic system, knowledge is the key for the spirit to escape its prison. The only person in *Blood Meridian* that seems to be capable of using his spirit is the Kid. In certain moments he seems to feel light in an otherwise uttermost dark world. In his essay "Why Believe the Judge," written for the revised version of *Notes on "Blood Meridian"* in 2008, Sepich connects the Judge with the conscious, and the Kid with the unconscious. But he also takes the comparison further, into the very core of the novel: "Mexico and the United States, Catholicism and Protestantism, the unconscious and the conscious, the irrational and the rational, the Kid and Holden, all quite real, all quite human, are layer upon layer in this book."[35]

Following Jungian ideas on the archetype, Sepich links the Judge with the alchemical figure of Mercurius. Originally the Roman God of trade and messengers, Mercurius (the Roman equivalent of Hermes) has various connotations with alchemy. The element mercury was seen as the secret transforming substance present in all living creatures. Often, Mercury has been approached as a divinity, combining in its being all opposites and presenting the working force or the fire for the whole process of life. Mercurius, who is associated with the wheel of life (*uroboros*), contains and unifies duality: he is a hermaphrodite, he is portrayed as a young and an old man, and he is

---

33. BM, 146–47.

34. This argument follows Daugherty, "Gravers False and True: *Blood Meridian* as Gnostic Tragedy."

35. Sepich, *Notes on "Blood Meridian,"* 149.

bride and groom; he contains the four elements and therefore is the quintessence of all:

> To the Christian mentality, the dark antagonist is always the devil. As I have shown, Mercurius escapes this prejudice by only a hair's breadth. But he escapes it, thanks to the fact that he scorns to carry on opposition at all costs. The magic of his name enables him, in spite of his ambiguity and duplicity, to keep outside the split (between Christ and the devil), for as an ancient pagan God he possesses a natural undividedness which is impervious to logical and moral contradiction.[36]

The key scene for this alchemical interpretation of the Judge is the first meeting of the Glanton gang with Holden: he sits on a single rock in the desert, with no equipment but his rifle, bearing the inscription *Et in Arcadia Ego*. The Renaissance proverb was used for memorial inscriptions for tombs and as graffiti under pictures of skulls. It translates as "Even in Arcadia there am I" and was used in Renaissance art to express the awareness of death and transience (*memento mori*). In the context of *Blood Meridian*, this proverb does not have an elegiac and self-reflexive connotation, but a threatening and sinister message: death is ubiquitous and the world is dark and pitiless, where killing is personified in the figure of the Judge. Sepich suggests that the stone of the Judge's appearance might be an analogue to the alchemist's philosopher's stone, a legendary substance that could supposedly turn metal into gold. The Judge uses "magic" to save the Glanton gang who are out of gun powder and are being chased by Apaches. He does not produce gold, but gunpowder, using saltpeter, charcoal, and sulphur, mixing it together with the urine of all the gang members, forming not only the substance to kill every one of the Indians, but also a "terrible covenant"[37] with Glanton and his gang, who are henceforth bound in a pact to ride with the Judge.

The Judge as Übermensch

> What is done out of love always takes place beyond good and evil.[38]

---

36. Jung, *Alchemical Studies*, 245.

37. BM, 126.

38. "Was aus Liebe getan wird, geschieht immer jenseits von Gut und Böse" (own translation from Nietzsche, *Jenseits von Gut und Böse*, Sprüche und Zwischenspiele, 153).

The Creative Eliminator

The Judge exists in the realm of historic and naturalistic law. Holden sees himself as an enlightened figure; the belief in any transcendence for him is superstition. He also rejects the ethical codes of society as a construct that holds back humanity's development:

> Moral law is an invention of mankind for the disenfranchisement of the powerful in favour of the weak. Historical law subverts it at every turn. A moral view can never be proven right or wrong by an ultimate test.[39]

Holden summarizes here the master-slave moral of Nietzsche and his challenge of the existence of objective morality. Cormac McCarthy's writing has been called Nietzschean and the figure of Judge Holden clearly shows parallels to Nietzsche's ideas. For our purpose, I will mention a few points relevant to the discussion of evil and the concept of reaching beyond a *moral* evil, mainly elaborated in *Thus Spoke Zarathustra, On the Genealogy of Morals,* and *Beyond Good and Evil*.[40]

Judge Holden and Nietzsche share the vision of a life beyond good and evil. Both criticize traditional morality and propagate an affirmative approach to life, including the creation of new values that would eventually create a higher existence. Both preach the renunciation of otherworldly values and focus their energies on the creation of a new value system, based on the natural world; as Nietzsche writes: "I love those who despise. Man, however, needs to be overcome."[41]

In that context, Nietzsche elaborated the concept of the *Übermensch*,[42] with a strong focus on the active will of the individual. The act of evil is therefore not defined through a moral framework, but more as a driving force behind the will to create:

> "Human beings are evil"—thus spoke all the wisest to comfort me. Oh, if only it were still true today! Because evil is a human being's best power. "Mankind must become better and more evil"—thus I teach. What is most evil is necessary for the overman's best.[43]

---

39. BM, 250.

40. For a discussion on Nietzsche's thought in Cormac McCarthy's work, see Donoghue, "Reading *Blood Meridian*," and Sepich, "The Dance of History in Cormac McCarthy's *Blood Meridian*," 16–31.

41. "Ich liebe die großen Verachtenden. Der Mensch aber ist etwas, das überwunden werden muss" (own translation from Nietzsche, *Also Sprach Zarathustra*, 505).

42. The term *Übermensch* and its translations are debated. Generally, it refers to the idea of an "ideal man" that humanity is aspiring to achieve.

43. Nietzsche, *Thus Spoke Zarathustra*, 234.

Part Two: Satanic Characters

The language of the novel shows parallels to the symbolism of *Thus Spoke Zarathustra*, in particular the references to dancing and the sun. The Judge is first encountered close to the meridian, just as the era of the *Übermensch* is referred to by Zarathustra as the "great noon":

> "Before God"—But now this god has died! You higher men, this god was your greatest danger. It is only now, since he lies in his grave, that you are resurrected. Only now the great noon comes, only now the higher man becomes—ruler.[44]

Dance was for Nietzsche the freedom and levity that is connected to the letting go of the old values; the Godlike dance is the affirmation of the earth and the possibility of physical change: "I would believe only in a God who could dance. And when I saw my devil I found him serious, thorough, profound, and solemn: it was the spirit of gravity—through him all things fall."[45]

Another parallel between McCarthy's character and Nietzsche's work is the reference to gambling. Both Holden and Chigurh (in *No Country for Old Men*), as discussed above, understand the gambler and the chance of the game as the only defining measure of behavior:

> For all things are baptized at the will of eternity and beyond good and evil; good and evil themselves, however, are only shadows in between and damp glooms and drift-clouds. . . .
>
> Oh sky above me, you pure, you exalted one! This your purity is to me now, that there is no eternal spider and spider web of reason:
>
> —that you are my dance floor for divine accident, that you are my gods' table for divine dice throws and dice players.[46]

Nietzsche's *Übermensch*, like Judge Holden, overcomes the slave moral of the Judeo-Christian belief system, most poignantly encountered in the notion of empathy:

> But it's their pity—
> —their pity is what I flee and why I flee to you . . .
> But you yourself—warn yourself too against *your* pitying! Because many are on their way to you, many who are suffering, doubting, despairing, drowning, freezing.—[47]

44. Ibid., 232.
45. Ibid., 29.
46. Ibid., 132.
47. Ibid., 214–15.

The Creative Eliminator

In that context, the reading of Judge Holden as *Übermensch* explains why the Judge had to dispose of the Kid, who has not totally overcome the feeling of empathy in favour of a new world order:

> Oh my brothers, am I perhaps cruel? But I say: if something is falling, one should also give it a push! Everything of today—it is falling, it is failing: who would want to stop it! But I—I want to push it too![48]

The Kid

"See the child"—with these words the novel starts, and the attention of the reader is drawn towards the Kid. McCarthy creates an interesting parallel in his novel's opening: "Ecce homo"—"Behold the man," the words Pilate uses to present the bound Jesus.[49] It is hard to establish why that attention should lie on the Kid—his character is not particularly developed and we do not know much about him: an illiterate whose mother died in childbirth, the Kid ran away from his alcoholic father at fourteen. Despite his unknown backstory, the Judge sets eyes on him and feels strangely concerned about him, possibly even threatened: the Kid offers a silent and passive resistance that has no chance against the Judge. Even though it remains unclear exactly what is happening to the Kid in the jakes of Fort Griffin, it is clear that the Kid is dying there, murdered by the Judge. Both are the only survivors of the Glanton gang and it seems inevitable that only one of them will dance in the end. The Judge disposes of the Kid, possibly because he is a potential threat, but more because the Kid has refused to accept the Judge as his surrogate father. Instead of obeying, he has shown resistance and refused to participate in the dance of the Judge. I want to argue that the Kid did so in two ways: he "kept in his heart some clemency for the heathen" and he stays silent so that he "would not be recognized"[50] and thus subverts the Judge's system of control, manifested in his notebook.

---

48. Ibid., 168.
49. John 19:5 (Latin from the Vulgate and English from the King James Version).
50. BM, 328.

Part Two: Satanic Characters

The Mimetic Cycle of Violence

With clemency for the heathen, Holden refers to the Kid's act of kindness and charity that put his own life in potential danger.[51] With his "moral" behavior, the Kid questions and subverts the Judge's system. The very few acts of kindness the Kid experiences interrupt the narrative as abruptly as the occasional thunderstorms over the desert night. Before he joins the scalp hunters, the kid meets herders on their way to a cattle market in Louisiana. He tells them that he has no outfit, no food, and no knife. He eats with them and when he sets out with his mule the following morning, he finds a small fiber bag tied to the animal's rope inside of which "was a cupful of dried beans and some peppers and an old greenriver knife with a handle made of string."[52] This act of kindness is the first step towards breaking the circle of violence. The Kid refuses to accept the teachings of the father, he refuses to dance, and he refuses to embrace the Judge's opinion on the inefficiency of moral law:

> Yet the kid does not, will not dance in the judge's ceremony meant to mimic the ritual of blood-letting war. . . . The kid's refusal to dance is not only a glaring resistance and affront to Holden but is also a blasphemous, heretical action of non-praise and a threat to the dogmatic orthodoxy of his war religion.[53]

The kid is not a hero: he shows ambivalence in his moral values. We know that the Kid has a violent disposition and he takes part in the mindless killings of the Glanton gang without showing any scruples. In the desert, the Kid has the chance to shoot the Judge, who is naked and vulnerable in front of the Kid's gun. Tobin encourages the Kid to shoot him, but he does not do so. It is here that the mimetic cycle of violence is broken. The enduring circle of war and violence can only be interrupted by the individual's choice to not surrender to it, even if this means death. I argue here that it is the Kid's empathy that makes him a threat to the Judge's world. Others in the Glanton gang show ambivalent reactions to the Judge, dependent on the circumstances, but these reactions are a result of learned moral and cultural behavior patterns rather than in a truly sympathetic emotion towards one's

---

51. Examples: After the Comanche attack on Captain White's filibusters, the Kid does not abandon his comrade Sproule who is badly injured and endangers the survival of the Kid. He refuses to "go on and save yourself," as suggested by Sproule. Later in the novel, the Kid refuses to kill the wounded Shelby, giving him water from his own canteen and hiding the man. Again, that action endangers the Kid's own life who finds himself shortly after in the snowy highlands without a horse.

52. Ibid., 21.

53. Clement, "The Last of the True," 50.

fellow human being: Tobin, disgusted by the Judge's sexual abuse and murder of the Apache boy, threatens the Judge with death, but at the same time does not hesitate to take part in the killing of men, women, and children in Indian settlements. The violence in *Blood Meridian* is unconstrained by pity. The only signs of human sympathy are shown by the Kid. An individual is only able to show *sympathy* (from Greek σύν πάθος, "with"/"together" and "suffering") if she is able to be aware of her own self, a certain self-consciousness. The Kid temporarily breaks the mimetic cycle of violence by showing empathy.

The cycle of mimetic violence is an expression used by French thinker René Girard in his book *I See Satan Fall like Lightning*, an approach to the origins of human violence and the biblical take on it. He uses the phrase to refer to the desire of people to be like the neighbor or to have what they have. That mimetic desire leads to conflict and violence through imitation and competition: as soon as a group of people encounter obstruction in its way to achieve what the model possesses, the group is turning the frustrated desire towards a victim/scapegoat who is blamed to have caused the "scandal."[54] The individual scandal is soon translated in a general cycle of violence: "When the first scandal occurs, it gives birth to others, and the result is mimetic crises, which spread without ceasing and become worse and worse."[55] The cycle of violence is broken by the victim and the ultimate victim is Jesus Christ on the cross:

> The single victim mechanism was [Satan's] personal property, his very own thing, the instrument of self-expulsion that put the world at his feet. But in the Cross this mechanism escapes once and for all from the control Satan exercised over it, and as a result the world looks completely different.[56]

The Kid is the last victim in *Blood Meridian*, but the reader is left in no doubt that there are many more to come. The Kid's death is ultimately meaningless, with redemption impossible. The kid's attempt to break the cycle of violence has failed, must fail in order to keep the eternal structure of nature that the Judge represents, intact:

> And the answer, said the judge. If God meant to interfere in the degeneracy of mankind would he not have done so by now? . . . This you see here, these ruins wondered at by tribes of

---

54. Girard refers to the translation of σκάνδαλον as *stumbling block*.
55. Girard, *I See Satan Fall Like Lightning*, 18.
56. Ibid., 151.

Part Two: Satanic Characters

> savages, do you not think that this will be again? Aye. And again. With other people, with other sons.[57]

And,

> It makes no difference what men think of war, said the judge. War endures. As well ask men what they think of stone. War was always here. Before man was, war waited for him. The ultimate trade awaiting its ultimate practitioner. That is the way it was and will be. . . . War is the ultimate game because war is at last a forcing of the unity of existence. War is God.[58]

Elimination of the Individual

The Kid's silence poses another resistance to the Judge: the Kid refuses to be included in Holden's sketchbook. He does not have a name, and thus poses a threat to the Judge for whom naming things means having control over them and eventually being able to destroy them. The Kid keeps his name safe; during the Tarot scene, the Judge attempts to name the Kid, he calls him *Blesarius*, but as nobody responds to that naming, he refers to him again as *el Joven*. The Kid thinks that silence will keep him out of the Judge's control and he is probably right, since the Judge himself says, during their last conversation in Fort Griffin, "Was it always your idea . . . that if you did not speak you would not be recognized?"[59] The Judge's aim is the annihilation of the individual, as is the aim of Glanton and his gang in the action of scalping itself.[60] The violence of *Blood Meridian* goes on after death: the Apaches of the war tribe that the Kid encounters while still riding with General White sodomize the dying and dead filibusters; the members of the Glanton gang find dismembered and castrated bodies. The social taboos are constantly violated in order to annihilate the other and to cut him off completely from the living and historic communities. When the group comes across ancient rock paintings, the Judge copies them into his notebook: "They were of men and animals and of the chase and there were curious birds and arcane maps and there were constructions of such singular vision as to justify every fear

---

57. BM, 146–47.
58. Ibid., 248–49.
59. Ibid., 328.
60. It was widely believed in the nineteenth-century American West that native spirituality held that being scalped barred the dead from entering the afterlife. See Sepich, "What Kind of Indians Was Them?" 125.

of man the things that are in him."⁶¹ When he is finished, he scratches away one of the designs completely, leaving only the raw stone where it had been. The Judge erases the memory, after having appropriated it.

The Kid is mutinous, but his resistance is not motivated by intellectual reflection or a conscious decision: he carries a Bible even though he cannot read; he does not shoot Judge Holden in the desert, but he kills his younger self, the young bone picker Elrod. We have no insight into the Kid's inner life, no reflection or self-conscious analysis is given. The Kid's only moment of reflection is his confession to a mummified woman, simultaneously showing an insight into his inner life and a selfless empathy towards a fellow human:

> He told her that he was an American and that he was a long way from the country of his birth and that he had no family and that he had travelled much and seen many things and had been at war and endured hardships. He told her that he would convey her to a safe place, some party of her countrypeople who would welcome her and that she should join them for he could not leave her in this place or she would surely die.⁶²

Summary: The Distant Pandemonium of the Declining Sun

The landscape of *Blood Meridian* is possibly more symbolic and reflective than its fictional characters: on their aimless journey west, towards the "distant pandemonium of the declining sun"⁶³ through a hostile and dangerous environment with heat, cold, thunderstorms, and quicksand, the group of scalp hunters come across several ruined churches, some just abandoned, others having been attacked by Indians. The churches do not offer comfort or refuge anymore; they have lost their meaning:

> Many of the people had been running toward the church where they knelt clutching the altar and from this refuge they were dragged howling one by one and one by one they were slain and scalped in the chancel floor.⁶⁴

---

61. BM, 173.
62. Ibid., 315.
63. Ibid., 185.
64. Ibid., 181.

Part Two: Satanic Characters

In the Christian concept, Satan cannot cross church walls; they are, like other holy places, a safe place for the believer. There is no safe place in *Blood Meridian*, "church walls cannot save man from man, and instead, serve as an ironic temple, parodying the golden role of neighbourly love."[65]

Glanton signed his terrible covenant in the desert, but the Kid was not part of that. The encounter between Kid and Judge is reminiscent of Jesus' temptation in the wilderness: the Judge tries to convince the Kid to join forces with him, to surrender to the power that rules the world. The relationship between the Judge and the Kid is central to the novel. Their dynamic is akin to a father-son relationship, shown when the Judge says "Don't you know that I'd loved you like a son?"[66] We know that the Kid is orphaned to such an extent that we do not even know his name. He is "divested of all that has been. His origins have become remote as his destiny."[67] The Judge takes a liking to him; the reader discovers in the course of the story that he molests and kills children, possibly equally attracted and threatened by their innocence. The relationship between the Judge and the Kid is mirrored in the encounter between the Judge and the Imbecile. The Judge tells the tale of the traveler who is murdered during his journey because of jealousy. The son is born without a father and is therefore deprived of the opportunity to take his life, the parricide that every son should be entitled to have: "The judge was seated upon the closet. He was naked and he rose up smiling and gathered him in his arms against his immense and terrible flesh and shot the wooden barlatch home behind him."[68]

Is the Kid the hero of *Blood Meridian*? The opposition of the Kid has no meaning, he who has no name will be forgotten after his death, his refusal to dance is a momentary glimpse, a flicker of light in the uttermost darkness of *Blood Meridian*. The Kid is not our hero, even though we desperately want him to be—he stands no chance against the Judge. He is, just as the Father and Son in *The Road*, carrying the fire in an unconscious attempt to oppose the utter darkness of a world after the sunset of humanity. Is Judge Holden a satanic figure? I would argue yes. McCarthy's allusions to the satanic figures of folklore and myth are deliberate. His Judge, however, transcends the usual role of Satan in narrative. There is no rebellious spirit in his actions, no aesthetic value in his appearance or musical talent, no tragic element in his personality, no psychological self-reflection, and no possible redemption through sympathy. Holden is an unleashed human being, void of anything

---

65. Clement, *The Last of the True*, 25.
66. BM, 396.
67. Ibid., 4.
68. Ibid., 333.

moral, beyond the boundaries of good and evil, solely following the power of his will. But he is a figure of evil, a literary attempt to approach the cruelty and violence of human behavior. He appears on the stage of the novel to perform his dance of horror and death, portraying the full extent of the human possibility to destroy. The landscape of *Blood Meridian* is full of ruined churches, the storyline mentions dead and absent fathers, the representatives of organized religion are either killed, like Reverend Green, or have fallen away, like former priest Tobin. McCarthy describes a world after the death of God, after the disintegration of moral structures that were closely connected with the Christian value system. The Christian Satan does not pose a threat in such a world; he has lost his status, but is replaced by something more monstrous and threatening: the Judge who takes the freedom of will and the absence of absolute moral values to its logical conclusion:

> The truth of the world, he said, is that anything is possible. . . . the order in creation which you see is that which you have put there, like a string in a maze, so that you shall not lose your way.[69]

---

69. Ibid., 245.

nine

The Stumbling Block

"Have you noticed that in this world God always keeps silent? It's only the devil who speaks. Or, at least, at least . . ." he went on, ". . . however carefully we listen, it's only the devil we can succeed in hearing. We have not the ears to hear the voice of God. The word of God! Have you ever wondered what it is like? . . . Oh! I don't mean the word that has been transferred into human language. . . . You remember the Gospel: 'In the beginning was the Word.' I have often thought that the word of God was the whole of creation. But the devil seized hold of it. His noise drowns out the voice of God. Oh! tell me, don't you think that all the same it's God who will end by having the last word? . . . And if, after death, time no longer exists, if we enter at once into eternity, do you think we shall be able to hear God then . . . directly?"[1]

The ruined churches of *Blood Meridian* are symbols for a world where institutionalized religion is in decline and the belief in metaphysical experiences is difficult to combine with the findings of empirical sciences. The death of personhood is closely connected to evil: wherever Being stops and Non-Being starts, there is space for negation and fear. The collapse of the house of religion in the West and the absence of a personal God contribute to a metaphysical void that is claimed by Satan who is the denier of any existence. The postmodern Satan appears without the attributes, both physical and behavioral that we have encountered in previous literary epochs. In keeping with postmodern tradition, Satan's character is deconstructed. The

---

1. Gide, *The Counterfeiters*, 395–96.

postmodern devil is aware of the satanic stereotypes and plays with them. There are no goat hooves, sulphurous smells, horns, or dubious contracts. Satan, in fact, shows in some texts disdain for the stereotypes attributed to him. Satan also appears tired of the big entries. The mundane and the ordinary become his new dwelling place.

Boredom and Evil

> Amongst the jackals, panthers, bitches,
> Apes, scorpions, vultures, serpents,
> Yelping, howling, snarling, groveling monsters,
> In the squalid menagerie of our vices,
> There is one uglier, filthier and most wicked!
> Although it manages no grand gestures or screams,
> It would gladly make the earth a shambles
> And swallow up the world with a yawn.
> Boredom!—involuntary tears burden its eye,
> As it dreams of gallows and smokes its hookah.
> Reader, you know this dainty monster well,
> Hypocrite reader—my match—my brother.[2]

For most existential philosophers in the nineteenth and twentieth century, boredom is an essential human condition. Martin Heidegger focused on boredom as a postmodern vice. Besides anxiety, boredom is the only mood that recognizes the human state of *Geworfensein*—being thrown into this world. But while, according to Heidegger,[3] anxiety and the feeling of being homeless constitute the meaning of our worldly dwelling by making room for ontological questioning, boredom is the indifference to worldly existence:

> No less than the anxious do the bored sense their alienation from the world and from themselves. Unlike the anxious, however, the bored forsake the quest for a home in the world. The world ceases to be a home in its familiar everydayness. But it also ceases to be an abode for ontological questioning. The absence of home is no longer experienced as a loss.[4]

---

2. Baudelaire, "Les Fleurs du Mal," 70–71.

3. Heidegger, *The Fundamental Concepts of Metaphysics*, 78–164, and Heidegger, "What Is Metaphysics?" 325–49.

4. Thiele, "Postmodernity and the Routinization of Novelty," 501.

Part Two: Satanic Characters

For Heidegger, the capacity for anxiety is essential to experience the question of Being and belonging. Boredom for him, however, is dangerous in so far as we do not face it, but try to ignore, resent or suppress it by means of modern technology.[5] *L'ennui* generally is regarded as a characteristic of postmodernity:

> As the century, and some speculate history itself, draws to a close, it becomes apparent that the former Age of Anxiety has given way to the Age of Boredom. The philosophic signs of these times are everywhere. Even the death of God has become all too familiar. It can no longer move us. In the postmodern world, the shock effect of nihilism has become boring and uninteresting. Armed with the most up-to-date boredom-swatters, the Last Man announces his indifference to unanswerable questions, and blinks.[6]

If we understand boredom as indifference to existence and as a lack of meaning and purpose, evil can be a way of filling the void in the human soul, of offering a thrill and a form of determination. If there is no meaning beyond human actions, then the actions themselves carry meaning.

But equally, evil itself is boring: "Evil is boring because it is lifeless. Its seductive allure is purely superficial. . . . It is boring because it keeps doing the same dreary thing, trapped between life and death."[7]

The texts we have discussed so far deal with the abyss of human existence, a reality of evil that is—luckily—mostly far removed from our everyday existence. But the reason why these texts work lies in the fact that they touch on the possibility of evil in everybody, expressed most poignantly in the idea of original sin. And often, evil appears in very mundane settings; it seems as if evil is more grey than black, more banal than extraordinary, more boring than flamboyant. In this aspect, the postmodern idea of evil forms a strong counterpoint to the Romantic idea of evil, which recognized evil as something extraordinary and rebellious. Boredom—or more generally

---

5. Technology in this context means not only machines or tools, but more generally the production and consumption of artefacts. Leslie Paul Thiele refers to the postmodern relationship towards time: "The essence of technological activity is efficiency. Its goal is to achieve given ends—such as the production of energy, artefacts, knowledge, wealth, power, or pleasure—with a minimum expenditure of resources. . . . This victory over time bears a price: humanity comes to relate to time as an obstacle and antagonist, as a recalcitrant force that demands harnessing. The effect of technological innovation, in other words, is not so much the saving of time as its conquest" ("Postmodernity and the Routinization of Novelty," 505).

6. Thiele, "Postmodernity and the Routinization of Novelty," 516.

7. Eagleton, *On Evil*, 124.

lack of purpose and deeper meaning to a personal existence—is a common motif in two contemporary novels that bring the figure of Satan *home* to the ordinary. Helmut Krausser's *The Great Bagarozy* (1997, English in 1998) and James Robertson's *The Testament of Gideon Mack* (2006) both describe an encounter with Satan that might as easily be identified as the fantasies of mentally ill people. Replacing theology, psychoanalysis is as close as it gets to a metaphysical construct to explain human existence, and both novels leave the reader without a clear answer on whether Satan was at work or the protagonist needs clinical help immediately. With those two texts, we return to the banal realities of domestic evil in everyday life and the question of what qualifies somebody or something as evil. The texts are set against the most recent book of Terry Eagleton, who defends the reality of evil against general views of it being an obsolete concept, and also Hannah Arendt's account of the *Banality of Evil*.

Mocking Satan

Helmut Krausser's novel *The Great Bagarozy* deals with the existential crisis of Satan in the postmodern world. It was published in 1997, translated into English in 1998, and made into a successful and critically acclaimed German movie in 1999. Krausser, who is a German novelist, playwright, poet, and lecturer, wrote *The Great Bagarozy* as a light-hearted and humoresque novella on the devil that plays with stereotypes and myths. Satan appears in form of Stanislaus Nagy. He is a strange young man and we first encounter him as a patient of psychiatrist Cora Dulz, who has just lost two of her clients to suicide. Nagy sees visions of the deceased opera diva Maria Callas who died in 1977. He is obsessed with her, but after a few sessions with Cora Dulz it becomes obvious that Nagy is by no means just a fan: he claims to be the devil himself who, in the guise of a black poodle, guided the life of the star. Cora is fascinated by the man and becomes increasingly attracted to him. She develops an interest that goes far beyond a medical examination and follows the story of how Nagy caused and witnessed the rise and fall of the greatest voice of the century. Eventually, the encounter and the conversations with Nagy lead to dramatic developments in Cora's own life: she kills her husband, blames Nagy, and gets away with it. She gives up her surgery, and rids herself from her old life, but she is not happy. She starts her aimless search for Nagy, but he has fulfilled his role in Cora's life. She only sees him once more, from a distance, but he does not see her.

Helmut Krausser's novel combines the old myth of the pact with the devil with a biography of Maria Callas and a critical analysis of the role of

Part Two: Satanic Characters

the devil in the late twentieth century. He creates a *ménage à trois* between Nagy, his analyst Cora, and the dead Callas.[8] It is through her life, her way to fame, and her downfall that Nagy defines himself and it is only through the story of Maria Callas that Cora learns anything at all from her patient. Nagy himself has no biography and no history. He uses the life of Maria Callas to communicate with Cora Dulz. It is through his obsession with Maria Callas, his love, adoration, jealousy, and hate, that Nagy becomes truly human. For Nagy, death would be welcome; he sees his existence as superfluous. It is the process of incarnation that Nagy describes to his therapist, and the necessary end of that process is destruction.

> I never was a child. In the beginning I was a thought. Later on came images. The images became flesh. At some point or other the process of personification was ... was overdue, probably.[9]

Helmut Krausser's Satan has lost his wings, his will to do evil and his glamor:

> My memory bore me away, along a flight-path of amber and gold, far back to the time when I still had wings. Beautiful wings.[10]

The Testament of Gideon Mack (2006) by the Scottish author James Robertson is the account of a Minister of the Church of Scotland in the fictional northeast town of Monimaskit, who is discovered dead in the mountains. A manuscript is found by a journalist who takes it to a publisher. The testament is Gideon's autobiography, but it is more than the memoirs of a Reverend who has lost his faith or rather never really had any to begin with. Shortly before his death, regarded by most as suicide, Gideon disappears for three days. By trying to rescue a friend's dog, he falls down a local gorge that is connected to local legends and has claimed many lives. After three days, he reappears and his safe return is celebrated as a miracle. Gideon reveals that down in the Black Jaws, he met the devil. The uninitiated observer would call it the moment in which Gideon's mental illness first manifests itself, particularly since he had just been involved in a local art installation concerned with the legends surrounding the Black Jaws and the devil. Gideon himself, however, describes his fall and the ensuing encounter as a moment of revelation and reconciliation. Gideon, coming from a Calvinist background and being a son of the manse, became a minister himself despite not believing in anything beyond the realities he can experience.

---

8. The opera star, born in New York, grew up in Greece during the Second World War and the Greek civil war, had an internationally successful career, and died in 1977.

9. GB, 42.

10. Ibid., 143.

The Stumbling Block

Even though he tries to be a good minister for his parish in Monimaskit, he is constantly fighting his inner demons: his marriage to Jenny is increasingly unhappy until she tragically dies in an accident, his mother suffers from Alzheimer's, he has a secret passion for his best friend's wife, and his relationship with his deceased father haunts him. The actual turning point in Gideon's life, however, is not the fall into the Black Jaws, but begins with his encounter with an eight foot stone in a clearing that has never been there before. His attempts to take photographic evidence or to show the stone to others are impeded and Gideon feels that this stone is a stumbling block[11] for him and has a deeper significance. In their subsequent encounter in the Black Jaws, the devil reveals that he himself has put the stone there, out of pure boredom, as he explains to the minister:

> I get so bored, Gideon. I have to do something to keep myself amused. I wanted to see what would happen. I like playing with people's minds. Crop circles, ghosts, poltergeists, UFOs, alien abductions. People need these things. If they didn't exist they'd invent them, if you see what I mean. So yes, I put the stone there.[12]

Gideon eventually confronts the public with his relationship with Satan and his new found beliefs at a funeral and is subsequently suspended from preaching and his post as a minister. He finishes his testament and leaves for his final encounter with the devil. The book finishes with an epilogue that is presented as the report of a journalist who enquires in Monimaskit about Gideon, revealing some more details about Gideon's life, but without providing conclusive proof for Gideon's story.

Both novels play with the traditional stereotypes of the Satan of Christian myth and folklore. The devil Gideon encounters in the abyss reveals his name, but only at the last pages of the testament. His initials are the same as Gideon's, GM, and they stand for Gil Martin, the devil in James Hogg's novel *The Memoirs and Confessions of a Justified Sinner*.[13] However, Gideon realizes much sooner with whom he is dealing. While he is in the abyss, in the devil's den, helpless due to a severe leg injury, he discovers the identity

---

11. The idea of the stumbling block will be discussed in more detail at the end of this chapter.

12. Robertson, *The Testament of Gideon Mack*, 293.

13. *The Testament of Gideon Mack* has many parallels to the nineteenth-century Scottish classic by James Hogg and through this short remark towards the end of the book, Robertson pays homage to his inspiration. He uses similar motifs and structure: like Hogg's novel, TGM is published as if it was a found document. Hogg's work is also one of the earliest works of fiction to employ the motif of the *Doppelganger*.

of his host. Trained as a theologian, Gideon is first looking for the obvious Satanic attributes:

> "Oh, for fuck's sake," he said. "What do you want me to do, show you a cloven hoof? Horns in my head, a forky tail and live coals for eyes? Is that what you want? Do you want me to take you up some mountain and show you my empire? Make loaves out of these stones? Throw myself off the steeple of your church and land without a scratch? I can do all these things. I can do anything you ask. Do you want me to speak in many tongues? I can do that. I know every language and every dialect that's ever existed on this earth. Do you want me to show you my supposed greatest achievements? Battlefields, wars, torture chambers, multiple rapes, mass murders? I can do that too, but what's the point? You know it all already and you don't believe I'm responsible for it. So what is it you want me to prove? That I exist? Look, here I am. Do you think I am doing this for fun?"[14]

Similarly, Stanislaus Nagy is described with attributes that are associated with the devil: he is pale, has dark, nearly violet eyes, dark hair, and has the figure of a dancer. His age is uncertain, sometimes his features lose plasticity and become transparent and he is of demonic beauty. In his therapy sessions with Cora, Nagy plays with the old stereotypes—he knows them, uses them and ridicules them: "I used to go around with goat's feet! With horns sticking out of my head! And no one bothered to explain the significance of that to me."[15]

As discussed before, satanic narratives refer to symbols established in folk and myth with roots in biblical stories and theological reflections. The satanic figures in the present texts play with these symbols—they appear lifeless and do not represent the true nature of the devil anymore. The symbolism, however, still plays a role in the perception of the protagonists: Gideon, knowledgeable in theology and literature, has heard the legends about the Black Jaws and the devil before: the apparition in the gorge is clearly associated with traditional images of the devil—he has superhuman strength, is sexually potent, multilingual, and is able to perform miracles. Both texts do not necessarily portray their satanic figure *without* devilish attributes, but they question and mock the traditional perception. Like other symbols in postmodernism, the attributes associated with Satan are deconstructed and put together without the metaphysical framework that used to regulate the perception of superhuman entities.

14. TGM, 282.
15. GB, 62.

The Metaphysical Search in Postmodernity

> There is something much bigger than religion going on in all that. Much bigger. The religion was just a phase, and it's coming to an end.[16]

> Evil, then, is a form of transcendence, even if from the view of good it is a transcendence gone awry. Perhaps it is the only form of transcendence left in a postreligious world.[17]

Gideon Mack and Cora Dulz both suffer from a lack of meaning in their lives. They experience a void that cannot be filled, an urge to escape mediocrity and at the same time they have strong feelings of longing that they find hard to identify. Cora Dulz is a woman in her mid-thirties, attractive, but bored and frustrated by her job and unhappy marriage. The encounter with Nagy brings a new excitement to her life. She is increasingly drawn to his strange attractiveness. Under the pretext of wanting to cure her patient's mental illness, she seeks his company, even outside her surgery. Stanislaus Nagy takes Cora to unusual places: he serves her champagne in a warehouse at night, leads her to gloomy and dangerous areas of the harbor, and meets her in a nightclub where he performs as the magician *Great Bagarozy*. Even though his intimate knowledge of her personal details is explained by her secretary's indiscretion, Cora Dulz is drawn into Nagy's story, until she is obsessed with her client, even possessed.[18] Nagy claims that he needs her in order to become a human being, but eventually rejects Cora's attempts to redeem him—whether through his satanic identity or through his own mental illness. For Cora, the idea of being without Nagy seems threatening:

> Say something. Give me your world and take mine away from me. Never have I fallen so deeply in love, nor will I ever do so again. Buy my soul, throw it away, do what you like, but do it to me. I'd love to destroy you, I'd really love to destroy you, to help you become human.[19]

It is this obsession that attracts Cora, the ability to be inflamed and enthusiastic about something. Cora herself has never shown any particular interest in anything.[20]

---

16. TGM, 227.
17. Eagleton, *On Evil*, 65.
18. "She felt like a woman possessed and it wasn't an unpleasant one" (GB, 51).
19. Ibid., 136.
20. For Nagy, the obsession with Maria Callas was the last big moment on this

Part Two: Satanic Characters

In the gorge, Gideon's situation is similar: he sees himself unable to experience true feelings. Even the death of his wife left him strangely detached. But his life also seems to lack good conversations; he misses the ability to be inflamed and enthused by something else than his solitary runs in the woods. To prove his existence, the devil decides to fix Gideon's badly wounded leg. Without any pain, he mends the broken bone with his hand and closes the wound. Gideon is convinced by this sign and his curiosity lets him get involved in a discussion with the devil. Gideon, who has all his life found it impossible to believe in the existence of God, seems to find all the answers he was looking for: "'Where's God in all of this?' I said. 'Now that is a good question,' said the Devil. 'Maybe you are God,' I said. 'Maybe you're God, and this is one big test.'"[21] Gideon, who has mocked prayer before and has rejected belief in anything beyond scientific facts and his own perception, engages in a theological discussion with the devil:

> "I'd say I was sick of apologising for you. I'm sick of the bloody mess. Something like that." "You'd blame me for it?" "Well, ultimately, who else is there to blame?" "Then you don't blame me? I mean, me the Devil. If that's who I am." "No," I said. "I don't blame you. You are just doing what you do. What do you do?" "That's another good question," the Devil said. "I used to have a purpose. We both had a purpose, God and me. Now? I just go from one window to another and stare out. Or stare in. Sometimes I do a few conjuring-tricks, push a button here, pull a lever there. But my heart's not in it. Basically, I don't do anything anymore. I despair, if you want the honest truth. I mean, the world doesn't need me. It's going to hell on a hand-cart, if you'll excuse the cliché, without any assistance from me."[22]

The devil in the Black Jaws mirrors Gideon's existential crisis and the perception that the world does not need the input from an evil transcendence, because the human capacity for evil is sufficient. The world is unhinged, the function of Satan as the force of chaos and disruption is obsolete.

God's story takes a similar direction:

---

earth, his last big challenge—but after her downfall and death, there is nothing left to hold him: "That's what happened to me with Maria. I suddenly found that I had become hooked on something, the way an unemployed man gets hooked on alcohol. Never before had I allowed my desire for beauty so much free rein. But then destruction was breaking all known records. There had to be a balance, a counterpart" (ibid., 49).

21. TGM, 294.
22. Ibid., 295.

> Maybe he's had enough. I keep thinking we're bound to run into another again but it doesn't happen. I reckon he's gone, Gideon. Taken early retirement. Packed up, pissed off, vamoosed, vanished, desaparecido. I think he's done the runner. And you know what? I don't blame him. I don't blame him at all.[23]

What kind of world is it that God and Satan both decide it is not worth caring about anymore? It is the world in which human beings have replaced any transcendence with their own existence. The postmodern world of deconstructed ideas and beliefs, the inevitable consequences of Descartes, Hegel, and Nietzsche, and the focus and trust in the individual and its position in the world.

Gideon is looking for sense and reason in life that he never found through faith in God. Both Gideon and Cora are searching for transcendence, for a meaning beyond the obvious, for a truth that is best experienced in legends and stories. Nagy, either as a patient with a severe personality disorder or the devil himself, expresses his disgust and disappointment about the man's unused potential:

> And if it were the case that I'm crazy, that there's a world inside me which isn't like yours; if it were the case that everything around was crying out IT ISN'T TRUE! YOU'RE SICK—WE'RE THE HEALTHY ONES, where would be the attraction in your healthiness? Where would its beauty lie? Once the earth was one big party for me, a ballroom, infinite scope, a nocturnal department store. And now? We're black and white comic strip heroes. Clichés tumbling from one ear to the next through a vast, grey void. I haven't discovered anything worth coming back to in your land. You're nothing but a noisy, lumbering mixture of decomposition gases! To say you're alive's a euphemism of the first order. There was so much you could have done to make something of yourself, so much. It's all purely academic now, or material for a hired Hollywood hack for whom no happy end can be too far-fetched, providing the money's good. Your body's a mass grave of wasted opportunities and stifled dreams, impossible to approach without an oxygen mask, and even then it makes one want to puke.[24]

After the decline of institutionalized religion in the West, the search for some kind of metaphysical truth remains. When Gideon falls into the Black Jaws, he falls metaphorically into the void of his soul. His need to find

---

23. Ibid., 296.
24. *GB*, 144–45.

Part Two: Satanic Characters

answers and something to hold on to is met by the figure in the gorge. The devil mends his broken limb, holds him in his arms to warm him, and the standing stone in the woods provides Gideon with a symbol that is both frightening and soothing: "The stone acquired a capital S in my mind. The stone became the Stone."[25]

> I would have to go back to check on the Stone. And there it would be, and I would be compelled to go and touch it. It was a comfort—a cold, wet comfort often enough, but that was how it felt, comfortable. Sometimes I'd lean with my back to it and close my eyes. Once I even fell asleep like that for a few minutes. It no longer felt alien or unfriendly. I liked it. And—there was no other way I can put this—I felt that it liked me.[26]

It is the conversation with the devil in the abyss that allows Gideon to make sense of the world and of himself for the first time. It is a spiritual encounter, a theological and philosophical discourse that Gideon has with the devil. After having lived a life dedicated to an absent God, Gideon has his first encounter with the supernatural. Gideon's life is remarkably normal for a twentieth- or twenty-first-century man in the Western hemisphere: he seems to have choices, but still feels forced into a certain direction, he has opportunities but cannot seize them, he wants to see a bigger plan behind his life but feels unable to see beyond his own circumstances. The encounter with the devil, his own personal descent into the abyss, changes something fundamentally in Gideon:

> In a sense, he was right. Without myth, cult, ritual and ethical living, the sense of the sacred dies. By making "God" a wholly notional truth, reached by the critical intellect alone, modern men and women had killed it for themselves. . . . But purely linear, logical and historical modes of thought have debarred many of us from therapies and devices that have enabled men and women to draw on the full resources of their humanity in order to live with the unacceptable.[27]

---

25. TGM, 34.
26. Ibid., 202.
27. Armstrong, *A Short History of Myth*, 132 and 134.

The Stumbling Block

The Absence of God and Death of God Theology

> You need to tell the end of the story in order to make it a true story.[28]

In both novels, the appearance of the satanic figure is associated with the experience of death: Gideon has lost his wife, sees a close friend dying, and struggles with the legacy of his dead father and sick mother. Cora, whose husband is obsessed with obituaries and finally encounters Death himself in a dream, has lost two clients to suicide and is confronted with her own transience. Maria Callas' death hour was Nagy's last moment of truth, a last glow of long gone days:

> Suddenly, we weren't in the kitchen any longer.... Before us was an ocean, dark, streaked with the first, hesitant grey of dawn. The sand we were sitting on was from hour-glasses that had stopped.[29]

Satan is no rebel angel, no passionate seducer, no personification of absolute horror, and no adversary anymore. In the world without God and a self-determined humanity, he has lost his place. With modernity, the image of Satan faded again. His centuries of triumph are over, he is no longer the rebel, the seducer, and the destroyer, but a sad and lonely figure with an identity crisis, abandoned on the stage by his eternal opponent who has been continuously declared dead. While the framework of the Christian world was still intact, Satan was the one to challenge it—the cosmos was organized and Satan was the chaotic force. In a world where everything is questioned and the cosmos is chaos itself, it seems that Satan is the point of reference, the static existence, a constant reminder of a worldview that had a clear understanding of good and bad. Satan works as a night watchman and as a magician in a scabby theatre. There is nothing left of the grand days of battles between heaven and hell:

> The old days. These were the days! People would call me up, secretly, I would arrive at midnight, they would offer me a soul for sale, I'd give the soul the once-over and name the price. Most were a bit disappointed at first, but soon realised they should be glad to get anything at all for a filthy black thing like that. The artists were the best! They really took themselves seriously![30]

28. GB, 162.
29. Ibid., 143.
30. Ibid., 62.

Part Two: Satanic Characters

The reason for the satanic crisis is the ultimate death, the death of God. Without the One to rebel against, the adversary has lost his meaning. The moment God left the world, the game was over:

> It was more fun when the white poodle was here. At the time I thought that when he went he would leave the field to me and that would be great. But without an opponent the game's not worth the candle.[31]

Nagy lets Cora know that the times of bitter fights for human souls between God and the devil are over:

> When God and I were still addicted to our little bets, for the odd soul or two, we used to fight like anything! Tooth and nail! As if the world might go up in flames, depending on the result, or at least the odd continent.[32]

Nagy is left on this world on his own, after God had left it.[33] God grew tired of this world and turned his back on it: "We haven't seen each other for a while now. The last time he looked pretty old. He'd had enough of the world."[34] In Krausser's novel, the tomb of the dead creator is the fridge in Nagy's house, decorated with burnt-down candles, a place of worship for the dead God:

> A huge deep-freeze, more suited to a hotel kitchen than this claustrophobic toilet with living-space. On top of it was an eighteen-inch mountain of candle wax, three colours of candle wax mingled together: red, black, and blue. Scraps of wick could be seen everywhere inside the dribbled mass, or sticking out like bristles. On the summit three candles were burning, slowly losing their cylindrical shape and melting into the wax massif.[35]

The figure of the postmodern Satan is even closer linked to story and narrative than in the centuries before. The disintegration of religious structures and worldviews climaxes in the twentieth century, after the experience of two World Wars and the Holocaust. And it is from this void that Satan returns. Theologically, this void has been characterized by the death of God theology, most closely linked to the American theologian Thomas J. J. Altizer:

31. Ibid., 112.
32. Ibid., 62.
33. "I should have left when God went. He always was a better loser" (ibid., 44).
34. Ibid., 47.
35. Ibid., 78.

> The modern Christian seer, whether a Blake or a Nietzsche, has proclaimed that the chaos lying upon our horizon is a nothingness evolving from the death of God, the tomb of the dead Creator.³⁶

The concept of the Death of God comes from German idealist Georg Wilhelm Friedrich Hegel (1770–1831) and finds its preparation and inspiration in the emphasis of reason and *Vernunft* of the eighteenth century. In his treatise *Wissen und Glaube* (1802), Hegel first formulated the idea of the death of God. The conviction of the death of God is the "infinite pain of the absence of God." Traditionally connected with Friedrich Nietzsche and his prophetic madman, the idea is no homogeneous movement.

There are, however, recurring issues and thoughts in the debate around the death of God:

> The poetic type of Satan has to a certain degree ended the cycle of his individual existence. He has passed from one form into another, until he has gone through the various forms and existences of all life. He has passed through all the rungs of the double ladder on which, according to the theory of the Hindu thinkers as well as of certain European pantheists, every nomad of the eternal existence must descend and remount. In the beginning Satan descended from the absolute to matter, from heaven to earth (the fall), where he was lowered to the rank of the New Testament, to enter into the bodies of the unclean animals. Then rising endlessly from a lower form to a higher form, he finally dematerialized himself in the works of our contemporary poets. He has conquered his attributes of an archangel and has entered again into the Infinite (the redemption).³⁷

The movement of Satan described in this passage is reminiscent of the theological movement of Jesus: the descent from the Absolute to matter (the Word becoming flesh), followed by the transcendence of the material through resurrection and ascension. According to Rudwin, the cycle of Word becoming flesh and then Word again, but in a transformed way, seems to apply to Satan as well: Christian narrative created the character of Satan, transformed him into a figure that at times was so real that his physical presence was unquestionable. His true power, however, lies wherever he transcends the physical existence and is read as the ever-present symbol for the existence of opposition. The decisive difference between the two

---

36. Altizer, *The Gospel of Christian Atheism*, 95.

37. Rudwin, *Devil Stories*, 308, quoting Polish writer Ignace Matuszewski's *Dyabel W Poezyi*.

movements is that of completion: the Christian belief is that Jesus' incarnation finds completion in his resurrection as the Christ. Satan on the other hand finds no completion and no redemption. I would argue that the poetic type of Satan has not ended his existence, but that Satan exists through the poetic.

Thomas Altizer, one of the most prominent Death of God theologians of the twentieth century sees the need to interrupt the cycle of word—flesh—word in order to maintain the meaningfulness of Christian faith in a postmodern world: "A new world or future can become real only by way of a total negation and reversal of the world of the past."[38] Altizer encourages modern Christians to say *No* to God, because he has ceased to be present in history and can only be present in his absence. According to him, God must really die in order to fulfill the Christian message. In other words, it is the downward movement that is important, not the upward movement—the Word becoming flesh, but not the transformation of the flesh. The human story ends with and in the flesh and only through the flesh is reconciliation thinkable:

> Can we now say that an eschatological movement of resurrection would be a descending movement from the "higher" level of Spirit to the "lower" level of flesh? . . . In other words, it would be an attempt to understand resurrection as incarnation, as the Word's becoming flesh. . . . But what if a radical faith were to transform the backward and upward movement of the ascension into the downward and forward movement of the Word's becoming flesh? . . . If the resurrection were understood as the consequence of a downward and forward movement of incarnation, then we could apprehend the divine process as passing from a past to a future form or mode in the resurrection. . . . No longer would resurrection be envisioned as a transition to a heavenly and transcendent "spiritual body," but rather as a movement from the transcendent realm of Spirit to the immanent realm of flesh, and hence as a transition to an earthly and immediate "physical body." . . . Symbolically speaking, this is no more and no less than a means of understanding or envisioning the resurrection of Christ as the descent into Hell.[39]

The idea of the death of God also affects the perception of Satan: if the resurrection of Christ is the descent into hell, we must envision an encounter between him and the adversary. However, such an encounter probably

---

38. Altizer, *The Descent into Hell*, 53.
39. Ibid., 116 ff.

goes beyond a meeting: Christ falls, the light-bearer descends into the realm of final fleshiness, of mortality and darkness. This is where he encounters the one fallen before him—reconciliation, happening through God becoming man, with the final consequences:

> Symbolically speaking, Hell is not simply other than Heaven. It is its inherent and intrinsic opposite: the realm of chaos, of suffering, and of death. . . . For only the loss of Heaven makes possible a transition to Hell. Consequently, to move from Heaven to Hell is not only to move from eternal life to eternal death but also to move from pure transcendence to its opposite.[40]

Altizer understands eschatological faith as a dying with Christ, which culminates in a downward and forward movement of resurrection:

> If descent and not ascent is our deeper primary image, it is the Descent into Hell and not the Ascension which is our primary symbolic ground, a Descent into Hell which is the Harrowing of Hell, or the sanctification of an ultimate abyss and darkness.[41]

According to Altizer, God passes into a satanic form and finally dies as Satan. The death of God and the death of Satan are therefore two aspects of the same thing: the descent of the Godhead into hell, the encounter between—or better, the merging of—Christ and Satan and then the final death that only in its conclusiveness fulfills the actual promise of the Christian message.

Altizer's reference points for the naming of God as Satan are both William Blake[42] and Friedrich Nietzsche:

40. Altizer, *The Descent into Hell*, 121.
41. Altizer, *Godhead and the Nothing*, 118.
42. Altizer's theology has been strongly influenced by William Blake (1757–1827) and his radical Christian visions: "In the light of Blake's vision, the fall is all, and, dialectically, the very fullness of his vision derives from the totality of its fallen ground: vision cannot reverse all things unless it initially knows them in a fallen form. An eschatological end can only follow a primordial beginning, but that beginning is not creation, it is fall. . . . We must rather recognize that it is precisely this act of dialectical inversion which prepares the way for the apocalyptic vision of genuine faith. Faith is vision, proclaims Blake and every seer. But vision can neither arise nor be consummated apart from a transformation of the totality of experience. If faith is to become real in this final sense, it must ground itself in a dialectical reversal of everything which has passed through the 'dark satanic Mills' of history and the cosmos" (Altizer, *Radical Theology and the Death of God*, 172).

According to Altizer, Blake depicted God as Satan on the eleventh plate of his illustrations for the book of Job to portray his own vision that "redemption can take place only after the transcendent and numinous God has been recognized as Satan or Selfhood." Altizer claims that "while the young Blake delighted in greeting Satan

> Hence the naming of God as Satan is absolutely essential for both Blake and Nietzsche. Only when Godhead itself is known and realized as absolute nothingness is such an absolute reversal possible.[43]

In his theological memoirs, Altizer summarizes the need to identify the abyss:

> Yes, the primary calling of the theologian is to name God, and to name that God who can actually be named by us, and if this calling has seemingly now ended, that could be because the theologian has not yet truly named our darkness, and thus not yet truly named God.[44]

That, of course, is reminiscent of the "naming spell": naming something means to give true existence and reality to it, but it equally means the loss of the magic that is connected with a secret name. Naming God therefore enables his final descent into the realm of human existence.

For Altizer, it is not possible to be a theologian without a voyage into darkness. In the context of Milton's *Paradise Lost*, Altizer talks about absolute evil, which is necessary for the epic drama:

> And this drama is a dialectical drama, impelled by the absolute opposites of Satan and the Messiah. Satan and the Son of God are not only dialectical opposites but dialectical polarities, each of whose deepest actions dialectically inverts and reverses the actions of the other, but in that very dialectical polarity each is absolutely necessary for the other.[45]

Altizer recognizes Hegel as the first philosopher to acknowledge the death of God and Milton as the first poet to envision a divine death in the crucifixion, that is eternal death in which "I in my selfhood am Satan," the self-annihilation of God in Christ is the self-annihilation of Satan:[46]

> Satan is our fullest image of an absolute darkness, but Satan is not decisively called forth in our history until the advent of apocalypticism, and Satan is our clearest image of an absolutely

---

as a redemptive figure, and an older Blake was overwhelmed and almost crushed by a realization of the deeper consequences of the divine identity of Satan, the regenerate Blake was finally able to name Satan as Jesus, thereby unveiling the redemptive goal of the fallen world of experience" (*Radical Theology and the Death of God*, 178).

43. Altizer, *Godhead and the Nothing*, 72.
44. Altizer, *Living the Death of God*, 177–78.
45. Altizer, *Godhead and the Nothing*, 77.
46. Altizer, *Living the Death of God*, 177–78.

The Stumbling Block

negative abyss. But only the Christian epic has fully envisioned Satan, and this envisionment only gradually evolves. It is not fully realized until the advent of the modern world, so that in *Paradise Lost* Satan is fully correlated with Christ, and in Blake's Milton and Jerusalem there occurs an ultimate conincidentia oppositorum between Christ and Satan.[47]

According to Christian theology, God needs to die in order to overcome the barriers between the deity and its creation. The death of God theology of the twentieth century has stated that the act of incarnation denies the return to a transcendent status of the deity and therefore resurrection—the death of God needs to be complete and irreversible.

God has left this world to the adversary, who is bored by it:

> Deep down inside me I'm not such a bad chap really, it's just everything's so boring, so mind-blowingly boring. So you play games. And in games there are winners and losers. You human beings have long since realised that. Wouldn't have it any other way.[48]

It is the devil of postmodernism, deconstructed, stripped in individual parts, deprived of any influence. It is no coincidence that Nagy contacts the psychiatrist Cora: he suffers from an existential crisis, has lost his old role and cannot find a new one. He knows that his existence is not necessary, not even possible any more:

> If you feel your heart-strings fluttering, you're no use as a devil any more. Sometimes I think Maria wanted me to slough my skin, as if something different might appear, instead of more snakes.[49]

Gideon's Satan in the Black Jaws is also aware of God's absence:

> But where was God? The devil hadn't seen him. God had gone missing. The Devil was tired, he was sick of what he was supposed to do, he was like you and me, a being without purpose, without hope. Everything had gone wrong with the grand design, the plan. There was no plan anymore. That was what I had learned in my three days with the Devil. There was no plan.

---

47. Altizer, *Godhead and the Nothing*, 145.
48. GB, 68.
49. Ibid., 42.

Part Two: Satanic Characters

> There was no redemption, no salvation, no system of debts and payments. But there was another life. There was more to come.[50]

God is absent in both novels. For Gideon, he had ceased existing in his childhood; for Cora, he appears as a faint memory, frozen and lifeless like the white poodle in the fridge. With God's absence, Satan's role is increasingly difficult. Traditionally, the adversary finds its *raison d'être* in opposing someone or something. Without God, Satan's character has lost its function.

Evil and the Ordinary

So far, the satanic figures in both texts are hardly personifications of evil: they represent resignation, boredom, and loss of purpose. Both satanic characters see themselves as obsolete in the world; their traditional function of destruction and opposition is carried out better and more efficiently by humankind. Cora hears from Nagy that this image—once sign of his triumph—was now only "shallow and sad, too black even for the devil."[51] The stage of the world does not need the devil anymore. It is as if the death of God has left Satan without a place in this world. According to Nagy, the beginning of the end for Satan was the Second World War:

> For the first time I had the feeling the human race didn't really need me any more, they could manage quite well on their own. They took over my role in the great game, only were more cruel and more single-minded than it would ever have occurred to me. It was the start of what you would call a "crisis of meaning."[52]

With the reign of evil in the hands of humans, boredom is all that is left for Satan:

> I don't enjoy evil any more. Everything's so boring. Every day you can hear in the news about torturers who are much more imaginative than me.[53]

Disguised as a black poodle, Nagy got to share the most private moments with Maria Callas, her raise to fame, her success on the stages of the world, her unhappy marriage to Onassis, and her downfall:

---

50. TGM, 342.
51. GB, 120.
52. Ibid., 49.
53. Ibid., 42.

> A stupid little beast. Easy to occupy. I often borrowed that dog. Just pulled him on like a glove, walked on all fours and wore a collar. That's how desperate I was to have Maria's fingers fondling me.[54]

The reality is darker and more evil than Nagy could ever depict: when Maria senses that Onassis intends to leave her, she fakes a pregnancy and bribes a doctor to simulate an abortion. But the doctor tells Onassis the truth and when Maria leaves the hospital, she is greeted by Onassis' derisive laughter. She is humiliated and betrayed, exposed to the cruelty of the one she loves.

For Gideon, the banality of evil manifests itself in the affair he has with his best friend's wife, but also in the consequences of his father's war memories, which left him traumatized. Evil very often has its roots in disappointments, humiliations, envy, and egoism in interpersonal relationships. Nagy's true defeat does not lie in the horrors of the world, but in his obsession with Maria. He helps build her fame, wants to be close to this perfect work of beauty, only to realize that she, like everything else, is not perfect and will decay and vanish:

> Maria was burning out before my very eyes! A Goddess, flogging herself to death, turning to ashes. She herself thought it was a temporary weakness. She fought against it, dogged as ever, only this time all the exertion of her will-power was in vain. *Tutta finite sulla terra* . . . that was the time when the white poodle left us. Left the future to me like a pile of rubbish. Didn't say goodbye to anyone.[55]

Nagy is disenchanted by people, but reminds Cora or rather himself that everybody is assigned a certain role in the play of life that cannot be escaped:

> Look at all these people. They make no demands on life that can't be satisfied with a full belly, a nice house and three orgasms per week. Plus health, death taking its time and good programmes on the box. And who can blame them? But when you remember that all the world's a stage, it's simply a non-starter. The human contract states we have to be actors for all and audience for all. And boredom's never very far away.[56]

54. Ibid., 79.
55. Ibid., 111.
56. Ibid., 39.

Part Two: Satanic Characters

In the discussed texts, evil is not portrayed through satanic figures, but through the human protagonists. It is not the evil of mass murder, genocide or war, but the destructive element that lies in malfunctioning relationships, loneliness of age, boredom, lack of communication, and envy. What is approached in the narratives is also the helplessness towards those feelings, the weakness of the human will, as expressed in Romans chapter 7: "For what I do is not the good I want to do; no, the evil I do not want to do—this I keep on doing."[57]

Terry Eagleton suggests that evil is rare and it should not be confused with broader definitions of the term, such as wickedness, depravity, and corruption of behavior. This is an important remark, especially in the context of a liberal world where derivations from moral behavior are generally not necessarily perceived as something negative. According to Eagleton, the traditional Satan, with his prototype in *Paradise Lost*, is not evil at all, judged from the contemporary understanding of the concept. His primary attributes are transgression, rebellion, and resilience—values that have positive connotation in modern society. In particular, transgression has become used increasingly affirmatively, and has therefore stopped being subversive.[58] I would agree with Eagleton on the fact that evil transcends moral categories, but I am not so sure about his remark that true evil is rare. It seems impossible to categorize evil—we would have to fall back to questions of motivation, extent of pain caused, understanding, and regret. Whenever the value and dignity of human existence is denied, we can speak of evil.

The famous expression the "banality of evil" was coined by Hannah Arendt, observing the Eichmann trials in Jerusalem and trying to understand the motivation behind the persons involved in historic evils and particularly in the Holocaust.[59] For Arendt, evil is not located in the realm of metaphysics, but needs to be approached through questions of moral responsibility and the reasoning powers of the individual. Her approach to evil is influenced by the thoughts of Immanuel Kant, and she refused any interpretation of collective guilt in her work. Arendt's thoughts are relevant in this context not just because of her thoughts on the banality of evil, but also for her theory on narrative:[60]

57. Rom 7:19.

58. Referring back to psychoanalyst Jacques Lacan, Eagleton observes that "if God is dead, nothing is permitted. For permission implies an authority that can grant you a licence; and if such an authority no longer functions, the idea of permission is bound to lose its force. Who in the age of 'permissiveness' is doing the permitting?" (Eagleton, *On Evil*, 121).

59. Arendt, *Eichmann in Jerusalem*.

60. Cf. Munz, "Banalität des Bösen—Erzählen vom Bösen."

In a methodical-hermeneutical way, telling a story is the most appropriate form of writing about evil, since it puts the events in the realm of human interpretation. Storytelling is a way of appropriating something which persistently evades any sense.... . Telling a story is an act that requires something which all "evildoers" in the world lack: empathy and the faculty of judgement of right from wrong.[61]

Arendt understands empathy as the absolute necessity of narrative. She sees the roots of evil and the inability to tell a story in the incapacity to take on a different perspective. Arendt, who witnessed the trials of Adolf Eichmann in Jerusalem, understands the Shoah as radical evil and as something that human beings can neither punish nor forgive, because it cannot be understood or explained. Arendt's observations show that there is no need for motives or even for a certain disposition to act in an evil manner. She discovered in Eichmann thoughtlessness, an inability to change perspectives, which resulted in both an entire lack of empathy towards his victims and also the inability to talk or communicate about their suffering. Arendt thinks in Kant's tradition when she affirms that every person has the positive ability *qua birth* to make conscious decisions and to understand the situation of the other. Narrating and reasoning are both social activities that require an ability to change perspective. This observation has an important implication for our discussion: we have established so far that evil is best expressed through narrative. However, at the same time, the process of telling the story of evil implies the ability to relate the singular event to a more general rule. In other words, storytelling is an expression of human empathy and respect of the individual's freedom. In her book *Vita Activa*,[62] Arendt argues that telling stories is a basic human activity. Through this, evil can be addressed and the empathy created through telling a story and listening to it a might bridge the distance and alienation connected to evil.

---

61. "*Methodisch-hermeneutisch gesehen ist das Erzählen die adäquate Form, über das Böse zu schreiben, denn es rückt das Geschehene in die Reichweite menschlicher Sinngebung. Erzählen ist eine Weise, sich das anzueignen, was sich gerade der Sinngebung so hartnäckig zu widersetzen scheint.... erzählen ist eine Tätigkeit, die das zur Voraussetzung hat, was den 'Bösen' dieser Welt mangelt: Einfühlungsvermögen und Urteilskraft, Recht und Unrecht voneinander zu scheiden*" (Munz, "Banalität des Bösen—Erzählen vom Bösen," 109, own translation).

62. Arendt, *Vita activa oder vom tätigen Leben*. English original (1958): *The Human Condition*.

Part Two: Satanic Characters

Summary—Satan as Stumbling Block

Both Cora and Gideon claim to have met Satan, but in both cases, it is left to the reader to decide whether this is truly the case or whether we are dealing with two individuals experiencing substantial midlife crises, paired up with psychotic episodes, severely distorted apperception, and sexual confusion. Both novels raise the question of where to set the fine line between reality and imagination, the question of whether evil is more than a misguided chemical reaction in the neurotransmitters of the human brain. Even though the situations of Cora and Gideon are far more domestic than the scenarios we have encountered in the previous literary examples, they both experience their own personal situation of conflict. They find themselves in the borderland of their psyche, entering uncharted territories of their souls. Satan appears as obstacle and stumbling block in the protagonist's way; he blocks their way as he blocked Balaam's way once. Satan as stumbling block also refers to the experience that, as well as being something deeply human, evil is experienced as something *outside* us. If we speak of evil, we refer to something beyond the secular ethics and moral values of society.[63] In myth and legend, Satan needs to be called and invited; the interaction with him involves an element of choice. The definition of evil also involves the freedom to choose it, to deny the possibility of turning away from sin. When Balaam finally sees what blocks his way, he is able to change his direction. The temptation through Satan also holds the opportunity to resist or to change a path. The freedom of will aspect has been crucial in the discussion of evil in the Christian world since Augustine, and it seems impossible to ignore it in any definition of evil. With the improved ability to understand human behavior psychologically and neurologically, the question arises of whether there is such a thing as *free will* at all, or whether any form of evil is just a deviation of the norm, an illness, as unavoidable as appendicitis. These statements do not give justice to the complex science of forensics and psychiatry, but in the light of increasingly detailed knowledge of the human brain and psyche, it seems important to keep in mind the element of voluntariness in any moral decision. It is important to acknowledge that a decision to act in a particular way is often pre-made by the individual's circumstances and previous decisions. However, it is crucial for any ethical understanding of humanity to hold firm the idea of the freedom of choice and will. In that context, Satan as stumbling block makes sense: he is the moment of doubt, the whisper of temptation that holds both the decision for and against personhood. In the end it will always be difficult or even

---

63. "Evil is a timeless condition rather than a matter of social circumstance" (Eagleton, *On Evil*, 53).

The Stumbling Block

impossible to fully understand how free the sinner was to turn away from sin. But for human life it is indispensable that we believe in the possibility of saying no to the temptations of evil.

We have characterized Satan as the stumbling block and in that context we cannot ignore the fact that Jesus himself is referred to or prophetically announced as stumbling block:

> He will become a rock one stumbles over—a trap and snare for the inhabitants of Jerusalem (Isa 8:14);
>
> A stone that makes them stumble, and a rock that makes them fall (1 Pet 2:8);
>
> They [the Israelites] have stumbled over the stumbling-stone (Rom 9:32).

Here we encounter Satan and Jesus in similar functions: as an obstacle that can interrupt a familiar path or test the righteousness of the traveler. This parallel is reminiscent of Satan's role in the Old Testament: Satan's function as adversary was part of the divine jurisdiction, his role as tester and accuser was acted out with the consent of God. This last aspect of the satanic character study takes us back to the biblical image of Satan and to the satanic proof of God's existence in twentieth-century Russia.

ten

The Transgressor

It's a legend; can a legend be true? Gideon Mack's question sets the scene for our last account of the satanic presence in narrative. The encounter with Satan opened Gideon's eyes to a metaphysical reality he had refused to believe in.[1] In a similar way, the encounter between the satanic figure of Woland and two Muscovites is described by him as the seventh proof of the existence of God: if you experience the reality of the devil, you will have to acknowledge the existence of God. The distinction between reality and imagination is one of the main themes of Bulgakov's novel *The Master and Margarita*. Woland, the satanic figure in the novel, has been the first inspiration for this work and shall conclude the study of twentieth-century narratives. In many ways, this novel brings together the satanic attributes we have already identified and thus leads towards our conclusion. Bulgakov's masterpiece was first published posthumously in the Soviet Union as a series between 1966 and 1967, and is considered one of the greatest novels of the twentieth century. Written between 1928 and 1940, the novel has three different plot strands that are connected through certain characters and themes. The first strand concerns the visit of Satan and his entourage to Soviet Moscow during the 1930s, the second is an apocryphal account of the encounter between Pontius Pilate and Jesus of Nazareth, and the third is the story of a Russian poet called Master and his lover Margarita, who interact with the characters of the other storylines, and bring all three strands together.

---

1. On one level, Gideon Mack could just been regarded as mentally ill, suffering from a schizophrenic disorder that suggests to him that he actually met the devil. But literature functions on another level; the story is able to transcend categories of the empirical world.

The Transgressor

The story starts with the devil's visit to Moscow during the 1930s. He and his demonic entourage cause havoc amongst the population, particularly for the literary elite of the city. The first to meet Woland is the young writer Ivan Ponyrew who writes under the pseudonym *Besdomny*, meaning homeless. Besdomny recognizes the mysterious nature of Woland and his entourage, and his attempts to warn the authorities brings him to the mental asylum of the city. There he meets the Master, the author of a historical novel about the encounter between Pontius Pilate and Jesus. His work having been rejected, the Master has burned the manuscript and left his lover Margarita. The Master's novel acts as the second storyline of the book: the setting is Jerusalem, where Pontius Pilate sentences the young Yeshua Ha-Nozri to death despite his deep-felt wish to converse with him about his belief that every person is good. The connection between the two storylines is embodied in the Master's lover, Margarita. She is asked by Woland to host his annual spring ball, where for one night the gates of hell are opened, and the sinners celebrate an extravagant and luxurious feast. Margarita, who has nothing to lose after the disappearance of her lover, agrees and turns into a witch, flying naked through the night and hosting the ball at Woland's side. As a reward for her fearless devotion, she is allowed to see the Master again, to live with him in love and poverty. The manuscript of the Master's novel is recovered and we hear from Woland that the encounter between Pontius Pilate and Jesus has been just as described in the Master's work. But neither Woland nor Yeshua, represented by his disciple and gospel writer Levi Matvei, see Moscow as a place for good people to live. Consequently, when Woland and his entourage leave Moscow on the morning of Easter Sunday, they take the Master and Margarita to spend eternity between heaven and hell, in a place of quiet peace, resembling the limbo in Dante's description.

The literary genre of *The Master and Margarita* is difficult to identify: political satire, historic novel, fantasy chronicle, philosophical tractate, or alternative gospel. The content is extremely complex and it is very difficult to give a coherent account of the plot, character, and the themes of the novel. The novel can be approached on many different levels and has been done so in many critical readings of Bulgakov's work. It is primarily regarded as a satire of the Soviet Union with its bureaucratic order, its greed and corruption, and of the regime of literary nepotism and censorship, generally read as an autobiographical reference to Bulgakov's own difficulties as a writer in Soviet Russia. In the following discussion, the political and sociological context of the novel will only be acknowledged as the narrative frame for the "fantastic" elements of the story—the appearance of Woland and his demonic entourage, and the dreamlike sequences of the Master's novel dealing with the encounter of Pontius Pilate and Jesus. The two main aspects I discuss are the role of Satan as executor or enforcer of the divine order, and the portrayal of Satan as transgressor between reality and fiction.

The Satanic in *The Master and Margarita*

The reader finds it easy to identify the character of Woland, who appears on the first pages of the novel as a satanic figure. The quote from Goethe's *Faust* acts as a prologue, leading the reader into the themes of the book with reference to the power that eternally wills evil and eternally works good. Furthermore, the stranger who meets the two Russian writers Berlioz and Besdomny "carries a stick with a black knob shaped like a poodle's head."[2] In some aspects, Woland is a straightforward Satanic character; he is equipped with a few well-known character traits, but also typically evades clear definition:

> Afterwards, when frankly speaking, it was already too late, various institutions presented reports describing this man. A comparison of them cannot but cause amazement. Thus, the first of them said that the man was short, had gold teeth, and limped on his right leg. The second, that the man was enormously tall, had platinum crowns, and limped on his left leg. The third laconically averred that the man had no distinguishing marks. It must be acknowledged that none of these reports is of any value.[3]

The name Woland is taken from *Faust*, but Voland or Wieland also occur as old German names for the devil.

But Woland also has some character traits that contradict the satanic stereotypes or that at least put another emphasis on the character. Woland is not the incarnation of evil, but the administrator of God's business on earth. In this context, he follows the tradition of the Old Testament that saw Satan as part of the divine court, ruler of the earth, and executioner of earthly things.[4] He has a globe in his room that shows the destruction in the world, and Abaddon, the Angel of Death, is in his service. Woland's position is subordinate to God—when Margarita asks him for mercy for the condemned sinner Frieda she met at the spring ball, Woland informs her that this is in the hands of a different department. Woland fulfills the functions of a traveler, tester, and tempter of human beings, and unwitting

2. Bulgakov, *The Master and Margarita*, 10.
3. MM, 10.
4. Cf. Part One, chapter 2.

The Transgressor

instrument of divine justice. He comes to Moscow in the form of a man, as a parody parallel to God's incarnation in Jesus. Satan's existence implies the existence of God. The role of Woland throughout the novel is to assert the reality of the supernatural: "Here is a devil who is at best a paradox: a source of both good and evil, he appears to be more the unerring judge of men and the agent of God's justice on earth than the incarnation of evil."[5]

Woland's entourage is also based on biblical sources, but Bulgakov's cosmology differs from the traditional Christian one. The characters, in fact, give a good summary of the different satanic attributes of Jewish-Christian myth: Behemoth's character, which throughout the novel appears as a giant tomcat that can walk on two legs, is a mythological beast, mentioned in Job 40:15–24. He is also linked to the Leviathan, the primeval monster and God's enemy. The cat—in particular the tomcat—has long been associated with witches and the witch's Sabbath. The Behemoth in *Master and Margarita* also fulfills the function of a joker, "a tom cat, amusing the Prince of Darkness . . . a demon page, the best jester who had ever existed in the world."[6] The character of Woland's fanged hitman, Azazello, is most likely related to the Azazel in the book of *1 Enoch*, where he is portrayed as one of the rebellious Watchers.[7] As one of the fallen angels, he taught men the art of warfare and women the art of deception using make-up.[8] In the *Apocalypse of Abraham*,[9] he is furthermore identified with the serpent, the great dragon, and hell:

> Azazel is no longer just a leader among the fallen angels but the leader of the demons. Figures originally separate have now fallen together while the various names have become only different aliases of the one devil.[10]

Koroviev or Fagot, "self-appointed interpreter to the mysterious consultant who needed no interpreting,"[11] appears as the devil's human representative. He is the one who leads the show of black magic in the Variety Theatre. He usually wears a checked suit, a jockey's cap, and a pince-nez. His dress-code has been linked to the appearance of the devil visiting Ivan Karamazov in Dostoevsky's *The Brothers Karamazov*. Koroviev

---

5. Weeks, "Hebraic Antecedents in *The Master and Margarita*," 226.
6. MM, 380.
7. Cf. Part One, chapter 2.
8. It is Azazello who gives Margarita the magic ointment that transforms her into a beautiful and powerful witch.
9. First century CE. Kulik, *Retroverting Slavonic Pseudepigrapha*, 2004.
10. Grabbe, "The Scapegoat Tradition," 158.
11. MM, 379.

also occasionally introduces himself as choirmaster,[12] possibly referring to the perception of Satan as a musician and composer. Hella is Woland's red-haired maidservant, who only ever appears completely naked. She is a female vampire, responsible for transforming Varenuhka into a vampire. Her role in Woland's entourage is that of support; she helps prepare Margarita and indeed Woland for the satanic spring ball. With the figure of Hella, Bulgakov links witchcraft to the devil. Hella has also been linked to Lilith, a female demon first accounted in the Sumerian period. Like Hella, Margarita is associated with the tradition of witchcraft and superstition, but in Margarita, we also find the element of *Faust*'s Gretchen. Abaddon appears as a minor figure, acting as the Angel of Death. He wears dark glasses, because a look into his eyes kills. Bulgakov took the figure from Revelation 9:11, "the angel of the bottomless pit," and also from the Hebrew word for destruction. In his work, Abaddon is of "rare impartiality and sympathizes equally with both sides of the fight."[13] He acts independently of Woland and appears infrequently in the novel. Nevertheless, death is part of what the satanic entourage brings, even if Bulgakov sees Abaddon essentially as an angel of God.

One last demonic or satanic element in Bulgakov's novel is the apocalyptical ride in chapter 32, entitled "Forgiveness and Eternal Refuge." The Master and Margarita leave Moscow with Woland and his entourage in the night before Easter Sunday. They ride into the air and the night exposes their true nature during that last flight towards the moon. The scene refers to the Apocalypse of St. John where in 6:1–8 the Lamb opens the first four of the seven seals and four horsemen appear bringing—according to the most common interpretation of the text—conquest, war, famine, and death. The association with the four riders is only a visual one, but Bulgakov clearly wanted to evoke an apocalyptic scenario in his last chapter. He not only brings the story of the Master and Margarita to an end, but also resolves the novel's central questions. Pilate is released from his platform and reunited with Ha-Nozri, and Satan and his entourage ride into the abyss:

> And when, from beyond the edge of the forest, the crimson and full moon began rising to meet them, all deceptions vanished, fell into the swamp, the unstable magic garments drowned in the mists.[14]

---

12. At the Patriarch's Pond.
13. MM, 259.
14. Ibid., 379.

The Transgressor

The true nature of the demonic characters is revealed,[15] and with their ride into hell, they bring the story to an end.

The Moscow apartment of the tragically deceased Berlioz becomes the dwelling place of the satanic entourage, and what is so interesting about Woland and his helpers is that together they portray most popular characteristics of the satanic image. Bulgakov borrows from other pieces of literature, biblical imagery, and folklore to create a colorful picture of the demonic elements visiting Moscow:

> There is a fundamental unity in the three major satanic characters. In demonology, the distinction between Satan himself, other fallen angels such as Azazel, and the primitive monster or serpent is far from clear: rather they are different facets of a single conception. The same is true of Bulgakov's unholy powers, whom we may regard as a satanic Trinity, in which Woland plays the major role.[16]

The figure of Woland alone is not what makes the novel so fascinating. It is the context into which he enters, the encounters he facilitates, the opportunities he offers, and the temptations he exposes to. In that respect, Bulgakov's character is as close as we will ever get to understanding the figure of Satan. As we have seen, Woland and his entourage come with the physical attributes that are ascribed to the demonic, but in the moonlight, they are unmasked and another, much deeper characterization of the satanic becomes obvious: Woland mocks the world, he tempts, and exposes. Evil exists without him, he only needs to administer the results.

The novel has a strong and indubitable Gnostic element. Woland does not appear as God's opponent, but more as his agent. He appears as an uninvited guest, exposing with his mockery the shadows of the Moscow society of the early twentieth century, but also the shortcomings of any society. The interplay with night and day, light and darkness, and also the search for "true" knowledge are important themes of the novel. The dialogue on the roof top between Woland and Matthew Levi that determines the fate of the Master and his lover, expresses the structure of power: Matthew Levi approaches Woland as yet another spirit in the divine realm, saying, "I have come to see you, spirit of evil and sovereign of shadows."[17] This encounter

---

15. The last book of the Christian Bible is called Revelation or Apocalypse, referring to the first word in the book in Koine Greek, ἀποκάλυψις, meaning "the lifting of the veil" or "revelation."

16. Wright, "An Approach to Bulgakov's *The Master and Margarita,*" 1167.

17. MM, 360.

creates a Satan similar to that of the Old Testament, that is, a member of the divine court. Satan acts as an instrument, he fulfills a function:

> The cosmology that emerges is more holistic in nature than the Christian one. Here the forces of good and evil are not in competition but coexist on more or less equal terms, each performing its natural function in the creation. Here evil is seen as an intrinsic part of the creation, the background against which good defines itself, and its presence is a prerequisite for life itself.[18]

In Gnosticism, the realization of knowledge—and in particular intuitive or esoteric knowledge—is the way to the salvation of the soul from the material world. The striving for knowledge is a prominent theme in *The Master and Margarita*. The novel shows parallels to the Faustian search for "Erkenntnis," knowledge that goes beyond the understanding of facts and reason. In John's Gospel, Pilate asks Jesus "What is truth?"[19] Like Faust, Margarita enters a pact with Satan[20] to find what she is searching for. Strangely, Satan acts as a warrantor for truth, truth conjured by devilish inspiration:[21]

> And as proof of this witness—the Devil, witness to the truth!—as proof to the disbelieving editor and poet who are about to part company, the Devil realizes his mad prediction: the editor slips under an oncoming tram, and loses his head. Truth emerging from madness, a familiar refrain—"matter and impertinency mixed."[22]

Satan—Reality or Fiction?

> Thus we come to the heart of what *The Master and Margarita* really is—an apocryphal text for the modern age.[23]

We have seen in the discussion around Satan's biography that the apocryphal texts had as much influence as the canonical Scripture on the development of the satanic character. The encounter between Pontius Pilate,

18. Weeks, "Hebraic Antecedents in *The Master and Margarita*," 232.
19. John 18:38.
20. "I would pawn my soul to the devil to find out whether he is alive or dead" (MM, 242).
21. Hass, *Poetics of Critique*, 38
22. Ibid., 37.
23. Weeks, 241.

the Procurator of Judea, and Jesus (referred to as Yeshua Ha-Nozri) in *The Master and Margarita* is yet another apocrypha, revealed in four chapters, narrated by three different characters in the novel: Woland was witness to the events, Ivan dreams it, and the Master tells the story in his manuscript. Bulgakov retells the gospel, using accurate geographic and historic settings, place names, and personal names. The story differs in detail, but does not ultimately change the fundamental message of the canonical Gospels:

> This is not to say that the Gospels are considered false, for a myth is always an expression of a basic truth. . . . In this, we might note, there is nothing contrary to the spirit of the New Testament, for the Gospels "are not histories or biographies, but didactic, apologetic, evangelical writings. Their main purpose is not to preserve a record of the past, but to set forth the common salvation."[24]

And so we conclude this work as we began, with a return to a biblical narrative, this time from the New Testament and without doubt as inspirational as Genesis.

The encounter between Jesus and Pontius Pilate, retold by a Russian author of the early twentieth century, summarizes the Christian message as Bulgakov understood it:

> A time will come when there shall be neither Caesars, nor any other rulers. Man will come into the Kingdom of truth and justice, where there will be no need for any authority.[25]

The emotional and physical consequences of Pilate's decision to act against his conscience are portrayed in his utter isolation. The true evil is therefore not experienced through the satanic Woland, but in the individual's decision to turn away from the possibility of love.

Woland takes on the role of a mediator between the immanent and the transcendent world, between the actual account of the encounter between Jesus and Pilate and the retelling through the novel:[26]

> Bulgakov's treatment of Gospel figures is the most controversial aspect of *The Master and Margarita* and has met with the greatest incomprehension. . . . By the deepest irony of all, the "prince of this world" stands as guarantor of the "other" world. It exists,

---

24. Wright, "An Approach to Bulgakov's *The Master and Margarita*," 1169.
25. MM, 30.
26. Woland brings together the different strands of the novel, and there are various parallels between the storylines: Jesus wants Levi Matvei to burn his manuscript, as the Master is burning his, but "Manuscripts don't burn," as Woland assures him.

> since he exists. But he says nothing directly about it. Apart from divine revelation, the only language able to speak of the "other" world is the language of parable.[27]

With *The Master and Margarita*, we return to the theology of the early church fathers, where the parameters of "reality" and "fiction" were not as distinct as the post-Enlightenment individual defines it. The question of what *really* happened has no place. The true ambivalence and the true power of the satanic character lies in its ambiguity and its ability to evade clear categorization. The question of who Satan really is cannot be answered; Bulgakov would argue that reality cannot be circumscribed by nature alone.

In the novel, the moon functions as a symbol marking the transit between the real and the fantastic world: most of the events happen "by the light of the moon, deceptive as it always is"[28] and which, as has been noted elsewhere,

> has no light of its own, but merely reflects and in a sense imitates, or parodies, the light of the sun. Thus, in *The Master and Margarita* events and characters are seen through the dim and inevitably distorting light of the moon.[29]

We also come back to the motif of the wanderer in the figure of Besdomny:

> The touchstone character of the novel is Ivan Homeless, who is there at the start, is radically changed by his encounters with Woland and the master, becomes the latter's "disciple" and continues his work, is present at almost every turn of the novel's action, and appears finally in the epilogue. He remains an uneasy inhabitant of "normal" reality, as a historian who "knows everything," but each year, with the coming of the spring full moon, he returns to the parable which for this world looks like folly.[30]

In his criticism of the pure materialism of the Soviet regime, Bulgakov created a satanic figure that only has limited powers to influence the moral decisions of individuals, but acts as a vehicle to approach more fundamental questions of truth, love, and faith. Margarita's love for the Master, Pilate's longing for Jesus' presence, the Master's passion for his writing, and

27. Pevear, introduction to MM, xix.
28. MM, 46.
29. Ericson, "The Satanic Incarnation," 22.
30. Pevear, introduction to MM, xxii.

Matthew Levi's commitment to the Word are beyond the realm of materialism and reason:

> Thus, the supernatural realm and the natural realm are inextricably bound together, and this is surely the main theme, the one which comprehends all others: Reality cannot be circumscribed by nature alone, and the naturalistic outlook is miserably inadequate.[31]

---

31. Ericson, "The Satanic Incarnation," 21.

Conclusion

Satan's Salvation or the Redemption Lies in the Text

> Then Jesus asked him, "What is your name?" "My name is Legion," he replied, "for we are many."[1]

The story of the possessed from Gadara is popular in art and fiction, in particular the demon's claim, "for we are many."[2] It implies not only the possible diversity of the satanic character, but also the power that stands behind him. The different characters discussed in this work are only a very small aspect of the satanic figure, but they were chosen to highlight the ambiguity of Satan's nature and to express the diversity of his appearance in the story. The origins of Satan lay, as we have seen, in his function as the stumbling block and the adversary, he appears as the one who challenges and provokes. Later, his character gained more influence; he grew to become a symbol of evil, expressing the need of the Christian belief system to blame the existence of negation on someone other than God. I would argue that we get closest to an understanding of the satanic character if we do not approach him ontologically, but phenomenologically, that is, if we are not trying to understand his being, but take a closer look at the roles he is playing in various stories and the function he serves in those stories. As a

---

1. Mark 5:9.
2. We have seen earlier that the connection between Satan and demons has been established relatively late in Christian theology and that the demonology of the Christian churches is far from concise. However, Satan is generally seen as the master of the demons and therefore "in charge" of possessions.

literary character, he fulfills different functions, and is used to facilitate the progress of the story.

In this conclusion, I wish to address three main objectives of the satanic functions that have been touched upon in the previous discussion.

1. Taking a closer look at the satanic attributes in the novels discussed, we find that the literary Satan *does* embody evil by portraying attributes that essentially negate life. As a fictional character, he is defined through personal and relational attributes. In the context of the story, Satan appears as a recognizable term of understanding for what is summarized as the experience of evil.

2. In the context of a dialogue between theology and literature I argue that Satan is the bridge between the two. Satan is not a theological character, but a fictional one. He defies theology's resistance to story by providing an understanding of evil that goes beyond the categories of dogmatics. As a character in the story, Satan opens the space for the other.

3. Satan's place is in the story and his functions of temptation, destruction, and trial are necessary for the story. He appears as the creative element and the driving force behind the narrative. Satan's existence is therefore a paradox, just as evil is: he is the "impossible possibility."[3]

Satan and the Borderland of the Soul

We have seen that the figure of Satan emerges in a vacuum, in the absence of relation. He exists outside the framework of explanation and defeats the clear separation between reality and fiction. He flourishes in the story, a shape-shifter, who is easily recognizable despite his changing appearances. The discussed narratives all show an element of fantasy. Satan exists outside the box of hermeneutics; he defeats the hermeneutical circle and flourishes in the excess. The themes of madness and insanity are elements in the discussed works; the encounter with Satan could easily be explained by the mental illness or delusion of the protagonists. It seems the only door left to enter is that leading to the realm of fantasy. The literary figure of Satan allows the transgression of the boundaries between reality and fantasy. His appearance questions those boundaries entirely and reintroduces a more holistic understanding to the phenomenon of evil:

---

3. Barth, *The Doctrine of Reconciliation*, 178.

Part Two: Satanic Characters

> [Satan] has developed through history and now appears to men in the twentieth century; men whose human natures, however, have changed little since the expulsion from the garden and since the days of the Roman Empire.[4]

The novels discussed in these chapters are very different yet offer some mutual points of reference. All the narratives are set in a *situation of conflict*. We are experiencing cultural shift, situations of political change and threat, and moments of personal and inner conflict. The plots are situated in historic realities, such as the borderlands of the American West in the late nineteenth century, the imperialist colonies of the early twentieth-century Congo, 1920s Moscow with its corruption and repression, the horrors of Nazi Germany, and the spiritual wasteland of the twenty-first century, where both God and institutionalized religion have died. The historic settings of the stories are, however, transcended by the introduction of a figure who is larger than reality: Satan is extracted from the normal world; he exists in the collapse of structure, in the absence of explanation, and in the borderlands between reality and fantasy, between normality and madness. In short, Satan enters into the void. He appears where the system of explanation, the codes of normality cease to work; he is the violation of the norm and exists in the excess:

> Wandering between two worlds, one dead the other powerless to be born,
> With nowhere yet to rest my head like these, on earth I wait forlorn.[5]

The Satan of the twenty-first century is characterized by boredom, destruction, and nihilism. He is the lost brother, the shadow, the alter ego that appears in personal and historical moments of doubt and pain. He is simultaneously fascinating and threatening; he who oversteps boundaries needs to be eliminated. The faces of Satan are very different in the discussed works, but he always appears as a human figure. As we have seen before, the nature of Satan is deeply *personal*; his nature is experienced in relation (or in absence of relation) to others. Kurtz's horror needs Marlow's discipleship to be fully recognized; Judge Holden dances on the grave of the Kid; Hitler's paranoid and fearful hate finds its climax in the murder of his son; Gideon Mack's Satan deep down in the gorge finds his way into the reality (or madness) of Gideon's life through conversation; and Woland needs Margarita to freely assist him in order to let hell loose for his spring ball. Satan is a shapeshifter, because he can be whoever we *want* him to be.

---

4. Wright, "Satan in Moscow," 1172.
5. Arnold, "Stanzas from the Grande Chartreuse," ll. 85–88.

Satan's Salvation or the Redemption Lies in the Text

Since the birth of psychoanalysis, the figure of Satan is generally regarded as the personification of the human psyche, a mere projection of the attributes that humans experience and fear. The subject of mental illness and madness plays a role in the discussed works—every experience of something that is not clearly part of the empirical world is ascribed to the realm of fantasy or madness. The figure of Satan is more complex than that. The boundaries between sanity and insanity are not clear and the figure of Satan comes from the borderlands of the human soul. The clear distinction between "reality" and "fantasy" leaves little room for many human emotions, and experiences often get blurred in fiction. The figure of Satan is a perfect example of this: he escapes clear definition, changes his shape and purpose constantly, and the essence of his existence is unknown outside of a particular narrative. Satan embodies aspects of what can be described as the experience of evil. Despite being used in the Christian tradition as a scapegoat, his existence does not help explain the existence of suffering and pain, since he is ultimately a divine creation himself and cannot act outside the framework of Christian monotheism. His character does, however, provide access to the understanding of evil through the stories he appears in: as a restless wanderer, he represents the experience of (self-)exile and alienation that is connected with evil. He appears as the alter ego or shadow, representing the individual's experience of evil as an omnipresent possibility and also the temptations of transgressing boundaries. Satan is a symbol of evil as nothingness, as the denial of existence, and at the same time, for the personal and relational experience of evil. Evil requires a counterpart; it relates to the experiences of the other. The literary Satan is an expression of evil as willful denial, the freely willed attempt to hurt or destroy another individual. Just as evil can be experienced in ordinary and banal circumstances, the satanic figures in the novels discussed appear more grey than black, and show why it is so difficult to talk about evil as an abstract concept in terms of a *good-bad* dualism.

The Impossibility of Redemption

The teachings of ἀποκατάστασις have been generally regarded as heresy by the Christian churches. The doctrine of universal salvation, first expressed by Origin in the third century, believes in the salvation of all because of a loving and merciful God. Other popular theologians dealing with the teaching of universal salvation were Clement of Alexandria and Gregory of Nyssa. The belief in the reconciliation of all living creatures has been rejected by most Christian denominations. The most obvious argument is the free will of human beings: if we have the power to decide, then we must also accept the possibility of consequences and the ultimate negation of God's grace. Yet sympathy and pity for the tragic figure of Satan have occurred throughout the history of Christian theology. Thomas Aquinas is said to have pitied Satan, thinking of the doom that awaited him and prayed on his behalf:

> All night Aquinas knelt alone, Alone with black and dreadful Night / Until before his pleading moan / The darkness ebbed away in light. / Then rose the saint, and "God" said he / "If darkness change to light with thee, The Devil may yet an angel be."[6]

Satan experienced his strongest sympathy from the French Romantics. Compassion and pity for the forsaken, the oppressed, and the unjustly treated were prominent emotions and motifs of Romantic writers. Among the Romantic writings were a few that went beyond pity for Satan and promoted the reconciliation of the Adversary:

> From the philosophical point of view, the conception of Satan's conversion and re-admission to heaven is the corollary of the faith in the perfectibility of man, and belief in the consequent end of evil on earth. This utopian hope for the final triumph of universal good, which was aroused in the minds of men during the eighteenth century, was still strengthened by the French Revolution. . . . Furthermore, many metaphysicians developed the theory of the Devil's repentance and return to heaven as part of their explanation of the origin and function of evil in the cosmic order.[7]

Looking at the doctrine of universal salvation from a non-dogmatic point of view shows us another reason why the teaching of a final reconciliation might not be favorable: a good story does not end but leaves its audience with the possibility of developing the narrative further. In regarding the teaching of universal salvation as heterodox, Christian theology recognizes the value of the story. It seems as if here might lay the answer for reconciliation between theology and literature: theology needs the illogical ferocity of literature, the lack of logical conclusion, the possibility of non-reconciliation. In the rejection of the teachings of universal salvation, Christian theology recognizes the importance of an open end. Satan is an unredeemed and ultimately unredeemable figure:

> It must be admitted, however, that this original and spiritual idea of the salvation of Satan, beautiful as it may be philosophically,

6. Call, "Aquinas," 115.
7. Rudwin, *Devil Stories*, 281.

Satan's Salvation or the Redemption Lies in the Text

is neither aesthetically nor theologically acceptable. Such a conception is inconsistent with the grandeur of the Personality of Evil. . . . All successful treatment of the Devil in literature and art, however, must be made to conform to the norm of popular belief and Catholic dogma. In art we are all orthodox, whatever our views may be in religion.[8]

The salvation of Satan is neither aesthetically nor theologically acceptable. The salvation of Satan in literature is not possible, since the dogmatic of Christian theology does not allow it. According to Rudwin, literature is therefore censored by theological dogma. I would argue that this observation is more successful if reversed: the final reconciliation of Satan is not possible in Christian theology because it does not work in story. Final reconciliation is unthinkable since it would imply the end of any story.

What does this observation mean for the relationship of literature and theology? We have seen in previous chapters that Satan is not a theological figure. Theological and doctrinal language struggles to express the meaning of Satan in the context of a Judeo-Christian worldview. It is through literature that the true being of personified evil can be expressed. Ultimate evil is not the subject of theological debate but to phenomenological experience. Postmodern thinkers see poets and authors as the new theologians. The need to find a new language has been expressed by many philosophers and theologians of the nineteenth and twentieth century. It seems as if some or even all concepts of traditional theology are far removed from the experiences in a postmodern world. The figure of Satan is certainly a good example of the inadequateness of theological language. Christian doctrine has always struggled to verbalize and systemize the existence of Satan. From the very beginning, Satan has been a myth more than a concept. He existed through narrative and his dwelling place is the story.

The Curse to Tell the Tale

Any worldview that eschews the reference to realities that transcend the natural world needs to see the roots of anything evil purely in the human mind. But we have seen that empirical science struggles to define and explain evil behavior. It is impossible to determine whether Satan exists as an independent personality or a transcendent being who is engaging in a cosmic battle with the forces of good, but he is a needful symbol of radical

---

8. Rudwin, *Devil Stories*, 281–82.

evil, because eventually "evil infinitely surpasses human evil."[9] We will never be able know the reality of Satan, the only thing we can truly understand is the human concept of Satan. From the viewpoint of practical theology, there seems to be a need for Satan;[10] to talk about Satan always means to talk of evil. The symbolic language of the devil implies the personal aspect of evil. The encounter with Satan describes the experience of evil as a transcendent reality that lies in us and is at the same time *more* than us. The narrative is the place where Satan can dwell and where we encounter evil as a truly personal and relational phenomenon. The relationship between the satanic and the story is symbiotic; one cannot exist without the other.

The *Mittagsfrau* (Midday Lady) is a female demon in Slavic mythology, known under that name in the Sorbian region of Eastern Germany. She appears on hot days during noon, during the time of harvest, causing confusion (referring to heat stroke), paralysis, and sometimes death. Carrying a scythe, she can appear as a beautiful young woman, an old hag, or a girl. She has black hair and is occasionally described as having a hoof. She wears the color white, associated in the Sorbian tradition with death and mourning. The only way to escape death is to tell her a story, without pausing, passing the stories of harvesting and spinning flax: of life and death. For one hour, or sometimes two, until the magic of noon has passed and the curse is gone. The myth of the *Mittagsfrau*[11] reminds us of the need to tell stories; otherwise, we are lost.[12] The demon drives us on to tell the tale, she is the one who inspires and torments at the same time. Satan is not just an object of the story, not just a literary figure, but also the poet and the inspiration. The nature of evil remains unknown to us; it touches us deeply and yet eludes our understanding. Wherever metaphysical systems have ceased to be in place, narrative is the only remaining way to transcend human reality and to deal with experiences that leave us speechless. As soon as we stop

---

9. Russell, *Mephistopheles*, 267.

10. This is an interesting thought that could be researched further. One example of a similar study is Leimgruber, *Kein Abschied vom Teufel*. Leimgruber's work is placed in the field of practical theology and explores the talk of the devil in contemporary Christian life.

11. In her award-winning novel *Die Mittagsfrau* (winner of the German Book Prize in 2007 and translated into English as *The Blind Side of the Heart*) author Julia Franck tells the story of Helene who abandons her eight-year-old son at a train station after the end of the Second World War. The reader of the novel looks for an answer, but there is none, apart from Helene's story. In Julia Franck's novel, the protagonist Helene loses her voice; the experience of war, rape, and loss turn her heart blind and cold, and she feels unable to engage with her child. When she realizes that she has no stories left for him, she leaves her son.

12. See also the myth of Scheherazade, who told 1001 stories to spare her life.

telling stories, we die. We deal with the satanic through our narratives and at the same time, it is the satanic that inspires us to tell them. Satan represents the unfinished, the broken, and the dark in human lives. He is the curse and simultaneously the inspiration of the story. The ability to tell the story and to hold on to it is expressed in the metaphorical fire that father and son carry through a post-apocalyptical America in Cormac McCarthy's *The Road*.

Again, we encounter the paradox: evil is best approached through the story, but equally, evil flourishes in the absence of an articulate narrative. During the trial of Adolf Eichmann, Hannah Arendt observed the connection between the inability to tell a story and the inability to empathize. The ability and the will to empathize, to change one's own perspective, and to listen to someone else's story is the only answer to evil we have.

The End

Satan is not a personification of evil but the result of our inadequacy to deal with evil. In the experience of the void, he is the one who fills it. Satan has no place outside the story. The Christian belief struggles with the existence of Satan and mostly refers to him through art and metaphor. He does not find a place in the system of Christian monotheistic theology and has consequently been outsourced to the realm of the story. There, he appears as the restless wanderer. He functions as a symbol for the will to oppose and destroy, as the eternal shadow. Satan personifies nothingness, the nothingness of evil that is abstract. Satan appears as possessor and parasite and appropriates the story. In that tangible form, he transgresses boundaries and provides access to the borderland of the soul. He functions as a scapegoat and as a facilitator, and shows us the banality of evil. As the serpent in Genesis or as Woland in the Variety Theatre, he makes us aware of our nakedness and reveals our weaknesses. As a shapeshifter, he constantly evades clear definition and thus defies categorization into reality or fiction. Satan is not an incarnation of evil, but an embodiment: in his physical and personal appearance, he provides access to the abstract concept of evil. His physical form can change, but his function in the story stays the same: Satan is a powerful literary figure, the eternal adversary, object and subject of the story. Without any real substance, he exists in the realm of the narrative, being at the same time destroyer and creator, the spirit that denies and the power that would the Evil ever do, and ever does the Good. Satan lends a face to what we experience as evil: the absence of relation, the exile of the soul, the loss of identity, the destruction of the other and the self. With the figure of Satan, we can encounter the experience of evil through the story, endure it in the story, and face it with the knowledge that the gift to change one's perspective is both necessary to tell a story and to feel connected with the suffering and the pain of others.

Bibliography

Fiction and Poetry

Alighieri, Dante. *The Inferno*. Translated by Robert Hollander. New York: Doubleday, 2000.
Arnold, Matthew. "Stanzas from the Grande Chartreuse." In *The Poems of Matthew Arnold*, edited by Kenneth Allott. 305. London: Longmans, 1965.
Baudelaire, Charles. "Les Fleurs du Mal." In *Complete Poems*, translated by Walter Martin, 70–71. Manchester: Carcanet, 1997.
Blake, William. *Complete Writings*. With Variant Readings, edited by Geoffrey Keynes. Oxford: Oxford University Press, 1972.
———. *Selected Poetry*. Edited by W. H. Stevenson. London: Penguin, 1988.
Bulgakov, Mikhail. *The Master and Margarita*. Translated by Richard Pevear and Larissa Volokhonsky. London: Penguin, 2007.
Byron, George Gordon. *The Major Works*. Edited by Jerome J. McGann. Oxford: Oxford University Press, 1986.
Call, Wathen Mark W. "Aquinas." In *Reverberations: Revised with a Chapter from my Autobiography*, 113–15. London: Trübner, 1876.
Conrad, Joseph. *Heart of Darkness*. Edited by Robert Hampson. London: Penguin, 1995.
Corelli, Marie. *The Sorrows of Satan*. New York: Elibron Classics, 2006.
Dostoyewsky, Fyodor. *The Brothers Karamazov*. Translated by David Magarshack, 1958. London: Penguin, 1982.
Franck, Julia. *Die Mittagsfrau*. 3. Auflage. Frankfurt: Fischer, 2007.
———. *The Blind Side of the Heart*. Translated by Anthea Bell. London: Harvill Secker, 2009.
Goethe, Johann Wolfgang von. *Faust. eine Tragödie; erster und zweiter Teil*. 3. Auflage. München: Dt. Taschenbuch-Verlag, 1980.
———. *Faust*. Translated by John R. Williams. Wordsworth Classics of World Literature. Ware, UK: Wordsworth Editions Limited, 1999.
———. *Faust*. Part One. Translated by Philip Wayne. London: Penguin, 1949.
Gide, André. *The Counterfeiters*. Translated from the French by Dorothy Bussy. London: Penguin, 1966.

Bibliography

Görling, Lars. *491*. Mit einem Vorwort von Prof. Ludwig Marcuse. Hamburg: Gala Verlag, 1965.
Gotthelf, Jeremias. *Geld und Geist: Bilder und Sagen aus der Schweiz*. Hamburg: tredition and Projekt Gutenberg-DE, 2011.
Heym, Stefan. *Ahasver*. 1981. Reprint. Frankfurt: Fischer Taschenbuch Verlag, 1992.
———. *The Wandering Jew*. New York: Hold, Rinehart, and Winston, 1984.
Hoffmann, E. T. A. *Die Elixiere des Teufels*. Frankfurt: Insel Verlag, 1978.
Hogg, James. *The Confessions of a Justified Sinner*. 1824; London: Panther, 1970.
Kazantzakis, Nikos. *The Last Temptation*. Translated by P. A. Bien. London: Faber and Faber, 1975.
Krausser, Helmut. *Der Große Bagarozy*. Hamburg: Rowohlt Verlag, 1997.
———. *The Great Bagarozy*. Translated by Mike Mitchell. Sawtry, UK: Dedalus, 1998.
Machen, Arthur. "The White People." In *The House of Souls*, 111–66. Knopf: New York, 1922.
Mailer, Norman. *The Castle in the Forest: A Novel*. London: Little, Brown, 2007.
McCarthy, Cormac. *Blood Meridian or The Evening Redness in the West*. London: Picador, 1990.
———. *The Border's Trilogy: All the Pretty Horses, the Crossing, Cities of the Plain*. New York: Everyman's Library, 1999.
———. *No Country for Old Men*. London: Picador, 2005.
———. *The Road*. London: Picador, 2007.
Mann, Thomas. *Doktor Faustus. Das Leben des deutschen Tonsetzers Adrian Leverkühn erzählt von einem Freunde*. Gesammelte Werke in zwölf Bänden, Band VI. Oldenburg: Fischer Verlag, 1960.
Milton, John. *Paradise Lost*. Edited with an Introduction and Notes by Stephen Orgel and Jonathan Goldberg. Oxford: Oxford University Press, 2004.
Mulisch, Harry. *Siegfried*. Translated by Paul Vincent. New York: Viking Penguin, 2003.
Robertson, James. *The Testament of Gideon Mack*. London: Penguin, 2007.
Sartre, Jean-Paul. *Huit-clos*. Paris: Gallimard, 1962.
Schubart, Christian Fr. Daniel. *Ahasver. Gedichte aus dem Kerker*. Zürich: 1785.
Shelley, Mary Wollstonecraft. *Frankenstein Or The Modern Prometheus*. Phoenix Science Fiction Classics. Rockville: Arc Manor, 2009.
Schlink, Bernhard. *Der Vorleser*. Zürich: Diogenes Verlag, 1997.
———. *The Reader*. Translated by Carol Brown Janeway. London: Phoenix House, 1997.
Stevenson, Robert Louis. *Dr Jekyll and Mr Hyde*. Foreword by Helen Dunmore. 1886. Reprint. London: Hesperus, 2003.

Theology, Theory, Commentary

Scripture, Commentaries, Doctrine

The Book of Enoch, or I Enoch: A New English Edition. Leiden: Brill, 1985.
The Book of Jubilees. Guides to Apocrypha and Pseudepigrapha. Edited by James C. Vanderkam. Sheffield, UK: Sheffield Academic, 2001.
Catechism of the Catholic Church. Rome: Libraria Editrice Vaticana, 1993.

The Dead Sea Scrolls Bible. Translated and with a commentary by Martin Abegg Jr., Peter Flint, Eugene Ulrich. Edinburgh: T. & T. Clark, 1999.
Dell, Katharine M. "Job." In *Eerdmans Bible Commentary*, edited by James D. G. Dunn and John William Rogerson, 337–63. Grand Rapids: Eerdmans, 2003.
Habel, Norman C. *The Book of Job.* Cambridge Bible Commentary on the New English Bible. London: Cambridge University Press, 1975.
The Holy Bible. Containing the Old and New Testament. New Revised Standard Version (NRSV). Oxford: Oxford University Press, 1995.
Hooks, Stephen M. *Job.* College Press NIV Commentary. Joplin, MO: College, 2007.
Schroeder, H. J. *Disciplinary Decrees of the General Councils: Text, Translation and Commentary.* St. Louis: Herder, 1937.

Monographs and Collections

Altizer, Thomas J. J. *The Descent into Hell.* Philadelphia: Lippcott, 1970.
———. *Godhead and the Nothing.* Albany, NY: State University of New York Press, 2003.
———. *The Gospel of Christian Atheism.* London: Collins, 1966.
———. *Living the Death of God: A Theological Memoir.* Foreword by Mark C. Taylor. Albany, NY: State University of New York Press, 2006.
Altizer, Thomas J. J., and William Hamilton. *Radical Theology and the Death of God.* Indianapolis: Bobbs-Merrill, 1966.
Arendt, Hannah. *Eichmann in Jerusalem: A Report in the Banality of Evil.* London: Penguin, 1994.
———. *Vita activa oder vom tätigen Leben.* München: Piper, 2002.
Armstrong, Karen. *A Short History of Myth.* Edinburgh: Canongate, 2006.
Arnold, Edwin T., and Dianne C. Luce, editors. *Perspectives on Cormac McCarthy.* Rev. ed. Jackson, MS: University Press of Mississippi, 1999.
Aschheim, Steven E. *Nietzsche und die Deutschen.* Stuttgart: Metzler, 2000.
Athanasius. *The Coptic Life of St Anthony.* Translated by Tim Vivian. San Francisco: International Scholars Publications, 1995.
Atze, Marcel. *"Unser Hitler." Der Hitler-Mythos im Spiegel der deutschsprachigen Literatur nach 1945.* Göttingen: Wallstein Verlag, 2003.
Augustine of Hippo. *Confessions and Enchiridion.* Newly translated and edited by Albert C. Outler. London: SCM, 1995.
Barasch-Rubinstein, Emanuela. *The Devil, The Saints, and the Church: Reading Hochhuth's The Deputy.* New York: Lang, 2004.
Barratt, Andrew. *Between Two Worlds: A Critical Introduction to The Master and Margarita.* Oxford: Clarendon, 1987.
Barth, Karl. *The Doctrine of Creation: Church Dogmatics.* Vol. III.3. Translated by Geoffrey William Bromiley and Thomas Forsyth Torrance. Reprint. London: T. & T. Clark, 2004.
———. *The Doctrine of Reconciliation. Church Dogmatics.* Vol. IV.3. Translated by Geoffrey William Bromiley and Thomas Forsyth Torrance. Reprint. London: T. & T. Clark, 2004.
———. *Kirchliche Dogmatik.* Zürich: Evangelischer Verlag Zollikon, 1957.
Bataille, George. *Literature and Evil.* London: Boyars, 2001.

Bibliography

Bonhoeffer, Dietrich. *Creation and Fall: A Theological Exposition of Genesis 1–3*. Edited by John W. de Gruchy. Translated by Douglas Stephen Bax. Minneapolis: Fortress, 1997.

Boureau, Alain. *Satan the Heretic: The Birth of Demonology in the Medieval West*. Translated by Teresa Lavender Fagan. Chicago: The University of Chicago Press, 2006.

Brall, Helmut, editor. *Von Sünde, Leidenschaft und Laster: Teufelsgeschichten aus tausend Jahren*. München: dtv, 1998.

Bründl, Jürgen. *Masken des Bösen: Eine Theologie des Teufels*. Bonner Dogmatische Studien. Würzburg: Echter, 2002.

Carus, Paul. *The History of the Devil*. 1900. Reprint. New York: Dover, 2008.

Clement, William Dean. "The Last of the True: The Kid's Place in Cormac McCarthy's *Blood Meridian*." MA thesis, University of Mississippi, 2009.

Cole, Philipp. *The Myth of Evil*. Edinburgh: Edinburgh University Press, 2006.

Connolly, Julian W. *The Intimate Stranger: Meetings with the Devil in 19th-Century Russian Literature*. New York: Lang, 2001.

Craze, Richard. *Hell: An Illustrated History of the Netherworld*. Berkeley: Conari, 1996.

Defoe, Daniel. *The History of the Devil. In two parts, the second being a Description of the Devils Dwelling Place, called Hell*. 6th ed. Philadelphia: Leary, Getz & Co, 1859.

Detweiler, Robert. *Breaking the Fall: Religious Readings of Contemporary Fiction*. San Francisco: Harper & Row, 1989.

Diamond, Stephen A. *Anger, Madness, and the Daimonic: The Psychological Genesis of Violence, Evil and Creativity*. Albany, NY: State University of New York Press, 1996.

Eagleton, Terry. *On Evil*. New Haven and London: Yale University Press, 2010.

Evans, C. Stephen, editor. *Exploring Kenotic Christology: The Self-Emptying of God*. Oxford: Oxford University Press, 2006.

Evil in English Literature. 23rd All-Turkey English Literature Conference Proceedings. Istanbul: Istanbul University, 2002.

Forsyth, Neil. *The Old Enemy: Satan and the Combat Myth*. Princeton: Princeton University Press, 1987.

———. *The Satanic Epic*. Princeton: Princeton University Press, 2003.

Fromm, Erich. *The Anatomy of Human Destructiveness*. Harmondsworth, UK: Penguin, 1977.

Girard, René. *I See Satan Fall Like Lightning*. Translated by James G. Williams. Maryknoll, NY: Orbis, 2001.

Graves, Kersey. *The Biography of Satan: Or, a Historical Exposition of the Devil and His Fiery Dominions*. 5th ed. Escondio, CA: The Book Tree, 1999.

Guetti, James. *The Limits of Metaphor: A Study of Melville, Conrad, and Faulkner*. Ithaca, NY: Cornell University Press, 1967.

Hass, Andrew. *Poetics of Critique: The Inderdisciplinarity of Textuality*. Aldershot, UK: Ashgate, 2003.

Hauke, Christopher. *Jung and the Postmodern: The Interpretation of Realities*. London: Routledge, 2000.

Hayter, Mary. *The New Eve in Christ*. London: SPCK, 1987.

Hegel, Georg Friedrich. *The Logic of Hegel. Translated from the Encyclopaedia of the Philosophical Sciences*. Translated by William Wallace. 2nd ed. Oxford: Oxford University Press, 1892.

———. *Phenomenology of Spirit*. Translated by A. V. Müller. Oxford: Oxford University Press, 1977.

Bibliography

Heidegger, Martin: *The Fundamental Concepts of Metaphysics: World, Finitude, Solitude.* Translated by William McNeill and Nicholas Walker. Bloomington, IN: Indiana University Press, 1995.

———. *Poetry, Language, Thought.* Translated by Albert Hofstädter. New York: Harper Colophon, 1971.

Hick, John. *Evil and the God of Love.* 2nd ed. London: MacMillan, 1985.

Hume, David. *Dialogues concerning Natural Religion.* Edited by Norman Kemp Smith. Oxford: Clarendon, 1935.

Janicaud, Dominique, et al. *Phenomenology and the "Theological Turn": The French Debate.* New York: Fordham University Press, 2000.

Jacobs, Alan. *A Theology of Reading: The Hermeneutics of Love.* Boulder, CO: Westview, 2001.

Jasper, David. *The Sacred Desert: Religion, Literature, Art, and Culture.* Oxford: Blackwell, 2004.

John Chrysostom. *Homilies on Genesis 1–17.* The Fathers of the Church Series 5. Washington, DC: Catholic University of America Press, 1985.

Johnson, Roger A. *The Origins of Demythologizing: Philosophy and Historiography in the Theology of Rudolf Bultmann.* Studies in the History of Religions. Leiden: Brill, 1974.

Jung, Carl Gustav. *Alchemical Studies.* Princeton: Princeton University Press, 1967.

———. *Civilisation in Transition.* Vol. 10 of *Collected Works.* London: Routledge & Kegan Paul, 1970.

———. *Modern Man in Search of a Soul.* Translated by W. S. Dell and Cary F. Baynes. London: Routledge, 2009.

Justin Martyr. *Justin, Philosopher and Martyr: Apologies.* Translated and edited by Denis Minns and Paul Parvis. Oxford Early Christian Texts. Oxford: Oxford University Press, 2009.

Kant, Immanuel. *Religion within the Limits of Reason Alone.* Translated by Theodore M. Greene and Hoyt H. Hudson. Chicago: Open Court, 1934.

Kasper, Walter, editor. *Lexikon für Theologie und Kirche.* 3rd ed. Freiburg: Herder, 1993–2001.

Kekes, John. *The Roots of Evil.* New York: Cornell University Press, 2005.

Kelly, Henry Ansgar. *Satan: A Biography.* Cambridge: Cambridge University Press, 2006.

Kelly, John Norman Davidson. *Early Christian Creeds.* London: Continuum, 2006.

Kirchhoff, Jochen. *Nietzsche, Hitler und die Deutschen: Die Perversion des Neuen Zeitalters.* Berlin: Edition Dionysos, 1990.

Kuhlmann, Helga, and Stefanie Schäfer-Bossert, editors. *Hat das Böse ein Geschlecht? Theologische und religionswissenschaftliche Verhältnisbestimmungen.* Stuttgart: Kohlhammer, 2006.

Kulik, Alexander. *Retroverting Slavonic Pseudepigrapha: Toward the Original of the Apocalypse of Abraham.* Leiden: Brill, 2004.

Kvam, Kirsten et al. *Eve and Adam: Jewish, Christian and Muslim readings on Genesis and Gender.* Bloomington, IN: Indiana University Press, 1999.

Leibniz, Gottfried Wilhelm. *Die Theodicee.* Berlin: Edition Holzinger, 2013.

Leimgruber, Ute. *Kein Abschied vom Teufel. Eine Untersuchung zur gegenwärtigen Rede vom Teufel im Volk Gottes.* Werkstatt Theologie—Praxisorientierte Studien und Diskurse, Vol. 2. Münster: Lit Verlag, 2004.

Bibliography

Lim, Timothy H., and John J. Collins, editors. *The Oxford Handbook of the Dead Sea Scrolls*. Oxford: Oxford University Press, 2010.

Marion, Jean-Luc. *Prolegomena to Charity*. Translated by Stephen Lewis. New York: Fordham University Press, 2002.

Marx, C. W. *The Devil's Rights and the Redemption in the Literature of Medieval England*. Cambridge: Brewer, 1995.

Maser, Werner. *Adolf Hitler: Legende—Mythos—Wirklichkeit*. Köln: Naumann & Göbel, 1971.

Middleton, Darren, editor. *God, Literature, and Process Thought*. Aldershot, UK: Ashgate, 2002.

Muchembled, Robert. *A History of the Devil: From the Middle Ages to the Present*. Cambridge: Polity, 2003.

Munz, Regine. *Banalität des Bösen—Erzählen vom Bösen: Der Beitrag Hannah Arendts*. Hat das Böse ein Geschlecht? Theologische und religionswissenschaftliche Verhältnisbestimmungen. Edited by Helga Kuhlmann and Stefanie Schäfer-Bossert. Kohlhammer: Stuttgart, 2006.

Murdoch, Iris. *The Sovereignty of Good*. London: Routledge & Kegan Paul, 1970.

Neiman, Susan. *Evil in Modern Thought: An Alternative History in Philosophy*. Princeton: Princeton University Press, 2002.

Neumann, Almut. *Verträge mit dem Teufel: Antike und mittelalterliche Vorstellungen im "Malleus maleficarum."* St. Ingbert, Germany: Röhrig, 1997.

Nichols, Sallie. *Jung and Tarot: An Archetypal Journey*. York Beach, ME: Weiser, 1980.

Nietzsche, Friedrich. *Also Sprach Zarathustra*. Werke, vol. 2. Edited by Karl Schlechta. München: Hanser Verlag, 1994.

———. *Jenseits von Gut und Böse: Vorspiel einer Philosophie der Zukunft*. Nietzsches Werke. Edited by Giorgio Colli and Mazzino Montinari. Berlin: de Gruyter, 1968.

———. *Thus Spoke Zarathustra*. Translated and edited by Adrian Del Caro and Robert B. Pippin. Cambridge: Cambridge University Press, 2006.

O'Grady, Joan. *The Prince of Darkness: The Devil in History, Religion, and the Psyche*. New York: Barnes & Noble, 1997.

Onions, C. T., editor. *The Oxford Dictionary of English Etymology*. Oxford: Oxford University Press, 1966.

Origen. *The Apology of Origen in Reply to Celsus: A Chapter in the History of Apologetics*. Edited by John Patrick. Edinburgh: Blackwood and Sons, 1892.

———. *Contra Celsum. Origen against Celsus*. Translated by James Bellamy. London: Mills, 1660.

Otto, Rudolf. *The Idea of the Holy: An Inquiry into the Non-rational Factor in the Idea of the Divine and Its Relation to the Rational*. Oxford: Oxford University Press, 1958.

Paffenroth, Kim. *Judas: Images of the Lost Disciple*. Louisville: Westminster John Knox, 2001.

Pagels, Elaine. *The Origins of Satan*. London: Penguin. 1996.

Palmer, Nigel F. *Visio Tnugdali. The German and Dutch Translations and Their Circulation in the Later Middle Ages*. Munich: Artemis Verlag, 1982.

Parker, Fred. *The Devil as Muse: Blake, Byron, and the Adversary*. Waco, TX: Baylor University Press, 2011.

Plato. *Republic 5*. Translated and edited by Stephen Halliwell. Warminster: Aris & Phillips, 1993.

Quinones, Ricardo J. *The Changes of Cain: Violence and the Lost Brother in Cain and Abel Literature*. Princeton: Princeton University Press, 1991.

Rahner, Karl, and Herbert Vorgrimler. *Kleines Konzilskompendium: Sämtliche Texte des Zweiten Vatikanums.* 27. Auflage. Freiburg: Herder Verlag, 1966.

———. *Kleines Theologisches Wörterbuch.* Freiburg: Herder Verlag, 1961.

Ricoeur, Paul. *The Symbolism of Evil.* Boston: Beacon, 1969.

———. *Time and Narrative.* Volume 1. Chicago: University of Chicago Press, 1984.

Rickels, Laurence A. *The Devil Notebooks.* Minneapolis: The University of Minnesota Press, 2008.

Robbins, Gregory Allen. *Genesis 1–3 in the History of Exegesis: Intrigue in the Garden.* Lewiston, NY: Mellen, 1988.

Rodin, R. Scott. *Evil and Theodicy in the Theology of Karl Barth.* Issues in Systematic Theology, Vol. 3. New York: Lang, 1997.

Roskoff, Gustav: *Geschichte des Teufels. Eine Kulturhistorische Satanologie von den Anfängen bis ins 18. Jahrhundert.* Köln: Melzer Verlag, 2004.

Roos, Keith L. *The Devil in the 16th-Century German Literature. The Teufelsbücher.* Bern: Lang, 1972.

Rudwin, Maximilian J., editor. *Devil Stories: An Anthology.* New York: Knopf, 1921.

Russell, Jeffrey Burton. *The Devil: Perceptions of Evil from Antiquity to Primitive Christianity.* New York: Cornell University Press, 1977.

———. *Lucifer: The Devil in the Middle Ages.* New York: Cornell University Press, 1984.

———. *Mephistopheles: The Devil in the Modern World.* New York: Cornell University Press, 1986.

———. *Paradise Mislaid: How We Lost Heaven and How We Can Regain It.* New York: Oxford University Press, 2006.

———. *The Prince of Darkness: Radical Evil and The Power of Good in History.* New York: Cornell University Press, 1988.

———. *Satan: The Early Christian Tradition.* New York: Cornell University Press, 1981.

Safranski, Rüdiger: *Das Böse oder Das Drama der Freiheit.* München: Hanser Verlag, 1997.

Schneider, Theodor, editor. *Handbuch der Dogmatik.* 2 Bände. Düsseldorf: Patmos, 2000.

Sepich, John. *Notes on "Blood Meridian."* Rev. ed. Foreword by Edwin T. Arnold. Austin, TX: University of Texas Press, 2008.

Seybold, Silke, editor. *All about Evil. Das Böse.* Ausstellungskatalog zur Ausstellung "All about Evil—Das Böse' im Überseemuseum Bremen. Mainz am Rhein: Verlag Philipp von Zabern, 2007.

Shelley, Percy Bysshe. "Essay on the Devil and Devils." In *Shelley's Prose*, edited by David Lee Clark, 264–75. Albuquerque: University of New Mexico Press, 1954.

Sorensen, Eric. *Possession and Exorcism in the New Testament and Early Christianity.* Wissenschaftliche Untersuchungen zum Neuen Testament 157. Tübingen: Mohr, 2002.

Sölle, Dorothee. *Realisation: Studien zum Verhältnis von Theologie und Dichtung nach der Aufklärung.* Darmstadt; Neuwied, Germany: Luchterhand, 1973.

Spufford, Francis. *The Vintage Book of the Devil.* London: Vintage, 1997.

Steiner, Rudolf. *Evil. Selected Lectures by Rudolf Steiner.* London: Rudolf Steiner, 1997.

———. *Knowledge of the Higher Worlds: How Is It Achieved?* London: Rudolf Steiner, 1969.

Stewart, John David. "Paul Ricoeur's Phenomenology of Evil." PhD diss., Rice University, 1965. Online: <http://scholarship.rice.edu/bitstream/handle/1911/14243/6510357.PDF?sequence=1>. Accessed 14 June 2013.

Bibliography

Strauß, David Friedrich. *Das Leben Jesu*. Tübingen: Osiander, 1838.
Temme, Marc. *Mythos als Gesellschaftskritik: Stefan Heyms "Ahasver."* Berlin: Dietz, 2000.
Tertullian. *On the Apparel of Women: The Ante-Nicene Fathers*. Translated and edited by Alexander Roberts and James Donaldson. Vol. 4. New York: Christian Literature Company, 1890.
Thomas Aquinas. *On Evil: Disputed Questions*. Translated by John A. Oesterle and Jean T. Oesterle. Notre Dame: University of Notre Dame Press, 1995.
———. *Quodlibetal questions 1 and 2*. Translated by Sandra Edwards. Toronto: Pontifical Institute of Medieval Studies, 1983.
———. *Summa Theologiae: Questions on God*. Edited by Brian Davies and Brian Leftow. Cambridge: Cambridge University Press, 2006.
Turner, Alice K. *The History of Hell*. Orlando: Harcourt Brace, 1993.
Van der Toorn, Karel et al., editors. *Dictionary of Demons and Deities in the Bible*. Leiden: Brill, 1999.
Vardy, Peter, and Julie Arliss. *The Thinker's Guide to Evil*. Hants, UK: O Books, 2003.
Von Balthasar, Hans Urs. *Glory, Grace, and Culture. The work of Hans Urs von Balthasar*. Edited by Ed Block Jr. Mahwah, NJ: Paulist, 2005.
Von der Osten-Sacken, Peter. *Gott und Belial: Traditionsgeschichtliche Untersuchugen zum Dualismus in den Texten aus Qumran*. Göttingen: Vandenhoeck & Ruprecht, 1969.
Vorgrimler, Herbert. *Geschichte der Hölle*. Munich: Fink, 1993.
Werblowsky, R. J. Zwi. *Lucifer and Prometheus: A Study of Milton's Satan*. London: Routledge, 1999.
Williams, David. *Deformed Discourse: The Function of the Monster in Medieval Thought and Literature*. Exeter, UK: University of Exeter Press, 1996.
Williams, Rowan. *Dostoevsky: Language, Faith and Fiction*. London: Continuum, 2008.
Wray, T. J., and Gregory Mobley. *The Birth of Satan: Tracing the Devil's Biblical Roots*. New York: Palgrave Macmillan, 2005.
Wright, Archie T. *The Origin of Evil Spirits: The Reception of Genesis 6.1–4 in Early Jewish Literature*. Wissenschaftliche Untersuchungen zum Neuen Testament, 2. Tübingen: Mohr Siebeck, 2005.
Zimbardo, Philip. *The Lucifer Effect: How Good People Turn Evil*. London: Rider, 2009.
Zirus, Werner. *Der ewige Jude in der Dichtung: Vornehmlich in der englischen und deutschen*. Leipzig: Mayer & Müller, 1928.

Articles, Essays, Book Chapters

Altizer, Thomas J. J. "An Absolutely New Space." *Literature and Theology* 21.4 (2007) 347–61.
Bultmann, Rudolf. "Neues Testament und Mythologie. Das Problem der Entmythologisierung der neutestamentlichen Verkündigung (1941)." In *Kerygma und Mythos: Ein theologisches Gespräch*, vol. 1, edited by H.-W. Bartsch, 15–48. Hamburg: Reich and Heidrich, 1948.
Burke, Colleen. "Joseph Conrad's *Heart of Darkness*: A Metaphor of Jungian Psychology." Lawrence University Freshman Studies Lecture, 1996. No pages. Online: <http://www.ljhammond.com/phlit/burke.htm>. Accessed 13 July 2011.

Bibliography

Cambers, Andrew. "Demonic Possession, Literacy and Superstition in Early Modern England." *Past and Present* 202 (2009) 3–35.

Cantor, Paul A. "Byron's Cain: A Romantic Version of the Fall." *The Kenyon Review* (New Series) 2.3 (1980) 50–71.

Cormac McCarthy Society. "A Translation of the Spanish in *Blood Meridian*." cormacmccarthy.com: The Official Web Site of the Cormac McCarthy Society. 1–4. Online: <http://cormacmccarthy.cookingwithmarty.com/wp-content/uploads/BMTrans.pdf>. Accessed 24 June 2013.

Crapanzano, Vincent. "Spirit Possession: An Overview." In *Encyclopedia of Religion*, vol. 13, edited by Lindsay Jones, 8687–94. Detroit: Macmillan Reference USA, 2005.

Daube, David. "Ahasver." *The Jewish Quarterly Review* (New Series) 45.3 (1955) 243–44.

"*Das Böse lebt in der Tat*". Interview with Hans-Ludwig Kröber, Charité Berlin. ZEIT Nr. 44, 22 October 2009. Hamburg: Zeitverlag Gerd Bucerius GmbH & Co. KG.

Daugherty, Leo. "Gravers False and True: *Blood Meridian* as Gnostic Tragedy." In *Perspectives on Cormac McCarthy*, rev. ed., edited by Edwin T. Arnold and Dianne C. Luce, 122–33. Jackson, MS: University Press of Mississippi, 1999.

Dorris, Michael. "The Mark of Cain." *The Threepenny Review* 67 (1996) 10–11.

Dickson, Paul. "The Phenomenology of Evil." *The Journal of Value Inquiry* 29 (1995) 5–17.

Donoghue, Denis. "Reading *Blood Meridian*." *The Sewanee Review* 105.3 (1997) 401–18.

Dryden, Linda. "To Boldly Go: *Heart of Darkness* and Popular Culture." In *Heart of Darkness* by Joseph Conrad, edited by Paul B. Armstrong, 500–506. Norton Critical Edition. New York: Norton, 2006.

DU 760—Der Teufel. Das Antlitz des Bösen. Zeitschrift für Kultur, Nr. 9, Oktober 2005. Online: http://www.du-magazin.com/archiv/detail/760.

Ericson, Edward E. "The Satanic Incarnation: Parody in Bulgakov's *The Master and Margarita*." *Russian Review* 33.1 (1974) 20–36.

Feder, Lillian. "Marlow's Descent into Hell." *Nineteenth-Century Fiction* 9.4 (1955) 280–92.

Guerard, Albert J. "The Journey Within." In *Heart of Darkness* by Joseph Conrad, edited by Paul B. Armstrong, Norton Critical Edition, 1–59. New York: Norton, 2006.

Grabbe, Lester L. "The Scapegoat Tradition: A Study in Early Jewish Interpretation." *Journal for the Study of Judaism* 18:2 (1987) 152–67.

Grimm, Heinrich. "Die deutschen Teufelsbücher des 16. Jahrhunderts." *Archiv für Geschichte des Buchwesens* 2 (1958–60) 513–70.

Hass, Andrew. "The Future of English Literature and Theology." In *The Oxford Handbook of English Literature and Theology*, edited by David Jasper, Elisabeth Jay, Andrew Hass, 841–58. Oxford: Oxford University Press, 2007.

Hall, Wade H., and Rick Wallach. "Judge Holden, *Blood Meridian*'s Evil Archon." In *Sacred Violence*, 1–13. El Paso, TX: Texas Western/University of Texas at El Paso, 2002.

Heidegger, Martin. "What is Metaphysics?" In *Existence and Being*, edited by W. Brock, 325–49. Chicago: Regnery, 1949.

Hick, John. "Evil and Incarnation." In *Incarnation and Myth: The Debate Continued*, edited by Michael Goulder, 77–84. London: SCM, 1979.

Hoeffe, Otfried. "Ein Thema wiedergewinnen: Kant über das Böse." In *Über das Wesen der menschlichen Freiheit*, edited by Otfried Hoeffe and Annemarie Pieper, 11–34. Berling: Akademie Verlag, 1995.

Bibliography

Holderness, Graham. "Half God, Half Man—Kazantzakis, Scorsese, and the Last Temptation." *Harvard Theological Review* 100.1 (2007) 65–96.

Isaac-Edersheim, E. "Ahasver—A Mythic Image of the Jew." In *The Wandering Jew: Essays in the Interpretation of a Christian Legend*, edited by Galit Hasan-Rokem and Alan Dundes, 195–219. Bloomington, IN: Indiana University Press, 1986.

James, Caryn. "Is Everybody Dead around Here?" *New York Times Book Review* 28, April 1985, section 7.31.

Jasper, David. "The Limits of Formalism and the Theology of Hope." *Literature and Theology* 1.1 (1987) 1–10.

———. "The Study of Literature and Theology." In *The Oxford Handbook of English Literature and Theology*, edited by David Jasper, Elisabeth Jay, Andrew Hass, 15–33. Oxford: Oxford University Press, 2007.

John Paul II. "General Audience: Wednesday 28 July 1999." §3. Online: <http://www.vatican.va/holy_father/john_paul_ii/audiences/1999/documents/hf_jp-ii_aud_28071999_en.html>. Accessed 14 June 2013.

Jung, Carl Gustav. "Instinct and the Unconscious." In *Collected Works*, vol. 8, 129–38. London: Routledge and Kegan Paul, 1970.

———. "On the Psychology of the Unconscious." In *Collected Works*, vol. 7, 3–119. London: Routledge and Kegan Paul, 1966.

Kerr, John. "The Devil's Elixirs, Jung's Theology, and the Dissolution of Freud's Poisoning Complex." In *Jung in Contexts*, edited by Paul Bishop, 125–53. London: Routledge, 1999.

Knowles, Owen. "Who's Afraid of Arthur Schopenhauer? A New Context for Conrad's *Heart of Darkness*." *Nineteenth-Century Literature* 49.1 (1994) 75–106.

Krause, Tilman. "Rezension zu Harry Mulischs *Siegfried*." *Die Welt* (die literarische Welt) 42.3, November 2001.

Levi, A. H. T. "The Relationship between Literature and Theology: An Historical Reflection." *Journal of Literature and Theology* 1.1 (1987) 11–18.

Lindsay, Mark. "Nothingness Revisited: Karl Barth's Doctrine of Radical Evil in the Wake of the Holocaust." *The Australian and New Zealand Theological Review* 34.1 (2002) 3–19.

Marion, Jean-Luc. "Metaphysics and Phenomenology: A Relief for Theology." Translated by Thomas A. Carlson. *Critical Inquiry* 20.4 (1994) 572–91.

Meisel, Perry. "Decentering *Heart of Darkness*." *Modern Language Studies* 8 (1978) 20–28.

Mills, Gene. "The Pneumatological Ekklesia: A Comparative and Constructive Work in Contemporary Ecclesiology." *Quodlibet Online Journal of Christian Theology and Philosophy* 4.2–3 (2002) no pages. Online: <http://www.quodlibet.net/articles/mills-tillich.shtml>. Accessed 21 February 2012.

Moberly, R. W. L. "The Mark of Cain—Revealed at Last?" *Harvard Theological Review* 100.1 (2007) 11–28.

Münkler, Herfried. "Der Pakt mit dem Teufel: Doktor Johann Georg Faust." In *Die Deutschen und ihre Mythen*, 109–47. Berlin: Rowohlt, 2009.

National Public Radio. "100 Best Characters in Fiction Since 1900." Talk of the Nation. No Pages. Online: <http://www.npr.org/programs/totn/features/2002/mar/020319.characters.html>. Accessed 5 June 2013.

Nietzsche, Friedrich. "Schopenhauer as Educator." In *Thoughts Out of Season*, Part II, 101–201. Edinburgh: Foulis, 1909. Online: <http://www.gutenberg.org/files/38226/38226-h/38226-h.htm#chapter9>. Accessed 4 June, 2013.

Olshewsky, Thomas M. "Between Science and Religion." *The Journal of Religion* 62.3 (1982) 242–60.

Orth, Stefan. "Antlitzlos und unbesprechbar? Neues Nachdenken über das Böse." *Herder Korrespondenz* 61 (2007) 144–49.

Ostriker, Alicia. "Dancing at the Devil's Party: Some Notes on Politics and Poetry." *Critical Inquiry* 13.3 (1987) 579–96.

Pevear, Richard. Introduction to *The Master and Margarita*, by Mikhail Bulgakov. xi–xxii. London: Penguin, 2007.

Ratzinger, Joseph. "Cardinal Ratzinger On Europe's Crisis of Culture." *Catholic Education Resource Center*. No Pages. Online: <http://www.catholiceducation.org/articles/politics/pg0143.html>. Accessed 4 June 2013.

———. "Hölle." In *Lexikon für Theologie und Kirche* (LthK), Band 5: Hermeneutik bis Kirchengemeinschaft, 2nd ed., 446–47. Freiburg: Herder, 1986.

Ricoeur, Paul. "The Hermeneutics of Symbols and Philosophical Reflection." *International Philosophical Quarterly* 2 (1962) 191–218.

Röhl, Wolfgang G. "Demons." In *Encyclopedia of Christianity*, vol. 1, edited by Erwin Fahlbusch et al., translated by Geoffrey W. Bromiley, 794–95. Grand Rapids: Eerdmans, 1999.

Sasso, James. "The Fragmented Will—Kant on Evil." In *Value Theory*, published by *Review Journal of Philosophy and Social Science* XXIX.1–2, 2004.

Sepich, John Emil. "The Dance of History in Cormac McCarthy's *Blood Meridian*." *The Southern Literary Journal* 24.1 (1991) 16–31.

———. "What Kind of Indians was them? Some Historical Sources in Cormac McCarthy's *Blood Meridian*." In *Perspectives on Cormac McCarthy*, edited by Edwin T. Arnold and Dianne C. Luce, 123–44. Southern Quarterly Series. Jackson, MS: University Press of Mississippi, 1999.

Smee, Jess. "Mailer's Young Hitler Novel Angers Germans." *The Guardian*, 29 January 2007. No pages. Online: <http://www.guardian.co.uk/world/2007/jan/29/books.secondworldwar>. Accessed 24 June 2013.

Smith, Ralph A. "John Joel Glanton, Lord of the Scalp Range." *Smoke Signal* (1962) 9–15.

Stephens, R. C. "*Heart of Darkness*: Marlow's Spectral Moonshine." *Essays in Criticism* 19 (1969) 273–84.

Thiele, Leslie Paul. "Postmodernity and the Routinization of Novelty: Heidegger on Boredom and Technology." *Polity* 29.4 (1997) 489–517.

Ulrich, Eugene. "Our Sharper Focus on the Bible and Theology, Thanks to the Dead Sea Scrolls." *Catholic Biblical Quarterly* 66 (2004)1–24.

Weeks, Laura D. "Hebraic Antecedents in *The Master and Margarita*: Woland and Company Revisited." *Slavic Review* 43 (1984) 224–41.

Wikipedia. "Mein Führer—Die wirklich wahrste Wahrheit über Adolf Hitler." No Pages. Online: <http://de.wikipedia.org/wiki/Mein_F%C3%BChrer_%E2%80%93_Die_wirklich_wahrste_Wahrheit_%C3%BCber_Adolf_Hitler>. Accessed 4 June 2013.

Other

Jagger, Mick, and Keith Richards. *Beggars Banquet*. The Rolling Stones. Decca Records, 1968.

www.ingramcontent.com/pod-product-compliance
Lightning Source LLC
Chambersburg PA
CBHW020838160426
43192CB00007B/704